THE
ECLIPSE OF CHRISTIANITY
IN ASIA

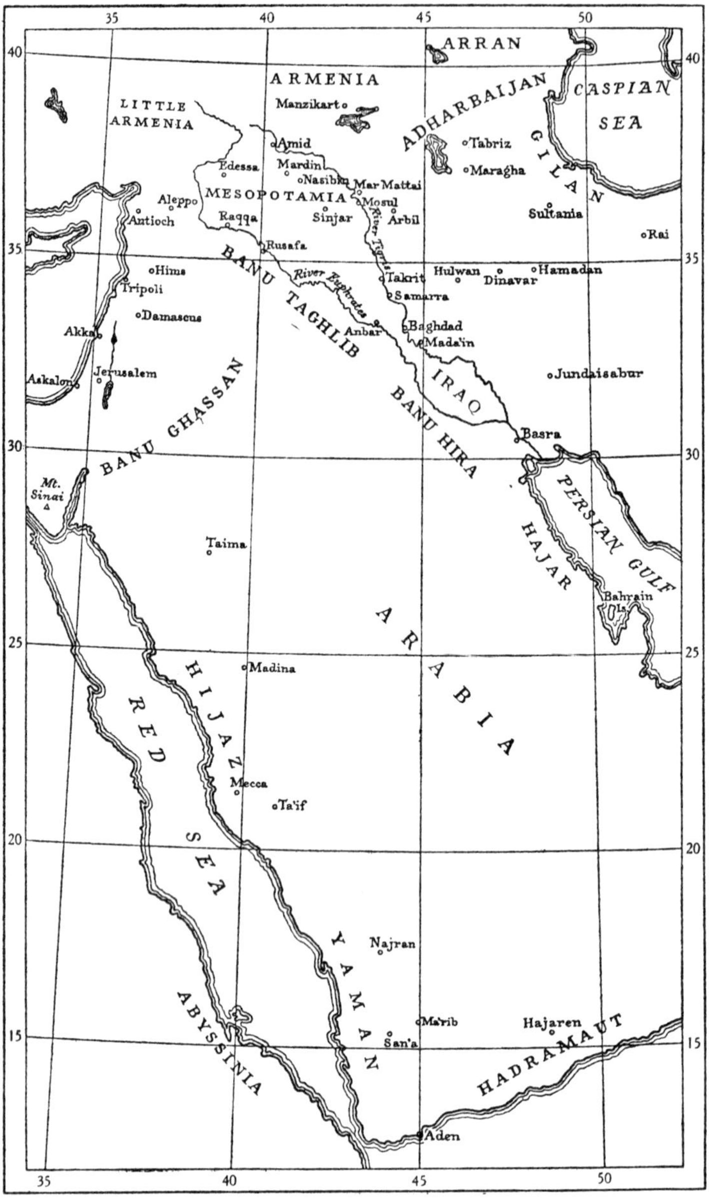

ARRAN
ARMENIA
LITTLE ARMENIA
ADHARBAIJAN
CASPIAN SEA
GILAN
Manzikart
Amid
Edessa
Mardin
Nasibin
Mar Mattai
MESOPOTAMIA
Aleppo
Antioch
Mosul
Arbil
Raqqa
Sinjar
River Tigris
Tabriz
Maragha
Sultania
Rai
Rusafa
Hims
Tripoli
Damascus
Akka
Jerusalem
Askalon
River Euphrates
Takrit
Hulwan
Dinavar
Hamadan
Samarra
Anbar
Baghdad
Mada'in
BANU TAGHLIB
IRAQ
Jundaisabur
BANU GHASSAN
BANU HIRA
Basra
Mt. Sinai
PERSIAN GULF
HAJAR
Taima
Bahrain Is.
ARABIA
Madina
HIJAZ
RED SEA
Mecca
Ta'if
Najran
YAMAN
ABYSSINIA
Ma'rib
San'a
Hajaren
HADRAMAUT
Aden

THE ECLIPSE OF CHRISTIANITY IN ASIA

From the time of Muhammad till the Fourteenth Century

BY

LAURENCE E. BROWNE, D.D.,

EMERITUS PROFESSOR OF THE UNIVERSITY OF LEEDS

NEW YORK

Howard Fertig

1967

First published in 1933 by the Cambridge University Press

HOWARD FERTIG, INC. EDITION 1967
Reprinted by permission of the Cambridge University Press.

Library of Congress Catalog Card Number: 67-13640

PRINTED IN THE UNITED STATES OF AMERICA
BY NOBLE OFFSET PRINTERS, INC.

IN MEMORY OF

WILLIAM HENRY BROWNE, LL.M., D.D.

FOR TWENTY-FOUR YEARS

PRIEST OF THE ARCHBISHOP'S MISSION

TO THE ASSYRIAN CHRISTIANS

WHO DIED AT QUDSHANIS

ON 14 SEPTEMBER 1910

PREFACE TO THE AMERICAN EDITION

When the first edition of this book was published I was on the staff of the Henry Martyn School of Islamic Studies in Lahore, which had been founded in 1930 as an interdenominational institution to further Christian missions to Islam. The book, which involved historical research, was intended to help Christian workers amongst Muslims by explaining how and why Christians in the past had failed to maintain their faith when they lived as a minority under Muslim rule. Now, thirty-three years later, I rejoice greatly that the opportunity has arisen for republication of the book in America, because I believe the book may still serve the purpose of furthering mutual understanding at a time when Christians and Muslims confront one another as never before. My studies of Islam and other religions were continued when I became the Professor of Comparative Religion at Manchester in 1941, and later when I became the Professor of Theology at Leeds in 1946. But, now that I am in retirement, I am no longer in a position to revise what I originally wrote, and for this reason I have asked Messrs Howard Fertig, Inc. to reprint the book without alteration. I would like to take this opportunity of thanking the Cambridge University Press for all that they have done for me through the years, from the time when they published my first small book on November 6th, 1913, up to their present kindness in arranging this American reprint.

August 4, 1966 LAURENCE E. BROWNE.

CONTENTS

Chapter I.	Christianity in the days of Muhammad	*page* 1
II.	Christian Influence on Muhammad	14
III.	Political Conditions	24
IV.	The Fate of the Christians at the time of the Muslim Conquest	28
V.	Christianity under the Caliphs	44
VI.	Christian Teaching and Life	64
VII.	Christian Missionary Expansion	93
VIII.	Polemic	109
IX.	The Muslim Reaction to Christian Life and Teaching	126
X.	The Turks and the Franks	137
XI.	Christianity under the Mongols	147
XII.	The Empty Triumph of Islam	179
Bibliography		187
Index		193

ERRATUM

Page 26, line 18: "June 20th" should read "July 15/16"

Chapter I

CHRISTIANITY IN THE DAYS OF MUHAMMAD

Christianity in Asia had a very different history from Christianity in Europe. In Europe Christianity found highly cultivated peoples whose religion had lagged behind their culture. The religion of Greece and Rome was already out of date, and had lost its hold on educated people, when Christianity appeared on the scene. The only serious rivals to Christianity in Europe were the Mystery Religions, themselves imported from Egypt and the East; and in the struggle that ensued the superior morality of Christianity, its historic foundation, and the adaptability of its system to the philosophy of the day, gave it the victory. Although emperors persecuted Christians for a while, the heathenism which they were trying to prop up was a lost cause, and hence it was inevitable that the day should come, as it did in the fourth century, when Christianity was accepted as the religion of the state. Once Christianity became the state religion, heathenism lost its secular support, and the tendency was for people to become adherents of Christianity as they became more civilised, so that the only non-Christians were the uncultured rustics, or pagans, and the inhabitants of the outskirts of the Empire where cultural influences were weaker. In the great code of laws of the Emperor Justinian, compiled less than a century before the time of Muhammad, it was enacted that heathen were to be baptised if they wished to enjoy the common rights of citizens, and this law was so administered that 70,000 so-called converts were added to the Christian Church in Asia Minor.

The moral battle for Christianity in Europe had been won in the early persecutions, and the intellectual battle in the days of the great Councils. The addition of numbers of converts when Christianity became the state religion added little to the victories of Christianity, and left for succeeding generations the task, as yet unfinished, of converting to Christianity the vast majority of nominal Christians. Even in a perfect Christian community there would be the task of converting to Christianity the children of each succeeding generation, but in a community of which only a small nucleus was really Christian the task was infinitely harder. The growth of Christianity in Europe since the fourth century has been a continual struggle against the forces of worldliness within the ranks of the Church.

In Asia the course of Christianity has been completely different. Never once until the thirteenth century was the favour of the state conferred on the Church. The religion of Persia was not a dying heathenism, but the highly organised and living religion of Zoroastrianism. The persecutions which burst from time to time on the Church can scarcely have been less intense than those of the Roman Empire, and they lasted longer. The first violent persecution, that of Sapor II, lasted for forty years in the fourth century (A.D. 339–79), when the Church in Europe had already won toleration and the favour of the court. Half a century later there was a two years' persecution under Bahram V (A.D. 420–2). A persecution again burst out about A.D. 428 under Yazdegerd II in which many were slain: we only have details from one province, but it probably extended throughout Persia. In the sixth century Chosroes I persecuted the Christians for five years (A.D. 540–5), and the end of the Sassanid rule was marked by the persecution of Chosroes II. The history of the Persian Church up to that time has been admirably written by Labourt and by Wigram,[1] in whose books full details can be read of these things. Christianity made great progress in spite of the persecutions. In the lulls between the storms vigorous evangelistic work was carried on, not only amongst the heathen, but even, in spite of the tremendous influence of the

[1] J. Labourt, *Le Christianisme dans l'Empire Perse*, and W. A. Wigram, *An Introduction to the History of the Assyrian Church.*

Magian priesthood, amongst Zoroastrians. Even in the midst of persecutions the boldness of the martyrs won converts to Christianity. In contrast to the Roman Empire there was no highly educated class to whom Christian apologies could be addressed, so that the Christians benefited little from the fact that they were better educated than others. Christianity made its way simply by the power of its higher morality. With the Muslim invasion the Zoroastrian state religion was replaced by Islam, even more firmly bound to the state. Throughout the whole period up to the Mongol invasion of the thirteenth century the Church was on the defensive, and the greater part of its energy was spent in the struggle against the religious forces which had the backing of the state. The result was that the course of Asiatic Christianity was very different from that of Europe, and a comparison of the apparent success in Europe with the apparent failure in Asia would be very unjust. The only worthy comparison between Christianity of the East and of the West would be made if we could imagine the fate of our Western Christianity if it had been subjected to the same conditions as the Eastern Churches. As a matter of fact, in spite of the eventual organisation of the Church in the Persian Empire apart from the Church in the Roman Empire, the affairs of the West had important effects upon the East, and in some cases, as we shall see, the Eastern Church suffered from the failures of the Church of the West to live up to its Christian standard. In so far as this was the case, Western Christianity must bear its share of the blame for the failure of the Church of the East. In one rather peculiar way the East suffered from the intellectual superiority of Europe. It has sometimes been noticed in a University that the presence of an outstanding figure in some branch of learning has hindered younger scholars from undertaking research in that subject. Somewhat similarly, the keen intellects of the Greeks soon got to grips with the intellectual problems of Christianity, while the Easterners were usually content to accept their results second-hand without themselves going through the intellectual discipline—not that they were always very much interested at the time, for it is strange to learn that the findings of the Council of Nicaea took a long time to get through to the East. Even the controversies about the person of Christ, which led to the sects of which the Easterners became such zealous partisans, really arose in the West. Burkitt, in his *Early Eastern Christianity*,[1] makes the interesting suggestion that one cause of the failure of Eastern Christianity may have been their intellectual cowardice.

From the time in the fourth century when Christianity became the religion of the Roman Empire, Christians were suspect in Persia as friends of the Romans, and it was no accident that the great persecution of Sapor II followed so soon after the official adoption of Christianity by the Roman Emperor. In order to overcome this natural suspicion of sympathy with a foreign power the Persian Christians organised themselves as a separate Church, distinct from the Church of the West, with the Bishop of Seleucia-Ctesiphon (which was afterwards called Al-Madā'in, i.e. The Cities, by the Arabs) as their Patriarch or Catholicus. Although the Catholicus frequently had communications with the Bishops of Antioch and of Europe, he never seems to have been subject to them. The status of the Persian Church as an independent national Church seems to have been gradually established, and was strengthened by political considerations, for it was natural that the Persian sovereigns should not wish their Christian subjects to be under the control of any foreign bishop. The Christians of Persia were always at pains to show that they were not allied to a foreign power, though in times of adversity they were apt to appeal for assistance to the Christian powers of the Roman Empire. Such appeals were at times successful, but created a bad impression in Persia, and in the end did more harm than good to the Church in Persia. The position of that Church as a body united under its Catholicus, and recognised by the state, was definitely settled at the Council of Seleucia in A.D. 410. This position of

[1] P. 189.

the Church, afterwards known as that of a *melet*, made the Church like a little state within the state, the Catholicus being responsible to the government for the behaviour of his people, and for such things as collecting taxes from them. It is to be noted that this establishment of the Persian Church in A.D. 410 was eighteen years before the outbreak of the Nestorian controversy. The followers of Nestorius were expelled from the Roman Empire; and the influx of Nestorian leaders into Persia led, towards the end of the fifth century, to the Persian Church becoming definitely Nestorian. The political advantage of being separated from the Church of the Roman Empire naturally encouraged Nestorianism, and the promoters of this separation were quite unaware of the loss the Persian Church would sustain by being cut off from their brethren in the West. About the middle of the fifth century a new direction was given to the Christological controversy by the teaching of Eutyches, which led eventually to the doctrine known as Monophysitism, which spread in Syria and Egypt. The Church of the Roman Empire repudiated both the Nestorian and the Monophysite doctrines as heresies, and called themselves Catholic or Orthodox. But as the same claim to be Catholic or Orthodox was also made by each of the other Churches, it will avoid confusion if we call the European Church by the name of Melkites, i.e. the king's men, the people who agreed with the Roman Emperor, the name by which they were always known in the East. It should be clearly understood that the use of the names Melkite, Nestorian and Jacobite for the three Churches is not intended to prejudice the question of their orthodoxy, but is only adopted to prevent ambiguity. The correct name of the Nestorian Church is the Church of the East, but the use of that name in a work of this kind might lead to confusion with the other Churches of Asia or with the Church of Eastern Europe.

For the purposes of this book it is scarcely necessary to go in any detail into the theological questions which led to the division of the Church into these three sects, especially because in the beginning of the seventh century, when our study commences, the divisions were already an accomplished fact, and were of greater political than of theological importance. It would of course be different if we could feel that the Melkite position was thoroughly sound and satisfactory, and that the other two positions were merely perverse errors. The fact is that all three started with the assumption that an unbridgeable gulf separated the divine and human natures, and yet that Christ was both human and divine. The assumption of the absolute distinction between the two natures was taken from a philosophy that did not know the incarnation; and it does not seem to have struck anyone to say that the fact of the incarnation proved that there was a kinship of the divine and human natures undreamt of by the philosophers. It would not perhaps be an unfair summary of the three positions to say that the Melkites accepted the incarnation as a fact and left unsolved the philosophical riddle; while the Nestorians and Monophysites made real attempts to solve the philosophical riddle, but in doing so failed to maintain the full truth of the incarnation. The Monophysites thought of our Lord as of one nature which was at the same time both human and divine, but, as they shared with the others the idea that the two natures were incompatible, their tendency was to emphasise His divinity at the expense of His humanity. In one way or another they failed to attribute to Him a full humanity, though they did not go so far as the ancient Docetists whc said that His humanity was only an outward appearance. The Nestorians in another way denied the incarnation, because they did not feel that the divine and human elements in our Lord had ever been truly brought together into a synthesis. Their tendency was to regard Him as two individuals temporarily bound together, so that He acted at one moment as God and at another moment as man. Religiously the Melkites were much sounder in putting at the forefront of their belief the fact of the incarnation; but philosophically their position was no better than that of the Nestorians or Monophysites. It is worth noticing in this connexion that the typical statement of the Melkite position was the Tome of Leo, and that the Latins never had the same interest in philosophy as the Greeks.

Whether Nestorius himself ever actually expressed his belief in the crude way that he is supposed to have done, and for which he was condemned, is a matter of dispute, and need not concern us here, for it is abundantly clear that the Nestorian Church never held the doctrine in that extreme form, and that as time went on its doctrine approximated more and more to what was known as orthodoxy in the West. Controversial writers continued to emphasise the differences, and a Jacobite writer could speak of Nestorians as "infidels".[1] But just as in the Mission Field to-day the divisions of Christendom are seen to be trivial compared with the truths held in common, so a broad-minded observer was able to recognise the essential unity of belief of these ancient Churches. A Nestorian writer of the ninth century, Ēlīyyā Jauharī, who was consecrated Bishop of Damascus in A.D. 893, said:

> They agree in observing the Sundays and Christian festivals. With regard to the offering of the Eucharist they are at one in saying that it is the Body and Blood of Christ. They uphold the confession of faith put forward by the 318 Fathers who were gathered together at Nicaea, which is repeated by all at every liturgy. They also agree in the truth of the priesthood in all its ranks, viz. the patriarchate, the episcopate, the presbyterate and the diaconate, and also in the water of baptism. There is no difference between them in blood nor in faith, but only in their party feelings [lit. passions]....And we see that all the Christians agree on the Gospel as the true book of God, and the book of Paul, and the Acts, and the books of the Old Testament, the Torah and the Prophets, and in the creed, and the Eucharist, and baptism, and the festivals and Sundays, and fasting, and the priesthood, and the cross, and belief in the day of resurrection and return and rising again from the dead, in the things that are lawful and unlawful, and in heaven and hell.[2]

[1] Nau, *Histoires d'Ahoudemmeh et de Marouta*, p. 19.

[2] Assemani, III, pt I, pp. 514–15.

After describing the different doctrines of the three Churches about the person of Christ, he concludes:

> So whereas they differ in word they agree in meaning; and although they contradict one another outwardly they agree inwardly. And all of them follow one faith, and believe in one Lord, and serve one Lord. There is no difference between them in that, nor any distinction except from the point of view of party feelings and strife.

It is worth while to record in this connexion the opinion of two modern Roman Catholic writers. Labourt says:

> Monophysitism in the sixth century was singularly refined, so much so that it is difficult to distinguish it from orthodoxy except by its refusal to admit the Council of Chalcedon and the Tome of Leo. Nestorianism accomplished a similar evolution, and the doctrine of Mar Aba [the great Nestorian Patriarch, A.D. 540–52] is not far removed from the Byzantine faith.[1]

Cheikho, in his preface to a collection of treatises by Melkites, Nestorians and Jacobites, dating from the ninth to the thirteenth centuries, says:

> Apart from a passage or two to which we have drawn attention, no one would suspect that these treatises are from the pen of people tarnished with Nestorian or Eutychian errors.[2]

In the time of Muhammad the Nestorian Church was the main branch of the Church in Persia. Its strength lay chiefly in Mesopotamia and 'Irāq, where it was divided into six provinces as follows:[3]

(1) Babylonia, with the see of the Catholicus at Seleucia-Ctesiphon or Madā'in.

(2) Susiana (Khūzistān), with the metropolitical see of Jundaisābūr (Syriac, Bēth Lāpāṭ). This town was the site of the great Nestorian medical school, and it was there that Arab medicine had its origin.

[1] *Christianisme dans l'Empire Perse*, p. 266.

[2] *Vingt Traités Théologiques*, Avant-propos, p. 2.

[3] Sachau, *Abhandlungen d. preuss. Akad. d. Wissenschaften*, 1919, Phil.-hist. Klasse, "Zur Ausbreitung des Christentums in Asien".

(3) Bēth 'Arbāyē, with the metropolitical see of Naṣībīn (Nisibis). The famous Nestorian theological school at Naṣībīn was founded towards the end of the fifth century by Barṣauma when the Nestorian pupils were driven from Edessa by the orders of the Emperor Zeno.

(4) Maishān, near the Persian Gulf, with the metropolitical see of Baṣra, a town which became of great importance as a centre of Islamic theological learning.

(5) Adiabene, with the metropolitical see of Arbīl.

(6) Garamaea (Bēth Garmai or Bājarmai) with the metropolitical see of Karkūk (Syriac, Karkhā dhe Bēth Selōkh).

The number of Christians in these six provinces must have been considerable. When 'Umar I made his first assessment for the taxation of non-Muslims in Babylonia, it was found that 500,000 people were liable to the tax. As these would only be men of fighting age, the total number of Christians and Jews would be about 1,500,000.[1] What proportion of these were Jews is not known, but presumably by far the greater part were Christians. With this number may be compared the total population of Mesopotamia and 'Irāq just before the Great War, which was estimated at the most at 1,500,000;[2] but of course the total population in the days of the Caliphate must have been considerably greater.

But these six provinces did not cover all the Christians of Persia. As early as A.D. 196 we find mention of Christians in Gīlān and Bactria. In the Canons of the Council of Seleucia in A.D. 410 there is mention of Bishops of Fārs, the islands of Baḥrain, Bēth Mādhāyē including the towns of Ḥulwān, Dīnavar and Hamadān, Bēth Rāzīkāyē including the city of Rai (near the modern Ṭihrān), and the district of Abrashahr (Nīshāpūr) in Khurāsān. In A.D. 424 Bishops of Rai, Nīshāpūr, Merv and Herāt were present at a Council. By A.D. 498 there were Christians among the Hephthalite Huns and Turks near the River Oxus, and a bishop was consecrated for them in A.D. 549. The bishopric of Herāt had become a

[1] Mez, *Renaissance des Islams*, p. 34.

[2] Baedeker, *Palestine and Syria*, 1912, p. 414.

metropolitical see by A.D. 588. Samarqand probably had a bishop, if not a metropolitan, before the time of Muhammad. There was a Nestorian community in China as early as A.D. 636.[1]

The Churches of Armenia, Syria, Egypt and Abyssinia were Monophysite. When the Nestorian scholars were driven from Edessa into Persia the Roman Empire was rid of the Nestorians; but it was not so easy to get rid of the Monophysites. By the middle of the fifth century the number of Monophysite bishops had been so much reduced that it seemed as if the Church must die out. But at that time, at the request of the Arab tribe of Banū Ghassān, and through the intervention of the Empress, two Monophysite bishops were consecrated for the Christian Arabs. One of these, Jacob Baradaeus,[2] was given the title of Bishop of Edessa; but actually he wandered about for thirty years reorganising the Monophysite Church, ordaining priests and consecrating bishops. It is after him that the Monophysite Church, particularly in Syria, was called Jacobite. Egypt practically entirely, and Syria for the most part, were Monophysite. The Christians of this Church in Egypt are known as Copts.

So long as the Monophysite faith was tolerated in the Roman Empire it could not get a footing in Persia; but when the Emperor Justin I (A.D. 518–27) began to persecute the Jacobites there was no longer any reason for the Persian government to exclude them. From their headquarters at Ṭūr ʿAbdīn (south of the Tigris, and north of Naṣībīn) they sent preachers everywhere, and especially tried to win over Roman and Syrian prisoners who were living in Mesopotamia and ʿIrāq. The monks of the monastery of Mar Mattai (north of Mosul, between the Tigris and the Great Zāb rivers) and the people of Takrīt (or Tagrīt, on the Tigris

[1] W. Barthold, *Zur Geschichte des Christentums in Mittel-Asien bis zur mongolischen Eroberung*; Mingana, *Early Spread of Christianity in Asia.*

[2] I.e. al-Barādaʿī, the man wearing a horse-cloth, one of his frequent disguises on his travels.

north of Sāmarrā) seem to have remained Monophysite and not to have adopted Nestorianism when Barṣauma introduced that faith into Persia. From these three centres, Ṭūr 'Abdīn, Takrīt and Mar Mattai, the Monophysite faith spread, but only with great difficulty owing to the opposition of the Nestorians. Mention must also be made of a Monophysite centre at Sinjār (or Shiggar, west of Mosul) which was noted for its scientific and medical studies. Political conditions at last allowed the Jacobites in Persia to organise themselves in A.D. 629, three years before the death of Muhammad. The Bishop of Takrīt was made into a Metropolitan with twelve bishops under him. At a later time the Bishops of Takrīt were given the special title of Maphrianus, and had charge over all the Jacobites in Persia.[1]

The most important Christian settlement in Arabia proper was the town of Najrān, on the northern border of Yaman. This town was on the trade route from the East which came up through South Arabia and then ran parallel with the coast through Mecca to Syria. The Christian community in Najrān was probably connected with this trade route, and may be regarded as an outpost of Syrian civilisation. Other places in Yaman, and even in Ḥaḍramaut, had Christian communities. Muslim historians tell of a great church at San'ā,[2] a city about halfway between Najrān and Aden. The capital of the Himyarite kingdom had been moved to San'ā from Ma'rib, probably in the fifth century when the great dyke of Ma'rib burst. *The Book of the Himyarites*, discovered in 1920, speaks of how "Christianity was sown in the town of Najrān and in the land of the Himyarites".[3] It also speaks of Christians in Ma'rib (55 miles east-north-east of San'ā), and in [Ha]jarēn, a town in Hadramaut some 280 miles north-east of Aden. There is also mention of a church in the town of Hadramaut, other-

[1] O'Leary, *Arabia before Muhammad*, pp. 138–41; Labourt, *Christianisme dans l'Empire Perse*, pp. 157, 198, 217, 240; Barthold, *op. cit.* p. 23.

[2] Ibn Hishām, I, 43.

[3] Moberg, *The Book of the Himyarites*, p. 31 *a*.

wise unknown but presumably at that time the chief town of the district;[1] and of a church in Ẓofār,[2] a town on the south coast, 650 miles from Aden, and nowadays just within the borders of 'Umān. All these churches were destroyed, and many Christians slain, in a persecution by a Jewish ruler in A.D. 523; but this by no means stamped out Christianity in the district, for the Abyssinian king, who took vengeance on the persecutor, "built many churches in that land, and appointed in them priests from those who were with him".[3] The origin of these Christian communities, as connected with the Syrian trade, would suggest that they were Monophysite, and this allegiance must have been strengthened by the influence of Abyssinia in Yaman. But the rivalry of the Persian and Roman Empires seems to have extended to attempts to capture the trade with the East, and before the time of Muhammad Persian influence was felt in Yaman. In A.D. 597 Yaman actually became a Persian province. It is probable that owing to this Persian influence the Christians of Yaman became Nestorians. The only direct evidence we have of this change is that the Nestorian Catholicus Timothy appointed a bishop for Yaman and San'ā at the end of the eighth century,[4] and a century later (A.D. 901) the Catholicus Yūḥannā b. 'Īsā is said to have written a letter to a priest in Yaman answering a number of questions he had asked.[5]

When we speak of Arabia we must think, not only of the great peninsula, but also of its northward prolongation into the desert area between Syria and 'Irāq. From the point of view of contact with civilised races this area was of great importance, because here on the borders of Syria and 'Irāq

[1] Moberg, *op. cit.* p. 5 *b*.

[2] *Op. cit.* pp. 7 *a*, 8 *b*, 19 *a*.

[3] *Op. cit.* p. 56 *a*.

[4] Budge, *Book of Governors*, II, 448; Assemani, III, pt II, DCIX; Tor Andrae, *Ursprung*, 1923, p. 170.

[5] This, and certain other statements about the later history of the Christians in Yaman, are quoted by Cheikho, *Christianisme en Arabie avant l'Islam*, p. 67, from MSS. in the Beyrouth Oriental Library, but he adds, "It is not possible to corroborate the traditions from this source by comparison with any other source".

Arab tribes, though still nomadic, came into touch with Christianity. Thus Ibn Hauqal says,

> They [the Arabs] settled down for the protection of Persia and Rūm, so that some of them became Christians and embraced the religion of the Christians, such as Taghlib from Rabī'a in the land of al-Jazīrah [Mesopotamia], and Ghassān and Bahrā and Tanūkh from Yaman in the land of Syria.[1]

The two tribes which were of the greatest importance as protecting the frontiers just before the time of Muhammad were the Banū Ghassān on the Syrian frontier, and the Banū Ḥīra on the Persian frontier. Of these the Banū Ghassān were all Monophysite Christians, and, as we have seen, it was they who were instrumental in getting Jacob Baradaeus consecrated as bishop. The Banū Ḥīra were not all Christian, but among them were certain clans called 'Ibād who were Christians, mostly Nestorian, though some were Monophysite, for Monophysite bishops are recorded in the sixth and seventh centuries.[2] The Banū Taghlib, who lived near the frontier of Mesopotamia, were entirely Christian. The tribe of Ṭai is interesting: originally coming from Yaman they migrated to Taima in Northern Hijāz, a town so closely in touch with Syria that it is mentioned several times in the Old Testament (Tema, Gen. xxv. 15, Isai. xxi. 14, Jer. xxv. 23). Here some of the tribe of Ṭai became Christians and others Jews, while the rest remained heathen. Owing to their proximity to Syria their name of Ṭai was often used by Syrian writers for Arabs in general.

In the Sinaitic peninsula there were numerous monasteries of the Melkites, so that Melkite influence must have entered Arabia from that side, along the trade route from Egypt; while Jacobite influence was exerted from Syria and from Yaman, and Nestorian influence from 'Irāq, and afterwards also from Yaman.

[1] *Al-masālik wal-mamālik*, ed. Leiden, 1870, p. 18, quoted by Cheikho, *op. cit.* p. 126. In pp. 124–41 Cheikho collects all the evidence for Christians among the different Arab tribes.

[2] Tor Andrae, *Ursprung*, 1923, p. 173.

Chapter II

CHRISTIAN INFLUENCE ON MUHAMMAD

With Christian influence pressing into Arabia along its three great trade routes, from Persia, Syria and Egypt, one would expect a general knowledge of what Christianity was. Arabia, it is true, is a vast country, but the towns where culture was likely to develop were mainly on the trade routes; and, apart from the Arabs permanently settled in these towns, many others paid them regular visits in the course of their trade. The old idea therefore that Arabia was completely cut off from civilisation can no longer be maintained. As yet uncivilised, it was certainly not closed to the influences of civilisation. Sura xcvi, 3–5, "Recite! for thy Lord is most beneficent, who hath taught the use of the pen, hath taught mankind that which he knew not", is Muhammad's appreciation of the value of the recent introduction to Mecca of the first element of culture, the art of reading and writing. That the art was new to Arabia is probably indicated by the fact that the Bible had not been translated into Arabic—a lamentable fact indeed, for if the Christians had been quick to seize the opportunity, and had made the first Arabic book the Bible instead of the Quran, the whole course of the religious history of the East might have been different.

Besides the Christians resident in Arabia there were also important settlements of Jews, and there has been considerable difference of opinion about the relative shares of Christianity and Judaism in influencing Muhammad. The tendency nowadays is to emphasise the former, and to regard Islam as a movement which grew up, if not in a Christian atmosphere, at least in an atmosphere in which Christianity was the main cultural element.

It must not, however, be supposed that, previous to Muhammad, Christianity had made much of an impression on the Arabs. Muhammad was a real pioneer, a pioneer of culture in Arabia, and particularly of that element of culture which is its strength and background, viz. religion. The only ground for supposing that the pagan Arabs had become familiar with Christianity, and that there was amongst them a tendency towards monotheism, is to be found in the pre-Islamic Arab poetry. In recent times a good deal of doubt has been cast on the genuineness of this poetry, and Prof. Margoliouth has brought strong arguments, as yet unanswered, to prove that the whole of this poetry is a later fabrication.[1] If it should finally be agreed that there is no extant pre-Islamic poetry, we shall have to consider Muhammad as even more of a religious pioneer than was formerly supposed, for, as Margoliouth points out, all the Arab inscriptions, of which many are now known, are purely pagan, and show none of that tendency towards monotheism which has been discerned in the poetry. On the other hand, if the pre-Islamic poets are unauthentic, one of the possible sources of Muhammad's misunderstandings of Christianity is ruled out.

As, however, the authenticity of the poets is still *sub judice*, it is only right to see what is the extent of the knowledge of Christianity and of monotheistic thought in Arabia to which they appear to witness. Considering the large amount of the poetry, the references to religion of any kind are few. The reason commonly given for this lack is that the stereotyped scheme of subject-matter in the poetry did not leave room for any mention of religion except by way of allusion or illustration. But if the Arabs had been religiously minded one may be sure that their religious ideas would have forced themselves into prominence in the poetry. We may therefore agree with the conclusion of Lyall:

> In the absence of proof that more passages bearing on the pagan worship originally formed part of the poems, it would seem a better warranted conclusion that the Arab of Central Arabia, in the days before al-Islam, interested himself little in religion of any

[1] "The Origins of Arabic Poetry" in *J.R.A.S.* July, 1925.

sort. A like character is given to the Bedawi of the present day, in spite of the mighty spiritual awakening wrought by Muhammad's preaching, by travellers who have lived in his company; and in this, as in many other things, it seems probable that he is a true descendant of his pagan forefathers.[1]

With but occasional references to religion of any sort, it is not surprising that there are not more indications, in the poetry, of monotheistic thought. Two examples will suffice:

Yea, the righteous shall keep the way of the righteous,
  And to God turn the steps of all that abideth;
And to God ye return, ye too: with Him only
  Rest the issues of things and all that they gather.

. . . . .

And the day when avails the sin-spotted only
  Prayer for pardon and grace to lead him to mercy,
And the good deeds he wrought to witness before Him,
  And the pity of Him who is compassion.

It boots not to hide from God aught evil within your breasts:
  It will not be hid—what men would hold back from God, He knows.
It may be its meed comes late: in the Book is the wrong set down
  For the Reckoning Day; it may be that vengeance is swift and stern.[2]

There is evidence from the pre-Islamic poets of some superficial knowledge of Christianity. The thing that struck their imagination most of all was the monk in his cell, e.g. Imru al-Qais begins a poem thus:

O Friend—see the lightning there! it flickered, and now is gone,
  As though flashed a pair of hands in the pillar of crowned cloud.
Nay, was it its blaze, or the lamps of a hermit that dwells alone,
  And pours o'er the twisted wicks the oil from his slender cruse?[3]

The frequent mention of the solitary monks is a reminder to us that Christian monasticism had greatly developed by the time of Muhammad, and that the religious influence of the hermits must be taken into account in addition to that of the

1 *Translations of ancient Arabian poetry*, p. xxvii.
2 Lyall, *op. cit.* p. 90 from Labīd, and p. 112 from Zuhair.
3 Lyall, *op. cit.* p. 103.

Christian Arab tribes. Some of the poets refer to Christian processions, the wooden bell calling to prayer, ivory pictures in marble niches, the myrtle twigs of Palm Sunday, and possibly to the Eucharistic cup.[1] It is not surprising to find that several of the poets who show some knowledge of Christianity were closely associated with one or other of the Christian tribes.[2]

The poems of Umayya b. abi 'ṣ-Ṣalt raise as many problems as they solve.[3] Umayya himself came from Ṭā'if near Mecca, was a contemporary of Muhammad, and up till his death remained hostile to Muhammad. The similarities to the Quran, and the differences, present difficulties; and the fact that some verses are certainly interpolations adds to the difficulty. Direct borrowing from one by the other is most unlikely. The fact that "in the legendary material, whether of Arabic or of Jewish-Christian origin, Umayya often has other or more exact information than Muhammad in the corresponding passages of the Quran"[4] seems to show that the poems cannot be merely later Muslim fabrications, for Muslims would not have been likely knowingly to have contradicted the Quran. The extract from No. xxxv, given below, even if not pre-Islamic, must have been written very early when Christianity, apart from the divinity of Christ, was looked upon as true. It suggests a frame of mind like that of Muhammad when, in the early Sura lxxxv. 10, he spoke of Christians as "believers". Here are a few short extracts from the poems attributed to Umayya:[5]

XV

O my soul! Thou hast no protector save Allah,
  Nor is there any other that surviveth the events of time.

[1] For examples see Bell, *Origin of Islam in its Christian environment*, pp. 43 ff., and Tor Andrae, *Ursprung*, 1923, p. 185.

[2] Lyall, *op. cit.* p. 93; Tor Andrae, *Ursprung*, 1923, p. 178.

[3] See Schulthess, *Umajja ibn Abi 's-Salt*; Power, *Umayya ibn Abi 's-Salt*, 1906 and 1912; Tor Andrae, *op. cit.*

[4] Schulthess, *op. cit.* p. 4.

[5] Text and German translation in Schulthess, *op. cit.*

XXIV

The heaven was not created, nor the stars,
Nor the sun—by whose side standeth the moon,
Whose measure the True and Immutable One hath decreed—
Nor the garden, nor paradise, nor joy,
Save by reason of His mighty will.

XXXV

O Lord, suffer me never to be an unbeliever.
Let faith be for ever the secret thought of my heart;
Let it pervade my frame, my skin,
My flesh and blood, so long as I live a man.
I take refuge with Him to whom the pilgrim makes pilgrimage,
And those who establish the religion of God,
Those who greet Him in their pilgrimage,
Seeking not God's reward as their prize.

. . . . . .

As for mankind, the event of the last hour tarries for them,
And all of them ask concerning the judgment, When?
In the days when their Christ meeteth the Christians among them,
And those who were His friends and associates.
They claimed Him, as they say, as their God,
And sent Him forth as an intermediary to learn the mystery.

LIII

Praise be to Allah who hath not taken
A son[1]; and hath appointed to His creatures their measure.
My countenance humbleth itself before Him, and all my being,
Among those who in thankfulness bow before His face.

Until those who have made a special study of the subject are in closer agreement it would be wise at least to bear in mind the possibility of learning from Umayya something of the movements of religious thought in the neighbourhood of Mecca in the days of Muhammad.

Even apart from Umayya we have seen that some of the other poets inclined towards monotheism; and if they were really pre-Islamic, this monotheism was probably chiefly due to Christian influence. But that these people constituted a sect, and that they were the people whom Muhammad called

[1] Or "sons". Both translations are possible. The reference may be either to Christ as the Son of God, or to Arabian polytheism.

hunafā is most unlikely: not only did he not like poets, but he did not want any rivals to himself as the Prophet of Arabia. The name *hunafā* is probably derived from the Syriac *hanᵉphē* "heathen", the name by which the Arabs were known to the Syrians. Muhammad seems to have believed that Arabia had had a primitive revelation of monotheism which in his day had become sadly corrupted, and he adopted the word *hunafā* (for which he formed a correct Arabic singular *hanīf*) as meaning the Arabs from Abraham to himself who had maintained the genuine Arabic revelation.[1] If this explanation of a much-discussed word is correct, Muhammad, in using the word *hanīf*, was thinking of the bearers of the old monotheistic tradition of his imagination; and was not thinking of any Arabs of his own day.

When we come to the study of the Quran itself we have to consider three possibilities for the main source of the borrowed ideas, either Judaism, or Christianity, or some heretical Christian sects. Now there is no doubt that the Biblical narratives appearing in the Quran are more nearly related to the form in which they appear in the Talmud and the apocryphal literature than to the original Bible stories. In so far as the similarity is greatest to the Talmud of course a Jewish origin is indicated; but in some cases the parallel is closest to the apocryphal literature. It must be remembered that even the Jewish apocryphal literature was preserved in Christian rather than in Jewish circles. There are still extant a considerable number of Christian apocryphal Gospels, and others doubtless are lost. These were probably the light and popular literature of the day in Christian circles, providing a greater amount of the purely miraculous element than the genuine Gospels. That these apocryphal Gospels were works of the imagination is obvious, as for instance the absurd tales of wonders wrought by Jesus in His childhood, which are referred to in Sura iii. 41, 43, but the fact of their being imaginative works does not make them necessarily heretical,

[1] Richard Bell, "Who were the Hanifs?" in the *Moslem World*, April, 1930.

and they were undoubtedly current in orthodox circles. There are, however, in the Quran certain statements about Christ which are distinctly heretical, and it is a question whether these were actually taught by any Christian sect in Muhammad's day. Of these the most serious is the denial of the death of Christ on the cross, which has resulted in a denial by Muslims up to the present day, not only of one of the most certain facts of history, but of the fact in history which is most vital to the human race. That there were Docetists in the early days of Christianity who denied the death of Christ on the cross is well known, but it is extremely doubtful whether any sect in Muhammad's day held that view, and it is almost certain that Muhammad's denial arose from a preconceived notion on his part that God would not have allowed a prophet to die such a shameful death. The second heretical statement is in Sura v. 116: "O Jesus, son of Mary, hast thou said unto mankind, 'Take me and my mother as two Gods beside God'?" The common explanation of this amazing charge is that some Christian heretical sect in the days of Muhammad believed in a Trinity consisting of God, Mary and Jesus. The only evidence for the existence of such a sect is a statement of Epiphanius about some people whom he called Collyridians. This was more than two centuries before the time of Muhammad, and it is scarcely conceivable that Muhammad could have found out the existence of a sect which was so unimportant in the seventh century that Church history is ignorant of it, and would then have brought the peculiar views of this sect as a charge against Christians in general. Al-Kindī, about two centuries after Muhammad, was unaware of any Christian sect that held these views, and could only suppose that "these misunderstandings have come to you [the Muslims] from the Jews when they tried to trap you thereby".[1] The Muslim theologian Ibn Ḥazm, who died in 1153, says that the belief that Jesus and His mother were two Gods beside God was held by the Borborians.[2] The fact

[1] *Risālat al-Kindī*, p. 37.
[2] I, 47.

that the only Christians he could find who had ever supported such a view were an obscure sect in Armenia goes to show that it was not held by any Christians with whom Muhammad could have come into contact. In fact, Ibn Ḥazm probably hit on the Borborians simply because their theological views were so little known that it would be difficult to disprove the charge. The Borborians were evidently a sect which was made the butt of nameless charges: Īshū'dād (Bishop of Hadatha, about A.D. 850) accused them of marrying their mothers and eating their children, and of some other abomination which he refrained from naming.[1] We may safely conclude that this curious Trinity of God, Mary and Jesus was simply a misunderstanding of Christian teaching on Muhammad's part. Two suggestions have been offered as to how this misunderstanding may have arisen. The one is that in Abyssinia the veneration for the Blessed Virgin Mary reached extraordinary proportions, and, as we know that Muhammad had close relations with Abyssinian Christians, the misunderstanding may have arisen in this way. The other suggestion is that the misunderstanding arose through the feminine gender of the Syriac word *rūḥā* for "spirit".[2] This grammatical fact had the peculiar result of causing some Syriac-speaking Christians to think of the Holy Spirit as "she". There was an early apocryphal Gospel called the *Gospel according to the Hebrews*, written probably in Aramaic, which was sufficiently like our canonical Gospel according to St Matthew to have been mistakenly supposed by some people in early days to be the original of it. This Gospel was quoted as late as the middle of the ninth century by Haimo of Auxerre in France, which shows how widely its use extended in both time and place. Origen (early third century) and Jerome (late fourth century) both on several occasions quoted a sentence from it, presumably referring to the

[1] *Commentaries of Isho'dad of Merv*, I, 270.

[2] This suggestion, and also the reference to the Gospel according to the Hebrews, was known to Gibbon (1787). See *Decline and Fall*, ch. L (Everyman's Library edition, V, 235 note).

Temptation, as follows:[1] "Even now did my Mother the Holy Spirit take me by one of mine hairs, and carried me away unto the great mountain Thabor". It is at least possible that while the Abyssinian veneration for the Virgin gave weight to the charge, the original ground of it was this passage from the Gospel according to the Hebrews or something based on it. For the idea was distinctly widespread: as late as the twelfth century a certain Egyptian priest, Mark ibn al-Qanbar, was accused (rightly or wrongly, it does not matter for our purpose) of calling the Holy Spirit feminine:

> He held that there was a feminine quality in the Godhead, and he taught that this feminine quality is proper to the Holy Spirit. He held that the eternal Word of God is born through all eternity from the Father and the Holy Spirit.[2]

The reason why in the past it has been difficult to believe that Muhammad was in touch with orthodox Christianity is that scholars scarcely realised what a strange development oriental Christianity had taken in the direction of monasticism. Tor Andrae has shown at length in his work, *Der Ursprung des Islams und das Christentum*, that Muhammad's emphasis on the fear of hell in the early part of his ministry is closely parallel to the monastic outlook of Syria and Egypt at the time. He says:

> There is scarcely any other form of Christianity in which the evangelical thought of the forgiveness of sins and our sonship of God is so completely quenched as in this Syrian monastic religion. The pious man has to earn his forgiveness of his own power by life-long penitence and self-torment.[3]

Muhammad favoured the Christians, and especially in his later life when he turned against the Jews he felt that the Christians were those with whom Muslims had most in common. This is surely an indication that he had learnt more from Christianity than from any other source. Also he approved

[1] M. R. James, *Apocryphal New Testament*, pp. 2–7.

[2] Abū Ṣāliḥ, *The Churches and Monasteries of Egypt*, ed. by B. T. A. Evetts, p. 40.

[3] 1924, p. 282.

of Christian monks, grouping them with others who served God:

> Thou wilt certainly find nearest in affection to them that believe those who say, "We are Christians". This is because some of them are priests and monks, and because they are free from pride [Sura v. 85]. Those who turn to God, those who serve, those who praise, wandering monks, those who bow down, those who prostrate themselves, those who enjoin what is right and forbid what is blameworthy, and keep to the bounds of God [Sura ix. 113].

But he did not approve of self-torture as a means of attaining salvation, and substituted for it the surrender of oneself once for all as a Muslim. In that sense the tradition, "There is no wandering monastic life in Islam", which was forged to counteract the growth of ascetic monasticism in Islam, truly expresses the mind of the Prophet. As little would he have approved of the ascetic practices of the Ebionites or other Jewish-Christian sects if such had been known to him, as many people have supposed. On this ground we can safely rule out Jewish-Christian sects as an important influence on Muhammad.

The conclusion to which we seem to be forced is that the main religious influence acting upon Muhammad was what passed for orthodox Christianity in his day. That is not to say that he had any clear or full idea of the life and teaching of contemporary Christians, but rather that, living and moving in places where Christians were frequently coming and going, he assimilated such Christian ideas as distilled over into the outward daily life and common thought of Christians. He was not accurately informed by experts in Christianity, but got his ideas from the common people. Even allowing for the misunderstandings that must have arisen through his hesitating to ask for correct information, and for his refusal to entertain some of the ideas held by all Christians, the general religious outlook he obtained is illustrative of the Christian outlook of the day.

Chapter III

POLITICAL CONDITIONS

The extraordinarily rapid conquests in the first days of Islam were due to a curious combination of circumstances. On the one hand the Arabs were for the first time united. Under the commanding influence of Muhammad their tribal jealousies were put away, and they were united by a bond which they had never known before—loyalty to a single God. Arabia, formerly more fertile, was no longer able to support its population, and the new politico-religious unity enabled the hungering masses to burst the bounds of the desert and seize the riches of more favoured races. On the other hand the two great empires of the day were weakened by long continued war with each other. Both were internally weakened by divided loyalties to rival claimants to the thrones; and the Roman Empire was further weakened by the religious strife of Melkites and Monophysites. The very name of Melkites is sufficient indication that those who were not Melkites had no loyalty to the Emperor.

In Persia the Emperor Hormizd IV, who had been reigning since A.D. 579, was deposed, and his son Chosroes (Khusrau) II placed on the throne in A.D. 590. But immediately on his accession Chosroes II found himself powerfully opposed by the Persian general Bahram. He therefore fled to Syria, and from there appealed for help to the Roman Emperor Maurice. It is a mark of the degradation of the Persian Empire that its ruler should have sought help against his own people from the ruler of their hereditary enemies. Maurice, seeing an opportunity of gaining a diplomatic victory over Persia, treated Chosroes well, and assisted him to regain his kingdom, receiving in return for this service a cession of Persian territory. For the moment it looked as if Persia was to become dependent on the Roman Empire; but a revolt in the

Roman Empire disappointed any such hopes. In A.D. 602 a rebel centurion Phocas seized the throne of Constantinople, and put Maurice to death. Chosroes at once saw an opportunity of freeing himself from Roman control. He denounced the treaty of peace, on the grounds that it had been made with the murdered monarch, and began a determined attack on the Roman Empire, first of all overrunning Armenia and then taking Edessa in A.D. 609.

Meanwhile a new rebellion broke out in the Roman Empire under Heraclius who was "Prefect of Africa" in Pentapolis. Heraclius himself set out for Constantinople, and while he was gathering reinforcements in the Greek islands his general Nicetas went to Egypt, stirred up rebellion there, and secured Egypt for Heraclius. In A.D. 610 Heraclius entered Constantinople, and was accepted as Emperor. The effort to gain the throne seems to have exhausted all his strength, and the Persians continued their attacks on the Roman Empire unhindered. Syria and Palestine were the first to fall. In A.D. 615 Chosroes took Jerusalem. Jerusalem was first surrendered by the Jews, but after it had been occupied the Christians rose up and slew the Persian garrison. Chosroes again took Jerusalem with the help of the Jews, and many thousands of the inhabitants were slaughtered and the city destroyed. It may have been in this connexion that Muhammad uttered Sura xxx. 1, "The Romans have been overcome by the Persians in the nearest part of the land; but after their defeat they shall overcome in a few years", or perhaps in connexion with some other victory nearer the time of the Hijra.[1] Although the Jews were at first favoured by Chosroes for assisting in the capture of Jerusalem, they afterwards fell into disfavour and were expelled from Jerusalem, while the Christians were allowed to rebuild their churches. In A.D. 617 the Persians invaded Egypt, first conquering the Delta and then turning to Alexandria. Most of the monasteries near Alexandria were destroyed and the monks slain. As in Syria, though the Persians had slain countless Christians in the

[1] Nöldeke-Schwally, *Geschichte des Qurans*, I, 150.

conquest, they afterwards showed religious toleration. In the same year the Persians invaded Asia Minor.

With the completion of the Persian conquests the Roman Empire was almost reduced to the city of Constantinople itself. Barbarian tribes pressed close upon the city on its westward side; while the Persians held Chalcedon, from which, looking across the narrow straits, they could see silhouetted against the sky the domes of the great city. But one thing the Persians had failed to do, and that was to get command of the sea, and this failure was to prove their undoing. Suddenly, perhaps at the instigation of Sergius the Patriarch of Constantinople, a change came over Heraclius: he awoke from his torpor, and determined to win back the Empire. Gathering together an enormous army he set sail on Easter Monday, A.D. 622, for Issus, only two or three months before that other more momentous journey in history—the Hijra of Muhammad to Madīna—which took place on June 20th of the same year. From Issus in the south and Trebizond in the north Heraclius cut the communications of the Persians in Asia Minor, and somewhere about A.D. 627 both Chalcedon and Alexandria were won back for the Empire. In A.D. 628 Heraclius took Dastagerd, 80 miles north of Madā'in, and Chosroes was captured and slain by his successor Siroes. The crowning triumph of Heraclius was the restoration to Jerusalem of the holy cross which had been taken by the Persians at the sack of Jerusalem. It was probably shortly before this event that Muhammad sent embassies to various sovereigns, including Heraclius and Chosroes, demanding their submission to Islam.

From the moment of his triumph Heraclius began a campaign of intolerance which was the ruin of his Empire. His first act was to drive the Jews from Jerusalem, and to sanction a general massacre of them, according to some authorities not only in Palestine and Syria but also in Egypt and Asia Minor. For several years he had been maturing a plan for bringing about a reconciliation of the Monophysites and Nestorians with the Melkites on a new basis of uniformity. The moving spirit on the Melkite side was Sergius of Constantinople. In counsel with him, and with Cyrus the Nestorian Bishop of Phasis (east coast of the Black Sea), and with Athanasius the Monophysite Bishop of Antioch, Heraclius put forward a new doctrine known as Monothelitism, which spoke of one will in Christ instead of speaking of one or two natures. The new doctrine was conceived, not with any desire to arrive at the truth, but merely to secure political peace by religious uniformity. But it failed completely of its object. Cyrus was sent to Egypt as Patriarch to enforce the new doctrine, and was also made the civil governor. The people of Egypt would have nothing to do with the new Monothelite doctrine. In order to enforce its acceptance Cyrus started a most terrible persecution of the Copts. All who could do so fled, including the Coptic Patriarch Benjamin, who did not come out of hiding till after the Arab conquest. Others went over to the Melkite side. Some pretended to do so, remaining Monophysite at heart. It may be that Cyrus went further than Heraclius had intended, but the Emperor cannot be absolved from responsibility. Thus it came about that his plans for achieving religious unity in the Empire resulted in stirring up in the hearts of the Syrians and Copts such hatred for himself and the Romans as was never forgotten. There is no doubt that this feeling of violent antagonism to the Empire and its ruler made the task of the Arab invaders easier. It must not, however, be supposed that the Copts submitted tamely to the Arab invasion. The deciding factor in the conquest was the treachery of Cyrus who, in his capacity as civil governor, handed over the country to the Arabs. Muslim historians refer to him as the Muqauqas, and many legends gathered round his name. The identification of Cyrus with the Muqauqas was first made by A. J. Butler and now seems to be gaining acceptance.[1]

[1] A. J. Butler, *Arab Conquest of Egypt*. See *Encyclopedia of Islam*, s.v. *Egypt* (II, 5), and S. Lane-Poole, *History of Egypt*, p. 5 n. 4.

Chapter IV

THE FATE OF THE CHRISTIANS AT THE TIME OF THE MUSLIM CONQUEST

The spectacular advance of the Muslim armies into Persia, Syria and Egypt was regarded by later Muslim writers as evidence of the hand of God. Muhammad himself regarded warfare in the cause of Islam as "fighting in the way of God". Too often in history has aggressive war been blessed in the name of religion for us to be surprised at it. It is true that it was the new monotheistic religion of Arabia which was the cord that bound together the Arab tribes and made their conquests possible. It is also true that wherever the armies went they called on people to join in their confederation which they called Islam. But we must not imagine that the call to Islam of those early conquerors was a call to religion in the sense of moral amendment of life. It was indeed a call to win heaven and escape hell, a felicitous end to be attained simply by joining the confederation. It was to solid material advantage that the call was made; and the vast booty that was gathered in during the first conquests was both a foretaste and a guarantee of the pleasures of heaven. It cannot be denied that the Arab tribes only joined wholeheartedly in the movement when they saw the booty coming in, and the promise of lands more fertile than Arabia. From their point of view this was an earnest of greater things to come: those who died fighting "in the way of God" attained the greater things sooner; those who survived enjoyed during their lifetime the riches of the conquered provinces. No consideration for the sufferings of the conquered races stayed the Muslims from draining them of their wealth, though they soon learnt not to tax them to extinction for fear that later generations of Muslims would have no sources of wealth to draw upon.[1] Only it was open to the conquered

[1] See Abū Yūsuf, *Kitāb al-kharāj*, p. 125, trans. p. 159.

peoples to share in the blessings of Islam by themselves joining in the movement, and so swelling the numbers of those who went out on the great career of conquest. In most cases such submission to Islam only came after defeat in battle, when their lands had already been devastated and their houses pillaged. All classes and sects must have suffered equally in this way, whether they accepted Islam or not. But when the conquest was complete the position of the subject peoples who retained their old religions was regularised by treaties, most of which were made locally with particular cities, districts or tribes. Our special interest is in the treatment meted out to the Christians. From what we learn from the Quran of Muhammad's feelings towards the "people of the book", and towards the Christians in particular, it is not surprising that the terms granted to Christians allowed them to continue the practice of their religion, and that they were not offered the alternatives of Islam or the sword.[1] Such terms were of course granted after the resistance had been broken down, and many Christians must have been slain in battle before the treaties were made. The distinction between the treatment of Arab and non-Arab, and between the treatment of people of the book and idolaters can scarcely be better described than in the words of Abū Yūsuf, who wrote between A.D. 786 and 798:

> The land of the Arabs is different from the land of the non-Arabs in this respect that the Arabs are only fought against to make them accept Islam. *Jizya* [i.e. the poll-tax] was not demanded of them, and nothing but the acceptance of Islam was accepted of them....But the ruling with regard to the Arabs is not the same as the ruling with regard to non-Arabs, for the non-Arabs are fought against for two reasons, that they should become Muslims or that they should pay the *jizya*, but the Arabs are not fought against except that they should become Muslims: either they should become Muslims or they should be killed. And we do not know that the Prophet of God or any one of his companions or

[1] The expression "Mohammed, with the sword in one hand and the Koran in the other" comes from Gibbon, *Decline and Fall*, ch. L (Everyman's Library edition, V, 207).

any one of the caliphs after him received *jizya* from the idolaters among the Arabs. It was only acceptance of Islam or death. And if they were conquered their women and children were taken captive, just as the Prophet of God on the day of Ḥunain led captive the women and children of Hawāzin, but afterwards he forgave them and let them go. But he only did this with the idolaters among them. As for the people of the book among the Arabs, they were in the same position as the non-Arabs: the *jizya* was accepted from them; just as 'Umar doubled the poor-tax for the Banū Taghlib in place of the *kharāj*, and as the Prophet of God imposed upon every adult man of the people of Yaman one dinar or its equivalent in Ma'āfirite cloth. And this in our opinion was like the case of the people of the book, and like the way in which peace was granted to the people of Najrān in exchange for a ransom. And as for the non-Arabs, the *jizya* is accepted from the people of the book among them, and from the polytheists, and the idolaters and the fire-worshippers, from their men. Now the Prophet of God had taken *jizya* from the Magians of the people of Hajar, and the Magians are polytheists and are not people of a book.[1]

In one point this ruling of Abū Yūsuf, who was of the legal school of Abu Ḥanīfa, was not followed by the later school of ash-Shāfi'ī, for he would not allow idolaters any alternative except the sword or Islam. Ash-Shāfi'ī, however, reckoned Zoroastrians as people of the book, for it was necessary to follow the precedent that Muhammad had accepted *jizya* from the Zoroastrians of Hajar on the west coast of the Persian Gulf, as stated above by Abū Yūsuf, and also from those of al-Yaman.[2] Baiḍāwi in his commentary on Sura ix. 29 says:

The meaning of the verse is that the *jizya* should be specially demanded from the people of the book; and it is established that 'Umar used not to take the *jizya* from the Magians until 'Abd ar-Raḥmān b. 'Auf witnessed in his presence that the Prophet had taken it from the Magians of Hajar, and that he said, "Treat them according to the rule of the people of the book", and that was because they have something like a book, so they are attached to the people of the book. But as for the rest of the unbelievers, *jizya* is not taken from them according to us; but according to Abu Ḥanīfa it is taken from them except from the idolaters of the

1 *Kitāb al-kharāj*, p. 79, trans. p. 100.

2 Al-Balādhurī, *Futūḥ al-buldān*, p. 78, trans. I, 110.

Arabs according to what is reported by az-Zuhrī that the Prophet made peace with the idol worshippers except those who were Arabs; and according to Mālik it is taken from all unbelievers except apostates.

The records that we have of the treaties actually made with Christians show that they were given the right to retain their religion in return for the payment of taxation. Thus, for instance, when the Muslim general Khālid had conquered the Banū Ḥīra he granted them security of their religion on the following terms:

This is the writing of Khālid b. al-Walīd to the people of Ḥīra. Abu Bakr as-Siddīq, the caliph of the Prophet of God, commanded me that when I returned from the people of Yemama I should go to the people of 'Irāq, both Arabs and non-Arabs, and invite them to God and His Prophet, and announce unto them Paradise and warn them of the Fire; and if they agreed they would have the same rights as Muslims and have the same charges imposed upon them. And I came to al-Ḥīra, and there came forth to meet me Iyās b. Qabīṣa aṭ-Ṭā'ī together with certain chiefs of the people of al-Ḥīra. And I invited them to God and His Prophet, and they refused to accept, so I put before them the *jizya* or the sword. And they said, "We have no strength to fight against thee, but make peace with us on the same conditions of paying *jizya* as the other people of the book". And I surveyed the number of them, and found their number to be 7000 men; then I examined them and found that there were 1000 men with chronic diseases, and I subtracted them from the total, so the number on whom the *jizya* fell was 6000. And they made peace with me on the basis of 60,000 [pieces of silver]. And I made an agreement with them that the pact and contract of God which was made in the case of the people of the Torah and the Injīl should be binding upon them, viz. that they should not raise opposition, nor assist an unbeliever against a Muslim, whether Arab or non-Arab, nor disclose to them the vulnerable places of the Muslims.[1]...

According to Yaḥyā b. Ādam[2] no treaties were made with the people of 'Irāq except with the Banū Ḥīra and the Banū Ṣalūbā, the rest of the land having been taken by force, the supposition being that treaties had only been granted to

[1] Abū Yūsuf, p. 171, trans. p. 222.
[2] Yaḥyā b. Ādam, *Kitāb al-kharāj*, pp. 32–5.

people who surrendered willingly. The town of Anbār, near the northern border which separated 'Irāq from al-Jazīrah or Mesopotamia, is specially mentioned as having no treaty. It is not surprising that 'Irāq, which bore the brunt of the first Muslim invasion, should have been taken by force, while the people of Mesopotamia should have surrendered in time to secure favourable terms.

Al-Balādhurī gives us in brief the terms granted to Christians in a number of towns of Mesopotamia. Thus:

> When 'Iyāḍ b. Ghanm, who was sent by Abū 'Ubaida, reduced ar-Ruhā [Edessa], he stood at its gate riding a brown horse; and the inhabitants made terms stipulating that they should keep their cathedral and the buildings around it, and agreeing not to start a new church other than what they already had, to give succour to the Muslims against their enemy, and to forfeit their right of protection in case they failed to keep any of these conditions. Similar terms to those of ar-Ruhā were made by the people of Mesopotamia.[1]
>
> This is what 'Iyāḍ b. Ghanm gave to the people of ar-Raqqah when he entered the city. He gave them security for their lives and possessions. Their churches shall not be destroyed or occupied, so long as they pay the tax assessed on them and enter into no intrigue. It is stipulated that they build no new church or place of worship, or publicly strike clappers [wooden boards used as church bells], or openly celebrate Easter Monday, or show the cross in public.[2]

Further conditions in other cases were that the Christians should guide Muslims who had lost their way, and that they should repair the roads and bridges.[3] The names of a number of towns are given which surrendered on similar terms, including towns in Armenia.[4]

The conditions imposed upon the Banū Taghlib were peculiar. They were so proud of their Arab blood that they did not wish to be treated as non-Muslims, and therefore objected to paying the *jizya*, but agreed to pay double the

[1] P. 179, trans. p. 269.
[2] P. 181, trans. p. 271.
[3] P. 182, trans. p. 273.
[4] P. 208, trans. p. 314.

amount of poor tax that the Muslims paid. At the same time they were unwilling themselves to give up their Christianity, though they agreed not to baptise their children. It is difficult to see why they agreed to this last condition. At any rate they appear to have ignored it, and to have continued to baptise their children. For the first half-century of Islam they remained a powerful tribe of which the great majority were Christian.[1] Abū Yūsuf records as follows:

> And 'Umar made peace with them [the Banū Taghlib] on the condition that they should not baptise [lit. "plunge into water"] any of their children into Christianity, and that their poor-tax should be doubled. And 'Ubāda used to say, "They did this without any covenant being imposed upon them; and that the *jizya* should not be charged to them".

Further he says,

> He [i.e. Ziyād, who had been sent to collect the taxes] said, And he ['Umar] commanded me to act sternly with the Christians of the Banū Taghlib, saying that they were Arabs and not people of the book, and perhaps they would become Muslims. He also said that 'Umar made a condition that the Christians of the Banū Taghlib should not make their children Christians.[2]

Balādhurī gives the two following records:

> Dā'ūd b. Kurdūs used to repeat that they had no claim to security [*dhimma*] because they used immersion in their ritual—referring to baptism,

and

> According to Mughirah, 'Alī used to repeat, If I should have time to deal with the Banū Taghlib, I would have my own way with them. Their fighters I would surely put to death, and their children I would take as captives, because by making their children Christians they violated the covenant and are no more in our trust [*dhimma*].[3]

[1] Lammens, *Journal Asiatique*, série ix, tome IV (1894), "Le Chantre des Omiades", pp. 97–9.

[2] Pp. 143–4, trans. pp. 184, 186.

[3] Pp. 190–1, trans. pp. 285–6.

One of several traditions about the Banū Taghlib collected by Yaḥyā b. Ādam runs as follows:

> ʻUmar b. al-Khaṭṭāb made peace with the Banū Taghlib on the condition that he should double their poor-tax, and that they should not prevent any one of them from becoming a Muslim, and that they should not immerse their children.[1]

Ṭabarī evidently knew the tradition in this last form, and took "their children" as meaning the children of those who had become Muslims, for he says that the condition was only "that they should not make Christian the children whose parents had become Muslims", thus trying to explain away an unusual and unreasonable condition.[2]

The Christians of Yaman and of Najrān were granted religious liberty on payment of a tax, which in their case took the form of a tribute of cloth. The rescript from Muhammad to the Christians of Najrān as given by Abū Yūsuf contained the following guarantee of freedom:

> Najrān shall have the patronage of God and the protection of Muhammad the Prophet, the Apostle of God, for their goods and their lives, their lands and their religion, their absent ones, their present ones, and their relatives, their churches, and all that is in their hands whether small or great.[3] A bishop shall not be moved from his bishopric, nor a monk from his monastic life, nor a priest from his priesthood.[4]

During the days of ʻUmar the people of the book were expelled from Arabia:

> ʻUmar b. al-Khaṭṭāb investigated until he found it certain and assured that the Prophet had said, There can be no two religions at the same time in the Arabian peninsula. Accordingly he expelled the Jews of Khaibar.[5]

Presumably as part of the same policy the Christians of Najrān were expelled and granted new lands in ʻIrāq. The excuse given for this breach of the treaty made by Muhammad was

[1] Pp. 47–8.
[2] I, 2482.
[3] Balādhurī, p. 72, trans. p. 100, adds "their camels, messengers and images".
[4] P. 86, trans. p. 109.
[5] Balādhurī, p. 34, trans. p. 48.

according to Abū Yūsuf,[1] "because 'Umar feared that they might harm the Muslims". This rather cryptic remark is explained by Al-Balādhurī as follows:[2] "they began to practise usury and became so numerous as to be considered by him a menace to Islam". The Christians of Yaman proper appear, however, not to have been expelled, perhaps because of their greater distance from Mecca, for there is evidence of the existence of a Christian community there in the eighth century.[3] They may even have continued for some centuries, for Cheikho says:

> In the sixteenth century the book of the Spaniard Ordeno de Cenaltos mentions that on his journey to the Maghrib he met some Arab tribes who surrounded him and asserted that they originated from Christian Arabs in Yaman. And the Capuchin missionaries in Aden in 1895 tell us that they found among certain people of Yaman traces which they had evidently inherited from their Christian ancestors.[4]

The expulsion of Christians was not completely carried out at first even in the Hijāz. A Christian Abu Zaid accompanied 'Uthmān as his confidant, and the Christian musician Ḥunain of Ḥīra was invited to Madīna by his fellow-musicians, and died there in the house of a great-granddaughter of Muhammad.[5] The later history of the Christians of Najrān in their new home in 'Irāq is instructive, as it shows the sort of treatment they received, and also their gradually decreasing numbers:

> When 'Uthmān b. 'Affān became Caliph he wrote to his governor in al-Kūfa...as follows, "Greetings. The civil ruler, the bishop and the nobles of Najrān have presented to me the written statement of the Prophet, and have shown me the recommendation of 'Umar. Having made enquiry concerning their case from 'Uthmān b. Ḥunaif, I learned that he had investigated their state and found it injurious to the great landlords [*dihqāns*] whom they prevented from possessing their land. I have therefore reduced

[1] P. 87, trans. p. 110.
[2] P. 72–3, trans. pp. 102–4.
[3] See above, p. 12.
[4] *Christianisme en Arabie*, p. 68.
[5] Lammens, "Le Chantre des Omiades", p. 236, referring to Aghani, XI, 24 and II, 127.

their taxation by 200 robes[1] for the sake of God and in place of their old lands. I recommend them to thee as they are included among the people entitled to our protection". When Mu'āwiya [or Yazīd b. Mu'āwiya] came into power they complained to him because of their dispersion, the death of some of them, and the conversion to Islam of others. They also presented the statement issued by 'Uthmān b. 'Affān for the reduction of the number of robes. To this they added, "And now we have still more decreased and become weaker". He then reduced the number by another 200 robes, thus reducing the original number by 400.

Al-Ḥajjāj, the tyrannical governor of 'Irāq, raised the tribute again to 1800 robes.

When 'Umar b. 'Abd al-'Azīz came into power [A.D. 717] they complained to him that they were in danger of extinction, that they were decreasing in number, that the continual raids of the Arabs overburdened them with heavy taxes for revictualling them, and that they suffered from the unjust treatment of al-Ḥajjāj. By 'Umar's orders their census was taken, and it was found that they were reduced to one-tenth of their original number, upon which 'Umar said, "I consider that the terms of this capitulation impose a tax upon their heads and not on their lands. The poll-tax of the dead and the Muslims, however, is annulled". He therefore held them responsible for 200 robes of the value of 8000 dirhems.[2]

The reduction of the number of Christians of Najrān from 40,000 to 4000 in the space of about eighty years is one of the few definite details we have of the diminution of Christians under Islam. It is not, however, to be supposed that non-Arab Christians diminished so rapidly, for it is evident that much more pressure was brought to bear upon Arab Christians to become Muslims, as we have seen, for instance, in the case of the Banū Taghlib.

There does not appear to have been any treaty with the Christians of the Banū Ghassān. Some of them became Muslims, for we read of them fighting on the side of Mar-

[1] The original tribute was 2000 robes. Abū Yūsuf, p. 88, trans. p. 112, gives the reduction of tribute under 'Uthmān as only 30 robes.

[2] Balādhurī, p. 73, trans. p. 102.

wān I in the battle of Marj Rāhiṭ in the year A.D. 684,[1] and it does not seem probable that Christians would have been allowed to fight in Muslim armies as late as that although they certainly did so in the first days of the conquest. But others of them remained Christians, and fled into Roman territory:

Jabalah b. al-Aiham sided with the Anṣār, saying, "Ye are our brethren and the sons of our fathers", and professed Islam. After the arrival of 'Umar b. al-Khaṭṭāb in Syria, in the year 17, Jabalah had a dispute with one of the Muzainah and knocked out his eye. 'Umar ordered that he be punished, upon which Jabalah said, "Is his eye like mine? Never, by God, shall I abide in a town where I am under authority". He then apostatised and went to the land of the Greeks. This Jabalah was the king of Ghassān and the successor of al-Ḥārith b. abi Shimr. According to another report, when Jabalah came to 'Umar b. al-Khaṭṭāb he was still a Christian. 'Umar asked him to accept Islam and pay the poor-tax; but he refused, saying, "I shall keep my faith and pay the poor-tax". 'Umar's answer was, "If thou keepest thy faith, thou hast to pay poll-tax". The man refused, and 'Umar added, "We have only three alternatives for thee, Islam, tax, or going whither thou willest". Accordingly Jabalah left with 30,000 men to the land of the Greeks [Asia Minor].[2]

One of the most surprising vicissitudes of history was that nearly two centuries later a Byzantine Emperor, Nicephorus I (A.D. 802–11), claimed to be a lineal descendant of this Jabalah of the Banū Ghassān.[3] Arnold says:

Many of the Arabs of the renowned tribe of the Banū Ghassān, Arabs of the purest blood, who embraced Christianity towards the end of the fourth century, still retain the Christian faith, and since their submission to the Church of Rome about two centuries ago employ the Arabic language in their religious services.[4]

[1] Muir, *Caliphate*, p. 319.

[2] Balādhurī, p. 142, trans. pp. 208–9.

[3] Finlay, *History of the Byzantine Empire* (Everyman's Library, p. 86).

[4] *Preaching of Islam*, p. 47, quoting from W. G. Palgrave, *Essays on Eastern Questions*, pp. 206–8.

A solitary example of forced conversion of Christians to Islam is found in the account of the occupation of the monastery of Mount Sinai by the Muslims, written, according to its editor, by a contemporary monk. The story goes that the servants of the monastery lived near the camp of Pharan, a place according to Cosmas Indicopleustes six miles from Sinai. The Muslims came and attacked the servants till the latter found that they were not strong enough to resist any longer, and became Muslims. One of them, however, preferring death to apostasy, determined to flee. His wife thereupon begged him not to leave her and her children to fall into the hands of the Saracens, but to kill them as an offering to God like Abraham. So he took a sword and slew them, and then fled. After wandering some time in the desert he reached the sacred Bush, which is inside the monastery of St Catherine. There he had a wonderful vision of holy fathers who at some earlier time had died as martyrs. The story ends thus:

It was, in my opinion at least, angelic troops which came to appear under the form of fathers who were martyred in this place and were reclothed with the crown of victory, in order to honour and escort him who had followed their example in the very place where they had dwelt, and had shown more affection and faith towards God than the saints who were before him.[1]

The general conditions made with the Christians and Jews at the time of the Muslim conquest are thus described by Abū Yūsuf:

As to thy question, O Commander of the Faithful, concerning the *dhimmis*, how it is that their synagogues and churches in the important towns or other places of the Muslim conquest have been left to them without being destroyed, and how it is that they have been allowed to continue to display their crosses at the time of their festivals, the reason thereof is that the arrangement made between the Muslims and the *dhimmis* only took place on condition that neither their churches nor their synagogues, whether within or without the walls, should be destroyed, that their lives should be respected, and that they should be allowed liberty to

[1] Nau, *Les Récits inédits du Moine Anastase.*

fight against and repel their enemies. Such are the conditions following the payment of the *jizya*, and under which the peace was concluded, and the written agreements demanded the non-erection of new churches or synagogues. It is thus that the whole of Syria and the great part of Ḥīra was conquered, which explains why the churches and synagogues have been respected.[1]

An example of these conditions of security is to be seen in the terms granted to Jerusalem:

The following are the terms of capitulation which I, 'Umar, the servant of God, the Commander of the Faithful, grant to the people of Jerusalem. I grant them security for their lives, their possessions, and their children, their churches, their crosses, and all that appertains to them in their integrity, and their lands, and to all of their religion. Their churches therein shall not be impoverished, nor destroyed, nor injured from among them; neither their endowments nor their dignity; and not a thing of their property; neither shall the inhabitants of Jerusalem be exposed to violence in following their religion; nor shall one of them be injured.[2]

For the Monophysites of Syria the predominant feeling at the Muslim invasion appears to have been a sense of relief that they were now able to practise their religion unhindered by the persecution of the Romans. Michael the Syrian, a Jacobite Patriarch of Antioch in the latter half of the twelfth century, says that the Emperor Heraclius

wrote throughout his Empire that anyone who would not adhere to the Council of Chalcedon was to have his nose and ears cut off and his house pillaged. This persecution lasted a long time... Heraclius did not permit the orthodox [i.e. the Jacobites] to present themselves before him, and would not receive their complaints with regard to the theft of their churches. That is why the God of vengeance, who is alone the almighty, who changes the empire of men according to His will, and raises to it the most humble, seeing the wickedness of the Romans who, wherever they ruled, cruelly robbed our churches and monasteries and condemned us without pity, raised from the region of the south the Children of Ishmael to deliver us by them from the hands of the Romans. And if, in truth, we suffered some loss because the

1 P. 164, trans. p. 213.

2 Quoted by Arnold, *Preaching of Islam*, p. 51.

catholic [i.e. Jacobite] churches which had been taken from us and had been given to the Chalcedonians [i.e. the Melkites] remained in their hands—because when the towns submitted to the Arabs they gave to each sect the temples which they found in its possession, and because at that time the great church at Edessa and that of Ḥarran had been taken from us—yet it was no light advantage for us to be delivered from the cruelty of the Romans, from their wickedness, from their anger, from their cruel zeal towards us, and to find ourselves at rest.[1]

Michael goes on to speak of the horrors of the Arab invasion, the capture of slaves, the pillaging, and the destruction of lands, but evidently regarded these things as the effects of war, and not as persecutions of Christians for their faith. The Monophysites of Egypt also remembered the Muslim invasion as a relief from persecution. A work written in Egypt at the beginning of the thirteenth century, and attributed to Abū Ṣāliḥ the Armenian, says:

This was the period during which the Emperor oppressed the orthodox people, and required them to conform to his creed, which was contrary to the truth. From these two men [i.e. Heraclius and the Muqauqas] the Christians suffered great persecution, yet they would not deny their faith. But in their time the Hanifite nation appeared, and humbled the Romans, and slew many of them, and took possession of the whole of the land of Egypt. Thus the Jacobite Christians were freed from the tyranny [of the Romans].[2]

Nestorian tradition also has it that the Christians were glad at the Arab invasion. An unknown Nestorian chronicler, who wrote somewhere between the ninth and the thirteenth centuries, says:

The countries were overthrown by the entry of the Arabs for the space of five years with uninterrupted evils and continual trials until the rule of the Arabs was established. And they demanded the *jizya* of the subject people, and they paid it. And they treated them well. And affairs prospered by the grace of

[1] *Chronique de Michel le Syrien*, II, 412–13.

[2] *The Churches and Monasteries of Egypt*, edited and translated by B. T. A. Evetts, pp. 230–1.

God most high. And the hearts of the Christians rejoiced over the domination of the Arabs (may God strengthen it and prosper it).[1]

In certain cases special diplomas were granted to the Nestorian Patriarchs. Thus the Nestorian chronicler Mari says that 'Umar gave a diploma to Īshū'yāb II "that no *jizya* should be exacted from his brothers and servants and adherents", and that this diploma was preserved to his day, i.e. about 1300;[2] and that 'Ali gave a similar diploma to the Patriarch Mārāma with regard to the Christians and with regard to observing the pact which assured their protection.[3] There was a natural tendency in later times to forge such diplomas in order to get better treatment from the Muslims. An example of an obviously forged diploma, supposed to have been addressed by Muhammad himself to the Christians of Najrān and all other Christians, is to be found in the *Chronique de Séert*.[4] But that the Nestorian Patriarchs did actually receive diplomas from the early caliphs is acknowledged by the Caliph al-Qāim in the diploma which he granted in the year 1075 to the Nestorian Catholicus 'Abdīshū', for he says:[5] "The noble diplomas in the days of the Rightly Guided Caliphs said this to thy predecessors in thy office". That the early caliphs were favourably disposed towards the Nestorian Church is also shown by a letter written by the Patriarch Īshū'yāb III to Simeon of Rēvardashīr in Fārs, in which he says:

> Those Tai, or Arabs, to whom God has granted the rule of the lands at this time, lo! they are with us as you know, but they have not attacked the Christian religion, but rather they have commended our faith, honoured our priests and the saints of the Lord, and conferred benefits on churches and monasteries.[6]

[1] *Chronique de Séert*, II, 261. [2] Mari, fol. 177 *b*.

[3] Mari, fol. 178 *a*, but unless this diploma was given before 'Alī succeeded to the Caliphate it must be an error, as Mārāma was Patriarch A.D. 647–50 or A.D. 644–7, and 'Alī did not succeed till A.D. 656.

[4] Part 2 (II), p. 602. See the editor's note on that page, and also Assemani, III, pt II, XCV.

[5] Mari, fol. 237 *b*. [6] Assemani, III, pt II, XCVI.

This patriarch reigned from A.D. 647 or 650–60, so the letter must have been written in the days of 'Uthmān or 'Alī.

Although the subject of this book is Christianity in Asia, it is not possible to leave Egypt out of account, owing to the close connexion between Egypt and Syria. With regard to the treatment of the Christians in Egypt we have some rather contradictory statements preserved by Al-Balādhurī:

> There is disagreement regarding the conquest of Miṣr [i.e. either Egypt or Cairo]. Some say it was conquered by force, and others by capitulation....The chief of Miṣr said to my father ['Amr b. al-'Āṣ], "We have heard of what you did in Syria, and how ye assessed poll-tax on the Christians and Jews, leaving the land in the hands of its owners to utilise it and pay its *kharāj*. If ye treat us in the same way, it would do you more good than to kill, capture and expel us...". Accordingly, he assessed on every adult, excepting the poor, two dinars as poll-tax, and on every land-owner in addition....To this end a statement was written, in which it was stipulated that, so long as they lived up to these terms, their women and children would neither be sold nor taken captives, and their possessions and treasures would be kept in their hands. This statement was submitted to 'Umar the Commander of the Faithful who endorsed it. Thus the whole land became *kharāj* land. Because, however, 'Amr signed the contract and the statement some people thought that Miṣr was taken by capitulation.
>
> I heard 'Amr b. al-'Aṣ say from the pulpit, "I have occupied this position and am bound to none of the Egyptian Copts by covenant or contract. If I want I can kill; if I want I can take one-fifth of the possessions; if I want I can sell captives. The people of Anṭābulus [Pentapolis] are excluded because they have a covenant which must be kept".
>
> The Egyptians had a covenant and a contract. 'Amr gave them a statement to the effect that they were secure with respect to their possessions, lives and children, and that none of them would be sold as slaves. He imposed upon them a *kharāj* not to be increased, and promised to expel all fear of attack by an enemy.[1]

Ṭabarī gives what professes to be a copy of the treaty made by 'Amr b. al-'Āṣ with the Egyptians, but it is probably a later composition. One clause permits partial remission of the

[1] Pp. 221–5, trans. pp. 338–43.

jizya if the Nile failed to rise normally, a concession not likely to have been made before the need for it arose.[1] The Copts themselves evidently felt that 'Amr had deceived them, and the two following quotations from John of Nikiu, who flourished towards the end of the seventh century, show the mixed feelings of the Copts towards 'Amr:

> 'Amr had no mercy on the Egyptians, and did not observe the covenant they had made with him, for he was of a barbaric race.
>
> And 'Amr became stronger every day in every field of his activity. And he exacted the taxes which had been determined upon, but he took none of the property of the churches, and he committed no act of spoliation or plunder, and he preserved them throughout all his days. And when he seized the city of Alexandria, he had the canal drained in accordance with the instructions given by the apostate Theodore. And he increased the taxes to the extent of twenty-two *batr* of gold till all the people hid themselves owing to the greatness of the tribulation, and could not find the wherewithal to pay.[2]

[1] Ṭabarī, I, 2588.

[2] *Chronicle of John, Bishop of Nikiu*, pp. 195 and 200. For the fate of Christianity in North Africa see Iselin, *Der Untergang der christlichen Kirche in Nordafrika*.

Chapter V

CHRISTIANITY UNDER THE CALIPHS

With the completion of the Arab conquest, the Christians, together with the Jews and Zoroastrians, entered into the position of protected subject people or *dhimmis*, each community being as it were a little state within the state. In later times these communities were known as *melets*, and the system continued under successive Muslim dynasties until its abolition in Turkey in 1923. The *dhimmis* were not only tolerated, but were entitled to the protection of the state. They were not allowed to fight in the army; and in lieu of military service were subject to a special tax known as the *jizya*. Synonymous at first with *kharāj*, the term *jizya* came to be applied solely to the poll-tax levied on *dhimmis*, while the term *kharāj* came to be used for the land tax which was levied on Muslims and non-Muslims alike. The amount of the *jizya* varied. At first it was normally one dinar annually (a gold coin of 4·25 grammes, i.e. a trifle more than the British half-sovereign which weighs 4 grammes), but this later became a minimum, and different amounts were charged to rich and poor. In accordance with the principle that the *jizya* was in lieu of military service, it was not exacted from women, children, aged men, or monks.[1] In imposing this extra tax on Christians the Muslims were following the example of their predecessors the Sassanian Emperors. We read that Sapor II, when he instituted his persecution A.D. 339–40, ordered Christians to pay double taxes as a contribution to the cost of the war, "for we have the troubles of the war, and they only have rest and pleasures",[2] and an additional poll-tax on Christians, who

[1] See *Encycl. of Islam*, s.v. *Dhimmi and Djizya*, and Tritton, *The Caliphs and their non-Muslim subjects*, ch. xv.

[2] Labourt, *Christianisme dans l'Empire Perse*, p. 46; Wigram, *Introduction to the History of the Assyrian Church*, p. 63.

did no military service, was part of the system of government established by Chosroes I, A.D. 531–78.[1] It is written in the Quran (Sura ix. 29), "Fight them that believe not in God and the last day, and who hold not as forbidden what God and His apostle have forbidden, and do not profess the true religion, those that have a scripture, until they pay the *jizya* in person in subjection". The Muslim law books use this text to justify, not only the payment of *jizya*, but also the humiliating conditions to which the *dhimmis* were subjected. The chief of these conditions were that the *dhimmi* must be distinguished by his dress, must not ride on horseback, or carry weapons; he was also under certain legal disabilities as regards testimony in the law courts, protection under criminal law, and marriage.[2] On the other hand the *dhimmis* were guaranteed security of life and property in the exercise of their religion. They might repair and rebuild existing churches, but not erect churches on new sites. The distinctive dress of Christians was not an innovation on the part of the Muslims, for there is evidence that it was in vogue in the sixth century.[3] Even the *melet* system was not an innovation of the Muslims. Ever since the Council of Seleucia in A.D. 410 the Christian Church in Persia had been officially recognised as a separate community under the authority of its own Patriarch, or Catholicus as he was generally called. At that Council Yazdegerd I issued a firman ordering that the decisions of the Catholicus and a certain bishop named Marutha, who acted as diplomatist and ambassador, were to be final, and would be enforced by the royal power.[4] Rules were not made at that Council for the appointment of the Catholicus, but were made later, "but, as a matter of fact, he was usually nominated by the Shah-in-shah",[5] a practice which the Muslim rulers themselves soon adopted. The most surprising of the conditions imposed on the Christians was that they should build

[1] Wigram, *op. cit.* p. 190.
[2] See Tritton, *op. cit.* pp. 186–90.
[3] Wigram, *op. cit.* p. 230. [4] Wigram, *op. cit.* p. 95.
[5] Wigram, *op. cit.* p. 99.

no new churches. It is extremely difficult to imagine why they should have agreed to such a condition unless they had already lost their evangelical zeal. Less than a century before, the great Patriarch Mar Aba (A.D. 540–55) refused to buy his freedom by promising to make no more converts,[1] and we cannot imagine a man of such a spirit signing an agreement to build no new churches. If, however, it is true that the agreements were made locally with particular towns in the first instance, the Christians may not have envisaged the possibility of needing more churches in their particular area. Then, at a later time, when lawyers codified these local agreements into a general system for the treatment of *dhimmis*, the number of Muslims had so greatly increased, and the number of heathen within the Empire had diminished to such an extent, that conversions to Christianity were very few, so that generally speaking there was no necessity to build new churches.

It must, however, be remembered that, though these legal regulations for the *dhimmis* were sometimes enforced with great severity, even with the addition of further disabilities not provided for in the law, at other times they fell into abeyance. Arnold gives a long list of new churches which were built from time to time, including examples from every century from the seventh to the twelfth.[2] Al-Māwardi, writing in the first half of the eleventh century A.D., did not regard these regulations as universally binding. He says:

> In the poll-tax contract there are two clauses, one of which is indispensable and the other commendable. The former includes six articles: (1) they must not attack nor pervert the sacred book, (2) nor accuse the Prophet of falsehood nor refer to him with contempt, (3) nor speak of the religion of Islam to blame or controvert it, (4) nor approach a Muslim woman with a view either to illicit relations or to marriage, (5) nor turn a Muslim from the faith, nor harm him in person or possessions, (6) nor help the enemies or receive any of their spies. These are the duties which are strictly obligatory on them, and to which they must conform. There is no need for them to be stipulated, and if that

[1] Wigram, *op. cit.* p. 207. [2] *Preaching of Islam*, pp. 58–59.

is done it is only to make them known, to corroborate the solemnity of the agreement imposed upon them and to make it perfectly clear that the commission henceforth of one of these acts will entail the breach of the treaty which has been agreed upon with them. The second clause, which is only commendable, also deals with six points: (1) change of external appearance by wearing a distinctive mark, the *ghiyār*, and the special waistbelt *zunnār*,[1] (2) prohibition of erecting buildings higher than those of the Muslims; they must only be of equal height or less, (3) prohibition of offending the ears of Muslims by the sound of the bell *nāqūs*, by reading their books, and by their claims concerning 'Uzair and the Messiah, (4) prohibition of drinking wine publicly and of displaying their crosses and swine, (5) the obligation to proceed secretly to the burial of their dead without a display of tears and lamentations, (6) prohibition of riding on horses, whether pure-bred or mixed, though they are allowed to use mules and asses. These six commendable prescriptions are not necessarily included in the contract of protection, unless they have been expressly stipulated, in which case they are strictly obligatory. The fact of contravening them where they have been stipulated does not entail breach of the contract, but the unbelievers are compelled by force to respect them, and are punished for having violated them. They do not incur punishment when nothing has been stipulated about it.[2]

As an example of the sporadic way in which the regulations were enforced, we read that between the years 1091 and 1105 the Christians in Baghdad were compelled to wear the distinctive dress. In 1105 an attempt was made by an over-zealous officer to enforce the same rule in Mosul, but the sudden death of the officer resulted in the order being rescinded both in Mosul and in Baghdad.[3] In the ninth century Abu 'Uthmān 'Amr b. Bahr al-Jāḥiẓ (who died A.D. 869) wrote a violent attack against the Christians which, even allowing for exaggeration, shows that the regulations were largely disregarded at that time. He said:

We do not disagree with the people with regard to the great wealth of the Christians, and that they have an established power, and that their water is pure, and that their business is reputable;

[1] ζωνάρη.

[2] *Les Statuts Gouvernmentaux*, trans. by Fagnan, pp. 305–6.

[3] Mari, fol. 244 *a*.

and we only disagree with regard to the difference there is between the two heresies and the two parties [i.e. between the Christians and the Jews], in the strength of the opposition and of the obstinacy, and the revenge against the people of Islam in all manner of trickery, to say nothing of the ignoble character of the origins and the vileness of the roots. And as for their power and their trade and their form, we know that they take hackney horses and racing steeds, and they gather crowds together, and smite with the mallet [i.e. on the board used as a church bell], and the citizens ogle at them, and they put on thick material and the overcoat, and they take hired servants, and they are called Ḥasan and Ḥusain and 'Abbas and Faḍl and 'Alī, and they all take these as surnames; and there is nothing left but that they should be called Muhammad and be surnamed Abu 'l-Qāsim. And the Muslims inclined towards them. And most of them gave up wearing the waist-belts, while others wore them under their clothes. And most of their great ones abstained from giving the *jizya*, and refused to pay it, although they were able to do so. And they hit him who hit them, and smote him who smote them. And they did not do what was in their power. And most of them, and our judges and our people, saw that the blood of the Catholicus and the Metropolitan and the Bishop was worth as much as the blood of Ja'far and 'Alī and al-'Abbas and Ḥamza.[1]

About the same time we have the evidence of the Melkite Patriarch of Jerusalem concerning the good reputation the Muslims had in the eyes of the Christians. In the same year that al-Jāḥiẓ died he wrote a letter to the Patriarch of Constantinople in which he said of the Muslims,[2] "They are just, and do us no wrong or violence of any kind". The treatment of Christians by Muslims is thus described by Ēlīyyā, Metropolitan of Naṣībīn 1008–1049:

What we believe concerning the Muslims is that their obedience and love impresses us more than the obedience of people of all other religions and kingdoms that are opposed to us, whether we are in their land or not, and whether they treat us well or not. And that is because the Muslims regard it as a matter of religion and duty to protect us, to honour us, and to treat us well. And whosoever of them oppresses us, their Master, i.e. their Prophet, will be his adversary on the day of resurrection. And their law

[1] *Three Essays*, edited by J. Finkel, p. 18.
[2] Bréhier, *Les Croisades*, p. 31.

approves of us and distinguishes us from the people of other religions, whether Magians or Hindus or Ṣabians or the others who are opposed to us.... It is clear also that the Muslims, when they have oppressed us and done us wrong, and then have turned to their law, find that it does not approve of their harming and oppressing us; but people of other religions, when they honour us and do us good, and turn to their law, find that it does not praise them for this. So the wrong doing of the Muslims towards us, and their enmity against us, and their confession that in treating us thus they are acting contrary to their law, is better for us than the good treatment of others who confess that it is contrary to their law to treat us well.[1]

We may suspect some element of flattery in the last sentence, for it is difficult to think what non-Christian non-Muslim rulers he was thinking of. He may have been thinking of the Christians living under Chinese, Mongolian, Tibetan, Turkish or Indian rulers, for we have remarkably little knowledge of how the Christians were treated who lived in those lands. His remarks would certainly gain point if the conjecture made below in Chapter VII is correct that Christianity in China had greatly diminished during the tenth century, and if that diminution was due to persecution by the Chinese authorities. Or he may have been merely thinking of the treatment of Christians by the Sassanian rulers of Persia before Islam. But even allowing for flattery, it is interesting evidence that oppression of the Christians, though taking place at times, was not countenanced by the Muslim lawyers.

One cause of the diminution of the Christian population in Western Asia, which must not be overlooked, was emigration into the territory of the Byzantine Empire. The Christians near the frontier suffered in the reign of Hārūn ar-Rashīd (A.D. 786–809) in consequence of his campaigns with the Emperor Nicephorus I, as we shall see presently, and the result was that 12,000 Armenians crossed the border and settled in Byzantine territory. The same thing happened again in the reign of al-Ma'mūn (A.D. 813–33). At that time

[1] *Dialogues with the Wazir al-Maghrabi*, in Cheikho, *Trois Traités*, pp. 66–7.

the country was thrown into disorder by the rebellion of Bābak, and large numbers of people, mostly Christian, fled for safety into Asia Minor and settled at Sinope on the coast of the Black Sea. So considerable was the immigration that the Emperor Theophilus (A.D. 829–42) enacted a law that the marriage of Persians and Romans should in no way derogate from the rights of those who were citizens of the Empire.[1] On the other hand, in the middle of the ninth century, the Christian schismatical sect of the Paulicians fled from the persecution of Michael III (A.D. 842–67) into Muslim territory, and joined with the Muslims in carrying out raids on Byzantine territory. But these Paulicians did not add to the strength of Christianity in Asia, because by their peculiar principles they did not recognise any Church order, and consequently could not join up with the Nestorian or Jacobite Churches. As Christians the Paulicians may quite possibly have shown a higher standard of religion and morality than the greater Churches, in spite of the Adoptionist heresy of their theology. But the persecution they suffered drove them into political rebellion. The Byzantine Emperor Basil (A.D. 867–86) eventually waged a successful campaign against them; and those who were not slain were scattered abroad in the Byzantine Empire and in Armenia.[2]

Before the coming of Islam, in the fifth century A.D., the Sassanids, when not engaged in persecuting the Christians, favoured the Nestorians above other Christians, because they were quite independent of the Christians in the Roman Empire. Then in the beginning of the sixth century, when the Emperor Justin I (A.D. 518–27) enforced the ruling of the Council of Chalcedon against the Jacobites, and persecuted them, the Sassanid rulers were more inclined to tolerate Jacobites, so that sometimes Nestorians and sometimes Jacobites had the advantage; but the Melkites were driven out of Persia before the time of Muhammad. When the Muslims first came they do not seem to have distinguished between the

[1] Finlay, *History of the Byzantine Empire*, pp. 85, 141–2.
[2] Finlay, *op. cit.* pp. 85, 155–6, 227–30, 314.

different Christian sects, so that we find Jacobite bishops for the first time in Sijistan and Herāt, and the Melkites were able once more to set foot in Persia and Central Asia.[1] Marwān II, the last of the Umayyad Caliphs, granted a diploma to the Jacobite Patriarch of Antioch John II in A.D. 744.[2] The agreement entered into, A.D. 797–800, between Charlemagne and Hārūn ar-Rashīd, commonly known as "the Frankish Protectorate of the Holy Land", was probably a similar diploma, giving Charlemagne the position of authority over the Melkites of Syria and Palestine. Eventually, however, the Muslims adopted the policy of their predecessors of favouring the Nestorians and keeping them under strict control. From A.D. 987 the Nestorian Catholicus was appointed by the Caliph even against the wish of the bishops, and three-quarters of a century later the Caliph put all the Jacobite and Melkite bishops under the Nestorian Catholicus.[3]

Nestorian culture was centred in three towns—Naṣībīn, where was the famous theological school, Jundaisābūr (Bēth Lāpāṭ) the medical school, and Merv. The medical school at Jundaisābūr played a great part in the development of Arabic medicine. The Nestorian doctors there were the teachers of the great Arabic scientists and philosophers, who in fact got their knowledge of Greek literature through Syriac translations.[4] Christians were in great demand for public offices because they alone were educated. Before the ninth century, not only were Christians in demand as accountants for the purposes of taxation, but all the doctors, astrologers and philosophers were Christians. By the ninth century, however, the Muslims were becoming educated, and resentment began to be felt at all the best appointments being held by Christians. In the passage quoted above from al-Jāḥiẓ it is

1 Barthold, *Zur Geschichte des Christentums in Mittel-Asien*, p. 24; Barhebraeus, *Chron. Eccles.* II, col. 126.

2 Barhebraeus, *ibid.* I, col. 309, and see the editors' note *ad loc.*

3 Mari, fol. 228 *b*; Assemani III, pt II, IC.

4 Barthold, *op. cit.* pp. 26–7.

clear that he was angered by the pretensions of the Christians. Here is another passage from the same work referring explicitly to their occupations:

From the honour that they have in the hearts of the people, and the love of the lowest of the people for them, it comes that some of them are scribes of the sultans, and chamberlains of the kings, and physicians of the nobles, and perfumers and bankers; and you will not find a Jew except as a dyer or a tanner or a barber [who applies leeches] or a flute-player or a mender of broken crockery.[1]

The Jews, who were mostly engaged in humbler trades, could be despised, but the Christians who held important posts could not be ignored, and this accounts for the anger and violent language of al-Jāḥiẓ against them. The result of Christians holding high positions at court was that they gained great political power; and it is said that in the eighth century almost every election of a patriarch was engineered by a Christian doctor or scribe at the court.[2] Naturally too they were able to find many lesser posts for Christians. Though it was possible thus for Christians to gain positions at the court and retain their faith, there must have been many, whose Christianity was feeble, who conformed outwardly to the state religion in order to gain the Caliph's favour. The Caliph al-Ma'mūn, in a speech delivered to his courtiers, said openly that there were many such around him:

By God, I know well that so-and-so and so-and-so—naming a number of his special companions—profess Islam outwardly, but are free from it, and act hypocritically towards me; and I know that their inner thoughts are opposed to what they profess. And that is because they are people who have not entered into Islam out of earnest desire for our religion, but desiring access to us and aggrandisement in the power of our realm. They have no inner conviction, and no desire for the truth of the religion into which they enter.... And indeed I know that so-and-so and so-and-so—naming a number of his companions—were Christians and became

[1] Finkel, *Three Essays*, p. 17.

[2] Labourt, *De Timotheo I Nestorianorum Patriarcha*, p. 34.

Muslims although they were averse to it, so they are neither Muslims nor Christians.[1]

However insincere such people may have been, they were lost to Christianity, and their children would be brought up as Muslims.

Assemani summarises the treatment of the Nestorian Christians under the Caliphs as follows:

> But although the Nestorians were furnished with royal diplomas, and although they held positions as scribes and doctors at the court, and very often became famous rulers of places, nevertheless they suffered vexations from the Muslims no less than other Christians. The cause of the evils may be gathered from those things which I shall shortly relate, the most important being the inconstancy of the Caliphs, the greed of the rulers, and the innate hatred of the Muhammadan doctors and people towards the Christians. But not rarely the tempest of persecution was aroused by the mutual jealousy of the Christians themselves, the licence of the priests, the arrogance of the leaders, the tyrannical power of the magnates, and especially the altercations of the physicians and scribes about the highest authority over their people [i.e. the appointment of the Catholicus].[2]

Examples may be given of persecutions stirred up by individuals who brought false charges, e.g.

> Ḥamdūn [apparently a Muslim] was attending upon ar-Rashīd [Caliph A.D. 786–809], and out of hatred for the Christians he told him that they worshipped and bowed down before the bones of the dead which were in their churches, and he destroyed the churches of Baṣra and Ubullah and others. And the Christians who were in the service of ar-Rashīd gathered together and informed him that the Christians did not worship nor bow down before the bones of dead men, but only honoured the bodies of martyrs and pious people and apostles, as is done with the tombs of prophets and their bodies. And he verified what they said to him, and commanded the churches to be rebuilt.[3]

During the same reign the monks of a monastery at Aleppo asked the Patriarch of Antioch to consecrate one of their

[1] *Risalat al-Kindī*, pp. 73–4. See Muir, *Apology of al-Kindy*, p. xii.

[2] III, pt II, C.

[3] Mari, fol. 188 *a*.

number as their bishop, but he refused and tried to foist another bishop on them. They were so angry that

> they went to the Caliph Hārūn ar-Rashīd at Marj Dābiq and defamed the Patriarch saying, "He is a spy of the Greeks in our land, and is sending letters and messengers". The Caliph was therefore angry, and commanded all the new church buildings to be destroyed. Then the Arabs acted tyrannically, and brought great calamities not only upon Tagra but also upon the district of Antioch and on Jerusalem, and destroyed many ancient churches. So great disaster befell the Christians.[1]

We read that about half a century later a certain Christian named

> Ibrāhīm b. Nūḥ began out of hatred to accuse him [the Patriarch Theodosius] before al-Mutawakkil [Caliph A.D. 847–61] for his behaviour and the guile of Bokhtīshū' in regard to him. And al-Mutawakkil was angry and commanded him to be deposed, and a month after his appointment sent to Baghdad and put him in prison, and proceeded to destroy the churches and monasteries in Surra-man-rā'a [Sāmarrā], and treated the Christians harshly, and forbade their employment in the royal service. And they suffered this patiently....And al-Mutawakkil turned against Bokhtīshū' because he acted deceitfully towards him, and laid hold on him and put him in bonds. And he imprisoned the Catholicus after one month in Baghdad and brought him to Surra-man-rā'a; and he destroyed the monastery in Durqona and he granted it to Muhammad b. Jamīl, the chief of police, to build it into a hospice....And he prevented the Christians from riding on horses, and he commanded them to wear dyed garments and to put a patch upon their shirts, and that none of them should be seen in the market on Friday, and that the graves of their dead should be destroyed, and that their children should not learn Arabic in the schools, and that their house-tax should be brought to the mosque, and that wooden images of devils should be erected on their gates, and a sound summoning them to prayer should not be heard, and a place should not be set apart for the liturgy; and he destroyed a number of churches and religious buildings.[2]

Even in this persecution no Christians were executed for their faith, for Īshū'dād of Merv, writing his commentary

[1] Barhebraeus, *Chron. Eccles.* I, col. 340.

[2] Mari, fol. 191*a*–191*b*. Compare Barhebraeus, *Chron. Eccles.* II, col. 192.

about A.D. 850, could find no examples to illustrate the text "And the hour cometh that everyone that killeth you will think that he bringeth an offering", except an ancient persecution stirred up against the Christians on account of the reported misdoings of the Borborians.[1]

At times riots occurred and considerable damage was done before the authorities stepped in to stop it, e.g. we have it on the authority of an author, who wrote within sixteen or eighteen years of the event,[2] that in the reign of the Caliph al-Muqtadir

> the Muslims rose up in ar-Ramleh and destroyed two Melkite churches, the church of Mar Cosmas and the church of Mar Cyriacus; and they destroyed the church of 'Asqalān [Askelon] and that of Caesarea. That took place in the month of Jumada II, A.H. 311 [A.D. 923]. And the Christians reported it to al-Muqtadir, and he commanded them to build what had been destroyed of theirs. And the Muslims rose up in Tanīs and destroyed the Melkite church outside of Ḥims in Tanīs which is called the church of Būthūr in the month of Rajab. Then the Christians built the church in Tanīs; and when it was nearly finished, the Muslims rose up again the second time and destroyed what they had built, and burnt it with fire. Then the Sultan helped the Christians till they had built the church....And the Muslims rose up in Damascus and destroyed the Catholic church of Mart Maryam, and it was a very great and beautiful church on which 200,000 dinars had been spent. And all that was in it was pillaged, both the building itself and also the ornaments and curtains. And monasteries were destroyed, especially the monastery of the women which was by the side of the church, and many churches of the Melkites were ransacked, and they destroyed the church of the Nestorians. That took place in the middle of the month of Rajab in A.H. 312 [A.D. 924]....And 'Alī b. 'Īsā came into Egypt at the beginning of the month of Rajab, and he seized the monks and bishops, and demanded the *jizya* from them—from all the monks and the feeble and the poor and from all the monasteries in the lower part of as-Sa'īd [Upper Egypt], and from the bishops and the monks who were in the monastery of Mīnā. And certain of the monks went forth to Irāq and sought help from al-Muqtadir. And he wrote to them that the *jizya* should not be taken from them, and that their affairs should be as of old.

[1] *Commentaries of Isho'dad of Merv*, I, 270.

[2] Eutychius, pt II, 82–3.

That this sort of thing should have happened in the reign of al-Muqtadir is not surprising: the Caliph had scarcely any authority; the Muslims had been engaged in a disastrous war with the Byzantines and had been obliged to pay heavy ransom for the release of the captives, which would quite sufficiently account for popular feeling against the Melkites; in Egypt a Fāṭimid invasion had been repulsed, and the country had been left in disorder. A graphic description is given us of a similar attack by a mob on a church, presumably at Baghdad, at a later time. It took place in the days of the Nestorian Catholicus Yūḥannā V, who died 1009:

The Muslims were excited because of a certain man who was found killed, and Abu Manṣūr b. al-Darājī was suspected of it, and they attacked the church of the Jacobites, called after Mar Thoma, and tore down its curtain, and one of them seized the strong wooden pole of the curtain, and went out towards the door. And it chanced that it got up against the door like a bolt, and by reason of the density of the crowd he could not turn it aside, and those who were entering did not know of this. And one of them took a long broom and held it up to the lamp, and the fire caught it, and he waved it about, illuminating some of the pillagers. And the fire caught some rush matting which was lying rolled up at the side of the sanctuary, and it caught a curtain which was in the women's part, and it reached the *bema* [platform]. And as it was all hung with old curtains, as inflammable as brimstone, the fire spread among the lattices and doors, and no one could extinguish it, and its flames reached up to the vaulted roof and its palm trunks and canes; and the fire spread to the courtyard, and many people perished; and as for those who took refuge at the well and climbed up it, the roof fell on them, the surrounding walls falling together. And as for those who fled out of the church, the Arabs stole their clothes, cleverly profiting by the opportunity. But it is, as they say, God's decree which saves a man, and it was His decree which prevented the same injustice befalling any of the other churches. And for a long time they were digging out their dead from under the ruins and debris, but most of them they did not recognise because of the effect of the fire upon them. And there were some wicked people who suggested that it ought to be turned into a martyr's shrine [i.e. of the Muslim who had been found murdered]; and they referred the matter to the lawyers of the day, viz. Abū Hāmid al-Isfahānī, Abū Bakr al-Khwarizmi, and al-Baiḍāwi, and others of the judges and lawyers; and the lawyers gave the decision that the man was guilty who had attacked the church, and that he had done what was not permitted in the law, and that the case of the guilty person must be referred to the Sultan that he should punish him, and so the matter was settled.[1]

Many of the troubles of the Christians were caused by their own leaders, who sought power by any means, giving and receiving bribes. Most of the appointments of patriarchs were the occasion for violent quarrels between the supporters of the rival candidates. For instance, the election of Timothy (Catholicus, A.D. 780–819) was largely influenced by his offering money to certain people, and pointing to some sacks full of stones as if they were full of money. When, after the consecration, they asked for the money, he showed them what the sacks contained, and said, "The priesthood is not sold for money".[2] The jealousy between the different Christian sects was such that they lost no opportunity for harming one another. For instance we read that early in the tenth century

many Greeks dwelt in the city of Baghdad, distinguished men, scribes and doctors, laymen, who asked Elias, Chalcedonian Patriarch of Antioch [Elias I, A.D. 907–34], to appoint a Metropolitan for them. He sent a certain John, who took his seat in a certain Greek church in Baghdad. Abraham, Catholicus of the Nestorians [Abraham III, A.D. 905–36], took it ill, and called the man to judgment before the wazir, and said, "We Nestorians are friends of the Arabs, and pray for victory for them. Why then is this foreigner, an enemy of the Arabs, made equal to us?" to which the wazir replied, "You Christians all hate us equally, and only love us in appearance". The Catholicus was silenced by this and could reply nothing against it; but he sought a patron of his cause, with a gift of a thousand nummi for his trouble, the chief doctor of the Arabs who attended him [the wazir]. He talked to the wazir and said, "Far be it from thee to put the Nestorians, who have no other king than the Arabs, in the same place as the Greeks whose kings never cease to stir up war against the Arabs,

[1] Mari, fol. 217 *a*–218 *a*.

[2] Mari, fol. 185 *b*, Amr, p. 64.

for they differ, as they say, as much as enemies from friends". When he had said this, the Arabs standing round went over to his opinion. It is said that Abraham the Catholicus spent two thousand golden nummi, till he had Elias, Patriarch of the Greeks, brought to Baghdad in the year 300 of the Arabs [A.D. 912] and forced from him a document in which he professed that it was not lawful in future for a Greek Catholicus or Metropolitan to remain in the city of Baghdad, or to fix his see there, but he ought to send there different bishops, one after another, who should visit the Greeks dwelling there and supply their needs, and then return to his own land.[1]

In the second half of the eleventh century the Nestorian Catholicus Sabarīshū' (1061–72) complained because the Jacobite bishop Thomas in Baghdad had married a Nestorian to a Jacobite.

Thomas said, "We are the heads of two peoples and two sects", in which he was making a claim to which he was not entitled.... So defence of the truth and protection of his position compelled him [Sabarīshū'] and he gathered together all the Christian people and their heads and leaders and physicians, and ordered that no scribe should enter his palace [i.e. Thomas's palace], and no physician the hospital, and no merchant his shop and dwelling-place.[2]

From time to time persecutions were initiated by the Caliphs. 'Umar II (A.D. 717–20) ordered the destruction of all recently constructed churches.[3] Under this heading mention must be made of the fate of the Christian tribe of the Banū Tanūkh. Shortly after the Muslim conquest some of the Christian Arab tribes appealed to the Byzantine Emperor for help, and he sent a fleet to Antioch and landed troops there in A.D. 638. The Christian tribes, including the Banū Tanūkh who were living in Qinnasrin south of Aleppo, rose in rebellion and joined the Greeks. The rebellion was put down by the Muslim forces. The Muslim general Abu 'Ubaida, hearing that the Banū Tanūkh had broken their

[1] Assemani, III, pt II, IIC–IC, quoting from Barhebraeus.
[2] Mari, fol. 228 *b*–229 *a*, quoted by Assemani, III, pt II, IC.
[3] Arnold, *Preaching of Islam*, p. 58.

pact and rebelled, called upon them, after their defeat, to accept Islam. Some of them did so, but one section of the tribe, the Banū Salīḥ, refused. They remained a Christian tribe for a long time. Nearly a century and a half later, in 779, we hear of the Caliph al-Mahdī compelling some of them to become Muslims. Even after that some remained Christian, for we hear of their goods being despoiled during the rebellion of Naṣr against the Caliph al-Ma'mūn in 823.[1] At the beginning of the ninth century Hārūn ar-Rashīd waged several campaigns against the Greek Emperor Nicephorus. Again and again the Emperor broke the treaties he had made with the Muslims, and this so enraged ar-Rashīd that when he eventually won a final victory he caused all the churches on the borderland to be cast down, and strictly enforced the rules as to dress, etc., with regard to the Christians.[2] In the year 825, in the absence of the Caliph al-Ma'mūn in Egypt, his brother destroyed a number of churches and religious buildings of the Jacobites and Melkites in Edessa. The Jacobite Patriarch appealed to the Caliph, who wrote a rescript with his own hand rebuking his brother and ordering him not to molest the Patriarch nor attack the churches.[3] The persecution of al-Mutawakkil, referred to above[4] as recorded by Mari as the result of the false charge of a Christian against the Patriarch, is explained by Muir[5] as the result of the return of Islamic orthodoxy and intolerance after the interval in which the Mu'tazilites had been in power.

[1] Balādhurī, p. 151, trans. I, 223; Muir, *Caliphate*, p. 140; Duval, "Histoire d'Édesse", in *Journal Asiatique*, série viii, tome XIX, p. 87 note.

[2] Muir, *Caliphate*, p. 478, who does not give his authority. It may be another version of the persecution recorded by Barhebraeus (see above, p. 54) as that persecution took place when ar-Rashīd was encamped against the Greeks at Marj Dabiq. For the breach of treaties by Nicephorus see Finlay, *History of the Byzantine Empire*, p. 95.

[3] Barhebraeus, *Chron. Eccles.* I, col. 360.

[4] P. 54.

[5] *Caliphate*, pp. 525–6.

Restrictions amounting to persecution appear to have been enforced under the Caliph al-Qadir (A.D. 991–1031):

And in his days [i.e. of Yūḥannā b. Bāzūk, 1012–20] the people [i.e. the Christians] were compelled to wear distinctive dress, and a number deserted the faith on account of the trials, woes and injuries [or "stonings"] that befell them. And the people of the Western parts were prevented from carrying out their funeral processions by day; and the people of the Third Quarter [in Baghdad], as many as were not religious, became Muslims, and there was great affliction. And part of the woodwork at the rear of the mosque of ar-Ruṣāfat was burnt; and it was laid to the charge of the Christians. But when the government of the Caliph al-Qadir learnt the truth of the matter, they prevented [the Muslims] from carrying out their design of attacking the Christians....And the people suffered trials, and made their prayers by night, and offered the prayers of Ascension Day by night. And the Christians were compelled to wear distinctive dress, and [only] to ride on mules and asses, and to dismiss the slaves and maidservants from their houses, and to put an order in writing concerning this which should be read from the *bema*.[1]

The most severe persecution of which we have record during the period of the Caliphate was that of the mad Fāṭimid Caliph al-Ḥākim which lasted 1009–20. A passage in Mari, probably interpolated, describes it as follows, under the life of Yūḥannā (1012–20):

And in his days the Christians of Egypt and Syria were persecuted, and the churches of Jerusalem were destroyed, and the furniture of the churches was spoiled, and the Christians were made to wear a wooden cross of five pounds weight round their necks, and a large number became Muslims; and hearts were torn with pity....And the bishop in Egypt related that in the western districts the number of churches destroyed reached about 40,000 churches and monasteries, and that only a few persons [Christians] remained.[2]

The general accuracy of this brief statement is borne out by other authorities. It appears that the motive of Ḥākim was

[1] Mari, fol. 220 *a*–221 *a*. Compare Barhebraeus, *Chron. Eccles.* II, col. 258.

[2] Mari, fol. 220 *a*–220 *b*.

zeal for Islam, and he was particularly angered against the Christians and Jews because of the important positions they held in the state and their insolent bearing towards the Muslims. As early as 1002 he executed a Christian named 'Īsā b. Nestorius who had been appointed to some important post by Ḥākim's predecessor. In 1004 he issued the first of his ordinances, not only against Christians and Jews, but also dealing with other matters in a manner which showed already a streak of madness: bathing without drawers was forbidden, the times of prayer were altered, and the eating of a particular vegetable was prohibited because it had been a favourite dish of 'Alī's opponent Mu'āwiya. Large numbers of Muslims also were deprived of their offices, tortured and slain. In 1007 he began confiscating the property of churches, and publicly burning crosses. About the same time he ordered little mosques to be built on the roofs of the churches. Two years later he issued an order for the destruction of the Church of the Holy Sepulchre at Jerusalem, and it is significant of the difficulty of carrying on the government without the help of Christians that the order for the demolition of this church had to be signed by a Christian wazir. Ḥākim's action against this church was the result of charges brought by a disaffected Christian who pretended to reveal the trick by which the holy fire was kindled in the sepulchre on Easter Eve. Soon afterwards Ḥākim ordered the destruction of all churches and the arrest of all bishops, and prohibited anyone from trading with Christians. The destruction of churches took place particularly from 1012 to 1014, and it was estimated that 30,000 were destroyed and pillaged in Egypt and Syria. The Jews suffered a like treatment. It is not surprising that large numbers of Christians became Muslims. But about 1013 Ḥākim permitted Christians to emigrate into Greek territory. This first sign of relaxation towards the Christians was no doubt due to the new attitude he was beginning to feel towards Islam; for in 1016 Darazi began to proclaim the divinity of Ḥākim. From that time Ḥākim began to oppose the ordinances of Islam, suppressing the poor-tax, the fast, and the pilgrimage to Mecca. In 1017 he granted liberty of conscience to Jews and Christians. It seems to have taken a little time before this liberty was made effective, and one can imagine that the Christians were not too ready to declare themselves openly and risk falling into his clutches or into the hands of the Muslim mob. But gradually the Christians were emboldened to come forward, and many who had embraced Islam returned to Christianity. The number of these apostates who returned was estimated at 6000. Finally in 1020 Ḥākim ordered the restoration of all the material of the demolished churches, removed the restrictions on the dress of Christians, and allowed them to sound the boards to call to worship. The blasphemous madness of allowing his name to be proclaimed in the mosque in the place of the name of Allah, "In the name of al-Ḥākim, the merciful, the compassionate", roused the Egyptians to fury. Darazi, who had encouraged him in this pretension, fled to the Lebanon where he founded the sect of the Druzes, who to this day worship Ḥākim as God. In Cairo violent revolts and rioting broke out. In 1021 the mad ruler disappeared, probably assassinated, though the circumstances of his death were never fully cleared up, and many people continued to believe that he was somewhere in hiding. His successor in the Fāṭimid Caliphate made a treaty with the Byzantine Empire confirming the permission to rebuild the Church of the Holy Sepulchre, and for the return to Christianity of those who had been forcibly converted to Islam.[1]

With the one exception of the persecution by the mad Caliph al-Ḥākim, it is evident that the Muslim government did not normally play the part of persecutor. The greater part of the sufferings of the Christians was due to personal quarrels. The principal blame that must attach to the government is that they were slow to suppress riots of the populace, and too ready to believe false accusations against the Chris-

[1] De Sacy, *Exposé de la Religion des Druzes*, I, cccii–cccxcix; Lane-Poole, *History of Egypt*, pp. 125–34; Bréhier, *Les Croisades*, pp. 35–9.

tians without enquiry. The restrictions imposed from time to time by the government were for the most part a natural result of the *melet* system, and were mostly a continuation of the restrictions which were current before the time of Islam. As the Muslims were governed by their *shari'a*, which included what we should call both civil and canon law, something like the *melet* system for non-Muslims was more or less inevitable. Though the disabilities under which the Christians lived were irksome and humiliating, and they suffered financially, there was no persecution to the death as had been the case under the Sassanids. One is therefore bound to conclude that the failure of the Christian community to hold their own, and increase in numbers, must have been due to the feebleness of their Christian faith. It has often been remarked that Muslims could not be converted to Christianity because the penalty for such an act was death. That would be a perfectly sufficient explanation if the subject under discussion had been anything other than Christianity. For Christ has conquered death, and persecution to the death cannot stop a real Christian movement. In the days before Muhammad the same penalty of death was in force in the case of apostates from Zoroastrianism to Christianity. Under that law many Christians were executed in Persia; and in the height of persecution the officer in charge of the persecution and of the executions was so struck by the bearing of the Christian martyrs that he suddenly stopped his work and confessed Christ, and was himself executed.[1] In those days Christianity was spreading in Persia, for nothing can stop that sort of spirit as has been proved over and over again in the great movements of Church history. It is therefore in the realm of Christian life that we must look for the reason of the fact that with the advent of Islam this spirit of victory seemed to desert the Church.

[1] Wigram, *op. cit.* p. 139; Labourt, *op. cit.* p. 127.

Chapter VI

CHRISTIAN TEACHING AND LIFE

The Nestorian Church accepted the creed of the Council of Nicaea, so that though refusing to accept the Council of Chalcedon they can scarcely be said to have been unorthodox, for the refusal was more on personal than on doctrinal grounds. In the writings of Eastern Christians, whether Nestorian, Jacobite or Melkite, there is but little with which we could quarrel from the point of view of credal orthodoxy. But it must be remembered that the conciliar creeds were framed to meet the errors of their own day, and were never supposed to be a full statement of what a Christian ought to believe and practise. For instance, Christians of all ages have known that it was their duty to love their neighbours as themselves, and the duty implies a belief that all men are our brothers; but none of the creeds mentions this beyond expressing our belief in the holy catholic Church. In order therefore to consider the way in which the Oriental Christians looked at Christianity, it is not sufficient to enquire about their theology, but we must go further and enquire how they regarded Christianity as a life, and how their theology worked out in its application to life.

Of the good works of Christ, and exhortations to imitate Him, we may quote the following: Theodore Abucara (Melkite, ninth century):

And since you accept the things we have mentioned, you are bound to know that these people [i.e. the Christians], who are five-sixths of mankind, only accepted Christ because of what they saw of these miracles which are mentioned in the Gospel and the books of the apostles, and by the power of the Holy Spirit who is spread abroad secretly in their hearts and satisfies them that Christ is God and the Son of God, as He said concerning Himself, and that He bore the sufferings and the cross which are spoken of in it [i.e. in the Gospel], and that He did not bear those sufferings out of weakness, or to no purpose, but for a good cause, and that was to bring him to light, by the Holy Spirit, whose heart was dark.[1]

Again, the same author says:

He came down from heaven, and appeared in our nature, and called us brethren and sons and friends, and mixed with us, both with small and great, for a few years, and gave us in Himself an example of the laws of all goodness—gentleness and humility and pardoning the sinner, and pointing out all goodness to all men, and removing all evil from all men, and that we should not repay evil for evil, and love to those whom we hate, and forgiveness of enemies, and renouncing wrong-doing and malice, and that we should not get the better of others, and prayer and humble supplication, and fasting, going hungry for forty days in which He hungered as an example for us to follow.[2]

The Apology of al-Kindi (Nestorian, about A.D. 830) says:

Then, after that, He began openly to preach to men until the day when He ascended to the heavens; and He urged them to repentance, and to abandon the world, and to fast in it, and to forsake people and children and possessions and attachment thereto, and to desire earnestly works of piety, and to abstain from iniquity, and to love to confer benefits on everyone, and to abstain from taking vengeance for wrongs, and to forgive them, and to do good to everyone. And He taught them that this would bring them near to God (blessed be His name!); and He urged them to do this that thereby they might be worthy of great reward and much recompense in the world to come.[3]

Abū ʿAlī ʿĪsā b. Iṣḥāq b. Zaraʿa, a Jacobite logician of Baghdad, who died 1007, says:

He has demanded of us to do good to our enemies and to pray for them, and to agree to what they demand of us, and to help them and love them; and this means that whatsoever works we propose towards them should be like what we propose towards those whom we love.[4]

[1] Cheikho, *Vingt Traités*, p. 87.

[2] Cheikho, *Vingt Traités*, pp. 111–12. This quotation is interesting as coming from a manuscript dated A.D. 877, which is said to be the oldest extant Arabic Christian manuscript.

[3] *Risālat*, p. 157.

[4] Sbath, *Vingt Traités*, p. 58.

Īshū'yāb b. Malkūn, Nestorian Bishop of Naṣībīn, who died in 1256, said:

> Verily we honour the cross because we depict the Saviour, because in this form He is presented to our senses; and He gave Himself in our stead, that we should imitate Him and give ourselves for the truth; and because it is His will to bring us by it [i.e. by the cross] to the resurrection.[1]

And again, the same author:

> But the Gospel calls us to what is contrary to the nature of men and their characteristics and manners, viz. love of enemies, doing good to those who wrong us, avoiding all desires, denying every inclination, and giving oneself up for the salvation of all mankind.[2]

The same author again:

> The Gospel calls to love. And love includes the believer and the unbeliever, the near and the far, the friend and the enemy. And this love is like unto the love of the Most High Creator in its characteristics, for He makes His sun to rise and sends down His rain upon the good and the wicked. And the Gospel incites both enemies and friends to good works, and urges enemies and friends to love, in the same way. And these are characteristics of the Most High Creator.[3]

These quotations, exhorting us to the path of gentleness and abstinence, are not so much wrong in themselves as in their false emphasis. When we read the Acts of the Apostles, we should never say that the chief characteristics of St Stephen, St Peter or St Paul were meekness, humiliation, and abandoning the world. Such a description would leave out the positive side of their character, the divine fire within them burning them up in service to God and men, denouncing sin and striving for righteousness. One is also struck by the idea in these quotations that to live the Christ-life is regarded as contrary to one's nature. This idea is part of the ascetic ideal which gained ground in the Eastern Church from the middle of the fourth century. Monks and hermits were regarded as people who were not merely following a special

[1] Sbath, *op. cit.* p. 158. [2] Sbath, *op. cit.* p. 155.
[3] Sbath, *op. cit.* p. 158.

calling, but as living a life which was intrinsically superior to normal human relationships, as if it were not possible to live the Christian life without fleeing from the rest of the world. In Edessa at the beginning of the fourth century only celibates were allowed to be baptised;[1] and, though that practice was soon abandoned, the preference for the celibate life was shown in the regulations about the marriage of the clergy. In the fifth century there was a movement against asceticism in the Nestorian Church: monks were allowed to marry, patriarchs and bishops were allowed to marry once, and ordinary clergy were allowed to take a second wife after the death of the first. A reaction, however, set in during the sixth century against the marriage of the higher clergy, and married men were forbidden to become bishops or patriarchs.[2] The Arabic tribes of Northern Mesopotamia, who were evangelised in the latter half of the sixth century by Aḥūdemmeh, the Jacobite Metropolitan of Takrīt, were much attracted to ascetic practices, and added an extra week to the beginning of Lent.[3] The Monastic History of Thomas of Marga, written about A.D. 840, exalts asceticism greatly, as one would expect from a monastic institution. In one place the author describes how Pythagoras, Homer and Plato attained their greatness through ascetic practices, and then proceeds:

> And if upon the heathen who are aliens, and who are remote from spiritual knowledge, God the Lord of all bestowed the wisdom which they sought after, or by reason of their affliction, or as it were for the benefit of others by the labour of the deepest tranquillity and silence and absence from mankind, made them glad, how much more to the holy men who keep His commandments, and who train themselves according to His will by hunger and thirst, and suffering, and tears, and prayer day and night, will He give not only the wisdom of this world, which they have not sought after, but the kingdom for which they suffer, and make them to enjoy the pledge of it here?[4]

1 Burkitt, *Early Eastern Christianity*, p. 125.
2 Barthold, *Zur Geschichte des Christentums in Mittel-Asien*, p. 28.
3 Nau, *Histoires d'Ahoudemmeh et de Marouta*, p. 28.
4 Wallis Budge, *Book of Governors*, II, 532.

The one thing above all for which Thomas throughout his work praises the various saints of the monastery is their asceticism, and one or two quotations would fail to give the impression that one gains from reading the whole book that to his mind asceticism is the chief mark of holiness. It is to be noticed that the extreme poverty and self-denial in which these holy men lived was quite unconnected with the changing fortunes of prosperity or poverty of the monastery, or the claims of the poor upon them, and thus differs entirely from the practice of St Paul who said:[1] "In everything and in all things have I learned the secret both to be filled and to be hungry, both to abound and to be in want". This thoroughgoing ascetic ideal was by no means restricted to the monasteries, but was generally held, as the following quotations will show: Ḥunain b. Iṣhāq, a Nestorian physician, who died A.D. 873, said:

> The invitation was not made from abasement to exaltation, nor from humiliation to honour, but from honour to humiliation, and yet it was so far accepted that he who accepted it delighted to die that he might live because of it.[2]

Yaḥyā b. 'Adī, a Jacobite philosopher, who died A.D. 974, said:

> The Gospel...bids us bear humiliation and leave off seeking honour and to prefer poverty, and to be patient in unbearable fatigue, and to leave the concessions of the law and its restrictions, and to command [people] to be brave in bearing sufferings, and to leave off seeking pleasures, and to leave off being afflicted by fears.[3]

Ēlīyyā, Nestorian Metropolitan of Naṣībīn (1008–49) said:

> The book that was in their hands commanded them to reject pleasure and food and drink, and to abandon the world and the rest of its blessings.[4]

[1] Phil. iv, 12.
[2] Cheikho, *Vingt Traités*, p. 145.
[3] Sbath, *op. cit.* p. 169.
[4] Cheikho, *Trois Traités*, p. 48.

Īshū'yāb b. Malkūn, who occupied the same see two centuries later (died 1256), said:

The Gospel calls to the acceptance of the noblest of the essences, viz. the essence of the Creator. And this is not achieved save by the best preparation. And the best preparation is the abandonment of the whole world, and the purifying of the soul from all defilement. And when this preparation comes to a man there shines upon him the essence of the Creator, and it dwells within his reasoning soul.[1]

This last passage is better than some, as it makes clear that asceticism is only a means to an end. But the thoroughly ascetic tone of Christianity is shown by the attack of al-Jāḥiẓ, the Mu'tazilite philosopher, who died A.D. 869, who can only explain it as a kinship to the Zindiqs (Manichaeans) who thought of matter as evil:

And when you hear their speech about pardon and forgiveness, and their talk of the wandering monastic life,[2] and their grumbling against anyone who eats flesh, and their preference for eating vegetables and not touching animal food, and their encouraging continence in marriage, and their neglecting to seek children, and their praise of the Catholicus and the Metropolitan and the Bishop and the monks for neglecting to marry and to seek offspring, and their honouring the chiefs, you know that between their religion and that of the Zindiqs there is an affinity, and that they have a natural leaning towards that religion.[3]

There was a sect of Christians called Muṣallīn, or Praying Men, known to the Greeks under the name of Euchites or Messalians. They sprang up in 'Irāq in the fourth century A.D., and spread thence to Syria and elsewhere, and their doctrines were current up to the twelfth century. It has recently been shown that the *Spiritual Homilies* attributed to Macarius were really written by one of this sect.[4] They believed that each man received from his ancestors at birth a

[1] Sbath, *op. cit.* p. 157.
[2] *as-siyāḥa*, the word used in the tradition quoted on p. 23.
[3] Finkel, *Three Essays*, p. 20.
[4] See G. L. Marriott, "The Homilies of Macarius" in the *Journal of Theological Studies*, XXII, 259.

demon which always led him on to evil. The only way to exorcise this demon was by continual prayer. They refused to do any kind of work, and abstained from meat and all other enjoyments of the senses, hoping in this way to attain perfect purity of soul, to raise themselves up by this means to heaven, to behold God, and to learn all mysteries. They believed that prayer and fasting would earn for them salvation, even (if Epiphanius is to be trusted) in spite of their immoral lives. The Nestorians regarded them as dangerous heretics, and took vigorous measures to suppress them,[1] but in Muslim eyes they were Nestorians,[2] and we may regard their teaching on asceticism as merely carrying to its logical conclusion the opinion of ordinary Nestorians on the subject.

There can be no doubt that the great urge towards asceticism came into Asia with Christian monasticism from Egypt; but in Asia it found congenial soil, and al-Jāḥiẓ was probably not very far wrong in seeing in it some kinship with Manichaeism, in which matter was regarded as evil. Not of course that any of the Christian writers went so far as to say that matter was evil, for they all confessed that God had created it, but subconsciously they seem to have felt that the body was a check to the soul, instead of being an instrument which the soul could use for its purposes. There was in Asia an old myth of the divine soul coming down to earth, and being clothed with the garment of humanity, and eventually freeing itself from this encumbrance and finding its way back again to its heavenly home. That myth is characteristic of Gnostic thought, and is beautifully expressed in the "Hymn of the Soul"[3] in the *Acts of Thomas*.

With this sort of idea in the air, and also the belief in the absolute gap between the Creator and the creature, it was very difficult for oriental writers to believe in a real union between God and man. Thus Theodore Abucara, the Melkite

[1] *Book of Governors*, II, 91, and the references given there.

[2] Shahrastāni, *Kitāb al-milal wan-niḥal*, p. 176, Haarbrücker's trans. I, 267.

[3] Translated in Burkitt's *Early Eastern Christianity*.

Bishop of Ḥarran, states the doctrine of the full humanity of Christ quite clearly in the following words:

He was not merely in the appearance of humanity, as He had appeared to those who had the first Law, but He was in our flesh, i.e. in the humanity which He had formed from the pure Virgin Mary, and our Lord came to us, and He in His own person undertook to call and save us.[1]

But a few pages further on in the same treatise he uses an illustration which appears to make the humanity of Christ merely a cloak of His divinity:

And the conquest of Satan, and the delivery of His people from his hand, is like a man who had some sheep, and there was near them a wolf, an enemy, who continually tore them and seized the sheep. And the man took a sheep's fleece from his flock and put it on, and then stood in the midst of the sheep as one of them, indistinguishable from them, till the wolf came, according to his custom, and jumped upon him, the disguised sheep, and drove him a long way, separating him from the flock; and when the wolf saw what strength the sheep showed, and the arrows the sheep shot at him, the wolf supposed that the sheep had changed their nature and become powerful like the wolves, and the wolf turned to flight. Such is the wisdom and craft of the creature. And God is wiser and craftier....But He showed His greatness by becoming united with Adam's nature, and in that nature fighting against the foe of the first man till he fled, and God delivered His people, just as the owner of the sheep drove away the wolf by wearing a fleece from a sheep of the flock till he fled and the victory over the wolf rested with the flock. Thus the wise *God concealed His divinity in Adam* [i.e. in humanity], and in it [i.e. in His divinity] opposed Satan the conqueror of Adam till he fled, and the victory was reckoned to Adam.[2]

With this last sentence compare the following from the Syriac version of the *Apology of Timothy I*, Nestorian Catholicus, A.D. 780–823:[3]

Christ is not two beings, O king, nor two sons, but Son and Christ are one; there are in Him two natures, one of which belongs

1 Cheikho, *Vingt Traités*, p. 113. 2 *Op. cit.* pp. 116–17.

3 *Woodbrooke Studies*, II, 19. The Arabic text as published by Cheikho in his *Trois Traités* is nearer the original than the Syriac. See *The Moslem World*, January, 1931. In this place the Arabic text has not the expression "clothed itself with the Word-God".

to the Word, and the other one which is from Mary clothed itself with the Word-God.

It is interesting to notice in the case of these two writers that when they get away from their technical terms they both show an imperfect conception of the true unity of God and man in Christ, and that this is as true of the Melkite as of the Nestorian. St John of Damascus accused the Nestorians of failing to believe in the unity of Christ:

> They [the Nestorians] attribute the humbler things wrought by the Lord in the days of His sojourn with us solely to His manhood; while the loftier and divine actions they attribute to God the Word; and they do not attribute both together to one and the same "person".[1]

And yet, as we have seen, St John's own pupil Theodore used language showing the same failure. We find in many of these Oriental writers that, however much they tried to express the perfect union between the divine and the human in Christ, they could scarcely get away from the idea that there were two sets of actions in Christ, some of which could be attributed to Him as divine, and some to Him as human; and the furthest they could go in uniting the two was to adopt the Western device known as the *communicatio idiomatum*, by which, merely as a trick of speech, the experiences of each of the two natures of Christ could be attributed to the other. For instance, Timothy says:

> Jesus, in that He is God, did not die, but He died in His human nature in that He is man. And as the dishonour is attributed to the king himself when his purple is torn in dishonour, or his royal garments rent in pieces, so the death of Jesus (on Him be peace) which befell Him in the body is attributed to His divine person.[2]

Ēlīyyā of Naṣībīn, in his dialogue with the Wazir al-Maghribi, was asked whether he believed in the confession of Nicaea. On his replying in the affirmative, the Wazir said:

> So then you must say that Jesus, the human, born of Mary, is God eternal and true, begotten of His Father before all times, and that He is not a creature, as the words require.

1 "De Haeresibus", Migne, *P.G.* XCIV, col. 740.
2 Arabic text of his Apology, Cheikho, *Trois Traités*, p. 17.

Ēlīyyā replied:

May God strengthen the Wazir! We are not obliged to say that, because the meaning which we indicate by saying "Jesus", which we show by saying "Lord" in this place, is the eternal Word. But what we mean by saying "Jesus" alone is the humanity which was taken from Mary; but the name "Lord" is added to "Jesus", and the name "Jesus" is added to "Lord" in a number of places because of the union. And what we mean by saying "Christ" is the two meanings together. So "Lord" is He who is the Word, eternal, creator; and "Jesus" is the temporal, who came into being. And our sentence "the only begotten Son of His Father before all times" is in apposition to "Lord" which is the Word, not to "Jesus" which is the humanity taken from Mary. And since this is so, it is absurd to say that Jesus who is human, who was taken from Mary, is eternal from of old, creator, begotten of His Father before all times, and uncreated.[1]

When it came to considering the sufferings of Christ even a Jacobite felt obliged to separate the two natures of Christ. Cyriacus, Jacobite Patriarch of Antioch, A.D. 793–817, said:[2]

And since the body was of our nature He was susceptible to sufferings like us; and for our sakes He truly suffered in the body

[1] Cheikho, *Trois Traités*, p. 36.

[2] Assemani, II, 117. But it should be noted that Monophysites were not always so careful in their language. One of the martyrs of Najrān, for instance, is reported to have said, "Thou shalt know that not only will I not say that Christ was a man, but I worship Him and praise Him because of all the benefits He has shown me. And I believe that He is God, maker of all creatures, and I take refuge in His cross" (Moberg, *Book of the Himyarites*, pp. 33 *b*–34 *a*). The aged monk whom Ibn Ṭūlūn met in Egypt spoke of a "crucified God" (see the passage quoted below, p. 82). The Nestorian Catholicus Īshū'yāb III said that "the Arabs cannot stand those who assert that God has been crucified" (quoted by Tor Andrae, *Ursprung*, 1923, p. 167). The Catholicus Timothy accused the Christians of Rūm, meaning the Jacobites, of "attributing sufferings and death to Him who absolutely does not suffer or die". (See the passage quoted below, p. 88). Ibn Ḥazm accused the Jacobites of saying "that Christ is God Most High Himself, and that God Most High (so great is their blasphemy) died and was crucified and slain; and that the world remained for three days without a ruler, and the firmament without a ruler; then He rose and returned as He was before" (I, 48).

the same pains as we do, i.e. the Word of God. But none of these things touched His divinity, for that would not be right. For how should He, who destroyed suffering and death with all its fear, be subject to death? And He only bore the sufferings in His body which was united to His divinity, i.e. the body of the Word, as we have said.

In connexion with the failure to grasp the full meaning of the incarnation, that God by becoming man had raised humanity to a new potential status in Christ, we may consider the practice of the veneration of images. The use of images in churches, and of veneration towards them, had developed into a regular cult by the sixth century, and had been steadily growing, in spite of occasional protests, until the eighth century. In A.D. 725 the Byzantine Emperor Leo the Isaurian issued his first edict against image worship as being idolatry. Only shortly before that date, about A.D. 722, Christians had been persecuted by the Caliph Yazīd II for their use of images,[1] and there can be little doubt that the movement in Europe was suggested by this action of the Caliph. In Europe a long controversy followed. Popular feeling in favour of the use of images was supported by the clergy. John of Damascus, living just outside the Emperor's dominions, was able to write in favour of images. The Emperor was succeeded by Constantine Copronymus, who convened a council of bishops at Constantinople in A.D. 753, who, under his orders, condemned the use of images, and persecutions followed. Eventually a council held at Nice in A.D. 787 permitted the veneration as opposed to the worship of images. The controversy as it was carried on in the West does not concern us here. Neither of the opposing parties made the best of their case: the iconoclasts might have emphasised the dangers of materialism; the anti-iconoclasts might have emphasised the loss to art if iconography and portraiture were forbidden.[2] Although in Muslim eyes the

[1] Assemani, II, 105, quoting from the *Chronicle of Dionysius* the Jacobite Patriarch, which was written about A.D. 775.

[2] For a presentation of the anti-iconoclastic case see Alice Gardner, *Theodore of Studium*, ch. ix.

veneration of any kind of image was idolatry, it must be noted that Christians did not attempt to depict the form of God, which is what we commonly understand by the word idolatry, but only that of Christ and the saints. The objection to the practice as stated by its opponents at Constantinople in A.D. 753 is extremely interesting: they said that it was only Monophysites or Nestorians who could logically make an image of Christ; for if they pretended to depict the whole Christ they were circumscribing the divinity and confounding it with the humanity, as the Monophysites did; or else they pretended to depict the humanity alone, which could only be done by Nestorians, who separated the two natures.[1] It is not certain that the Melkites themselves were so free from separating the natures that they would have felt any difficulty, on that score, in depicting the manhood alone. In fact, John of Damascus taught that the use of images resulted from the incarnation, and that it was a testimony against the merely docetic view of our Lord's human nature.[2] There was of course some truth in the last clause, for no Docetist would have wished to depict the form of Christ. But the main need in Asia at that time was for a protest, not against Docetism, but against the Muslim view of Christ, i.e. that He was a mere man.

If we look at the question, not from the point of view of the ancient controversialists, but simply asking ourselves whether the veneration of pictures or images of Christ does tend to an understanding of the incarnation, we are bound to answer in the negative. The incarnation is a union of God with the whole man, and not merely with the material part of man. It is a culmination of creation in three stages, (1) the taking up of matter into the sphere of life, whereby matter attains to new powers and freedom which it had not had before, (2) the taking up of living bodies into the human sphere, whereby the animal attains to new powers and freedom which it had not had before, and (3) the taking up of man

[1] Tixeront, *Histoire des Dogmes*, III, 463–4.
[2] Kidd, *Churches of Eastern Christendom*, p. 147.

into the divine sphere, whereby man attains to new powers and freedom which he had not had before. This is the theme of that great theological work *The Incarnate Lord* by Lionel Thornton. It is difficult to find a passage in that book which can be quoted apart from its context, but the following will perhaps serve the purpose:

> The highest law of being in His [Christ's] case is the law of being proper to deity. There is no abrogation of other laws of being. In His organism are all the laws of being which exist in each of us. But even the highest of these, that which constitutes Him "the man Christ Jesus", is not the highest law of His Being. It is not, therefore, that principle of unity which determines His status. His human organism has the creaturely status which is proper to humanity, just as the constituent parts and elements in our complex organisms each have their proper status in the cosmic series, notwithstanding their being built into a spiritual organism. The human body is not less physical because it is taken up into a spiritual organism and has become an organ of spirit. Neither is the human organism less human because it is taken up into union with the eternal Logos and has become the organ of His deity. Just the reverse. Each level of the series reaches its cosmic fulfilment by passage towards the eternal order.[1]

The significance of this outlook upon the question of the cult of images is this: Christ did not take matter up directly into the divine sphere, but only in so far as matter was already taken up into the sphere of animal life, and animal life was already taken up into the sphere of humanity. The claim that the use of images of Christ is a logical result of a belief in the incarnation is not true, for the image is only material. We must look to see the incarnate Christ shown forth, not in some merely material symbol, but in human life, in the life of regenerate humanity, i.e. of Christians in whom Christ is born.

> As the "image" of the creative Word is impressed upon the spirit of man in the first creation, so the "image" of the Incarnate Lord is impressed upon the spirit of man in the new creation.[2]

It is exactly this fact which the Oriental Christians failed to realise. The great Greek anti-iconoclast Theodore of Studium

[1] P. 238. [2] Thornton, *op. cit.* pp. 446–7.

said,[1] "The true Christian is nothing but a copy or impression of Christ", but entirely failed to see the logical result that the proper object of reverence was not a material picture of Christ but a true Christian.[2] It is therefore probably true to say that the imperfect conception of the implications of the incarnation was the cause of the prevalence of this practice, which did almost more than anything else to offend the Muslims. That it was a real stumbling-block to Muslims cannot be denied; and one cannot help feeling that if the Nestorians had had a more Christian spirit they would have abandoned the cult of images out of respect for the feelings of the Muslims, even though they believed the cult permissible for themselves, in the same way that St Paul dealt with the question of eating meat offered to idols.

A curious attack by a Nestorian, living some time after A.D. 1000, on Melkites and Jacobites for having too many images, and for putting them in places where they could not properly be venerated, seems to indicate that the Nestorians at that time were paying a more superstitious veneration to images than the other sects, even though the number of images might be less. The passage comes as a section of a chapter entitled, "Reply to him who disapproves of our abhorring the communion of the Melkites and Jacobites", and runs as follows:

> They multiply images in their churches, and say that they all ought to be worshipped, but as a matter of fact they despise the image of Christ and our Lady for they put it in baths and other unclean places.[3]

1 Gardner, *op. cit.* p. 153.

2 It should be noticed that the parallel often drawn between ikons and sacraments is false. The sacraments have their validity (apart from the express command of our Lord) through the activity of the elements—the bread and wine *nourish*, the water *washes*—which are the symbols or channels of divine activity in the recipient There is no such activity which can be attributed to an ikon.

3 Tract by an anonymous author against Muhammadans, Jews, Jacobites and Melkites, entitled, "Book of proof of the true faith", attached to the epistles of Īshū'yāb b. Malkūn of Naṣībīn (Assemani, III, pt I, p. 305).

As late as the thirteenth and fourteenth centuries Christian writers defended the veneration of images against Muslim objections, explaining the difference between veneration and adoration, and showing that the veneration of the image was only intended to do honour to Him who was depicted by it, just as one might kiss the hem of the king's robe, or the carpet that was before his throne. A treatise to this effect was written by Sophronius, Coptic Patriarch of Alexandria (850–61),[1] and another by Īshū'yāb b. Malkūn, Nestorian Bishop of Naṣībīn, who died in 1258.[2] From the latter it appears that the Nestorians not only had crosses and images of Christ, but also images and pictures of the saints. These images of the saints were kissed by the people, and incense was offered before them, and before relics of the saints. Altars were set up there, and Eucharists offered in memory of the saints. People used to take mementoes from their graves and oil from their lamps, and large crowds gathered together for their memorial festivals.[3] Paul Rāhib, the Melkite Bishop of Sidon, wrote on the same lines towards the end of the same century.[4] An Archbishop of Sulṭānīyya, writing about 1330 of the Nestorian Christians in China, said:[5] "They have very handsome and devoutly ordered churches with crosses and images in honour of God and the saints". 'Amr b. Mattai, who flourished about 1340, after describing the origin of the Iconoclasts, says:

As for what may rightly be said on this matter, i.e. the portrayal by the Christians of pictures in their churches and sanctuaries, and their honouring them, it is not that they worship them according to the calumnies of ignorant men. Know therefore that their depicting them is not vanity nor ignorance, nor honouring the substance of the medicaments and colours; but the intention is to remember every one of the saints so depicted in time of need, for their intercession in the time of trouble, and by them to attain to

[1] Eutychius, pt II, p. 64.
[2] Sbath, *Vingt Traités*, p. 158.
[3] *Op. cit.* p. 165.
[4] Cheikho, *Vingt Traités*, p. 12.
[5] Yule, *Cathay*, I, 249; Yule-Cordier, III, 102.

the will of the Most High God, since they are more honoured by God and nearer to Him. And if anyone, by reason of the distance of the places, or intervening mountains, or terrible seas, cannot go to their graves and the resting places of their bodies to seek their intercession, they depict their forms, and underneath each picture write the miracles that were wrought by their hands. And likewise they depict the objects of nature of the heaven and the earth, and all that therein is, from the beginning of the creation, such as the judgment of the Deluge, and Noah's ark, and the tower of Babel, and the sacrifice of Isaac, and such like, that the ignorant who cannot read and write may understand it, and that understanding may reach him whose knowledge precludes him from understanding a book, so that all men may embrace this knowledge.[1]

Thus we can trace the use of ikons in the Nestorian Church well on into the Mongol period. In modern times the Nestorians alone of all the Eastern Churches have abandoned the use of images, only using the cross to which they pay the greatest reverence.[2] The use of the plain cross without the figure of Christ on it goes back at least as far as the middle of the thirteenth century, for William of Rubruck, in his journey across Asia from Southern Russia as far as the town of Karakorum, mentions several times that the Armenians and Nestorians whom he met used the cross but not the crucifix. In response to Rubruck's questions they could only reply that it was their custom. Whatever the cause may have been it was apparently not due to any dislike of images or pictures in general.[3] When the Roman Catholic missionaries went to Malabar they found that the Nestorian Christians there did not use images and said, "We are Christians. We do not worship idols".[4] Probably they gave up the use of images in view of the prevalence of Hindu idolatry. One can

[1] Assemani, III, pt II, CCCLIII, quoting from Liber Turris.

[2] Adrian Fortescue, art. "Iconoclasm" in *E.R.E.* For a defence of the adoration of the cross see 'Abdīshū', Metropolitan of Soba or Naṣībīn, who died in 1318, in his *Book of the Pearl concerning the true faith* (Assemani, III, pt I, p. 359).

[3] *William of Rubruck*, pp. 104, 142, 191.

[4] Assemani, III, pt II, CCCXLIX.

only conjecture the reasons which led the Nestorian Church elsewhere to abandon the cult. Possibly the Mongols, after they had become Muslims, forcibly compelled them to abandon it. There is reason to think that this may have been the case, because Ghāzān, the Mongol Emperor of Persia 1295–1304, of whom we shall speak later as the initiator of the real persecution of the Christians, felt very strongly about idolatry. He said:

> There are sins which God never forgives. The greatest of these is the worship of idols. I have been guilty of this myself through ignorance [when he was a Buddhist], but God has enlightened me.[1]

When we compare the Nestorian Church with the Church of the apostolic age, the most noticeable difference is the absence in the Nestorian Church of that spiritual power which was the mark of the early Church. Looking back to the origins of Christianity, Eastern writers continually claimed that Christianity had made its way by the overwhelming power of the miracles of Christ and the apostles, e.g. the Nestorian Catholicus Ḥanānīshū' I (A.D. 686–700) was asked one day by the Caliph, "What do you think of the religion of the Arabs?" and he promptly replied, "It is a kingdom founded on the sword, not a faith confirmed by divine miracles like the Christian faith and the Mosaic faith of old".[2] Theodore Abucara said:

> Likewise Christ our God, the Wisdom, the Truth, did not begin any teaching until He had made clear His divine power by miracles, and there came to Him those who were suffering from all kinds of sickness and diseases.[3]

Al-Kindi says:

> Thou shouldst know that we only believe the prophets and accept their words because they bring us the conditions of prophethood and the proofs of apostleship and the signs of inspiration, not by conquest and victory, not by family pride nor patriotism,

[1] Howorth, *History of the Mongols*, III, 397.
[2] Barhebraeus, *Chron. Eccles.* II, col. 136.
[3] Sbath, *Vingt Traités*, p. 81.

not by individual or ancestral dignity, not by size of family nor by the strength of their power and abundance of goods, not by the simplicity of laws and customs, not by giving way to the passions of the body, not out of fear of the government nor dread of the sword and whip, but by the wonderful signs which men are not capable of, nor have they strength to do the like of them: these are clear divine proofs, like the signs of the prophets, and the marvels of our Lord Christ, and the deeds of His disciples the apostles, whereby the intelligence of the philosophers and the wisdom of the wise are confounded. Therefore we accept their words and all that they bring, and believe them, and recognise that it is a truth which has come down from God.[1]

Ḥunain b. Iṣḥāq, a Nestorian physician who died A.D. 873, gives as the first reason for which the truth is received, "if the recipient sees signs whereby man's power is enfeebled".[2] Yaḥyā b. ʿAdī, a Jacobite philosopher who died A.D. 974, said:

It must be that it [Christianity] is only received and believed in by the signs and miracles which its missionaries showed.... The acceptance by those who received it must have been because of the witness of what the missionaries did in the way of signs opposed to human nature.[3]

An extremely interesting defence of Christianity is recorded by Masʿūdī.[4] He says that there was an aged Christian monk, 130 years old, whom Aḥmad b. Ṭūlūn met in Egypt in A.D. 873. This man supplied Ibn Ṭūlūn with much information about Egypt, and in response to a question about Christianity boldly confessed that Christianity was incapable of intellectual proof, and in fact from the intellectual point of view it contained irreconcilable contradictions. That being so, the aged Copt could only suppose that the acceptance of Christianity by mighty kings and intelligent people must be accounted for by miracles which overwhelm the intellect. The passage is as follows:

And this monk was one of the Copts of Egypt who profess the Jacobite faith, and he was a Jacobite; and Sultan Aḥmad b. Ṭūlūn

[1] *Risālat*, p. 79.
[2] Cheikho, *Vingt Traités*, p. 144. [3] Sbath, *op. cit.* pp. 170–1.
[4] *Kitāb murūj adh-dhahab*, edited by de Meynard, "Les Prairies d'Or", pp. 386–8.

on a certain day commanded a philosopher who was present in the assembly to ask him concerning the proofs of the Christian religion. So he asked him about it, and the Copt said, "I find the proof of the truth of Christianity in its contradictions and inconsistencies which are rejected by intelligence and repelled by the mind because of their difference and contrast. Analysis cannot strengthen it, and syllogism cannot establish it, and proof cannot help it, though the intelligence and perception enquire and search into it. In spite of that, I have seen that many peoples and mighty kings endowed with knowledge and of sound judgment have submitted to it and practise it; and so I know, in view of the intellectual contradictions which I have mentioned, that they do not accept it or practise it except for proofs which they have witnessed, signs which they have known, and miracles which they have recognised, which compelled them to submit to it and practise it". His questioner said to him, "What are the contrasts in Christianity?" He said, "Can one understand them or know their limits? Among them is their saying that the One is three, and the three are One; and their explanation of the persons and the essence which are the Trinity; and do the persons individually exercise power and knowledge or not? and concerning the union of their eternal Lord with created man; and the events of His birth and crucifixion and being killed; and is there anything more dreadful and detestable than a crucified God, and His face being spat upon, and a crown of thorns being put upon His head, and His head being smitten with a stick, and His hands being nailed, and His sides being pierced with lances and wood, and His asking for water, and His being given vinegar to drink in a gourd of colocynth?"

It is characteristic of the Islam of that period that the confession that Christianity was incapable of intellectual proof was regarded as tantamount to a confession of its falsehood. Thus the narrative concludes:

So they ceased from discussing with him, and desisted from disputing with him, because he admitted to them the contradictions of his religion and its corruption and feebleness.

Ēlīyyā of Naṣībīn, writing in the eleventh century, attributes to miracles the conversion, not only of the early Christians, but also of the nations that received Christianity in later generations:

And when I saw that, and found that there entered into the

Christian religion philosophers of the Greeks and their wise men and many peoples and different sects and divers provinces, like the Greeks and the Franks and the Bulgars and the Copts and the Nubians and the Armenians and the Syrians and the Persians and the Turks and the people of China and others of the peoples, not from something that they feared or from something that they hoped for, I knew that they could not have entered into it for any other reason than the divine miracles which led them to it.[1]

So firmly were people convinced that miracles were necessary to convert men to Christianity that Thomas of Marga, in describing the missionary work of Yabalāhā and Qardagh in Gīlān and Dailām and the regions beyond, although no records of miracles had reached him, still felt they must have happened:

When the blessed men had received this permission from the Patriarch, they ordained and made Thomas, Zacchaeus, Shem, Ephraim, Simon, Ananias and David, bishops of the countries which had been taught by their hands, through the signs and mighty deeds which had been manifested by them, no one of which, on account of their number and the remoteness of the countries in which they were wrought and completed, have we been able to distinguish clearly how it was worked, or in what village or city, or in whom a healing was performed, or from whom devils and sicknesses were expelled.... But now if thou wishest to learn in part concerning the wonderful deeds which took place at their hands, consider in thy mind that not without cause and simply through words divorced from deeds did those barbarian nations of daring thieves, and plunderers, and worshippers of devils turn from their polluted religions, which were established without the labour of fasting and prayer, and despise the customary acts of the service of hateful things, and bow their necks to the submission of the yoke of fasting and of prayer, of vigil by nights, and of abstinence from every kind of food on the stated fasts and holy festivals.[2]

It is perfectly true that the miracles of the first age were a tremendously strong evidence for the truth of the gospel, but the power of the Spirit was seen among them in other, and even more impressive, ways than by physical miracles,

[1] Cheikho, *Trois Traités*, p. 49.
[2] *Book of Governors*, II, 491–2.

particularly in the fact of conversion and the vitality and heroism of the Christian converts.

> The unique characteristic of nascent Christianity was its power. "Power" is the word harped upon throughout the New Testament and the Fathers; power to translate ideals into action; and that not only in the hearts of the refined few, but of the vulgar many; weak women, ignorant children, uncultivated slaves; power to convert the grossest of sinners into miracles of sanctity and martyrs for their faith. It was this power which stirred society to its depths and revolutionised the world. And the same creative power has continued through the ages, and is at work, as a fact of experience, in the world to-day. Nor has this power merely affected the personal lives of its possessors. It has worked through them outwards; and by degrees, and at the cost of many a martyrdom, raised the entire spiritual standard of the world.[1]

Of this kind of power the Eastern writers seem to have had little experience. Proselytes to Christianity were indeed made in vast numbers among the heathen outside Muslim territory —but in such numbers that it is difficult to believe that many of them were spiritually converted. We have no records of Muslims being converted to Christianity, nor even of Christians passing through the spiritual experience of conversion, the nearest approach to this being cases of men who refused episcopal dignity and cares and retired to a monastery or hermit's cell. We find, it is true, miracles recorded of Christians, but they were not so much works remarkable for their spiritual power as wonders and signs of the sort that our Lord refused to give to the Jews. The *Monastic History* of Thomas of Marga is full of wonders of this type, which were attributed to former members of the monastery, and one may be permitted to suspect that some of these, like the miracles of Yabalāhā and Qardagh, had their origin in the author's fertile brain. Al-Kindi, who was contemporary with Thomas of Marga, claimed that miracles did occasionally happen in his day, but he could give no examples, and was at great pains to give reasons why miracles were not common as in the apostolic age. Of these reasons the most

[1] Illingworth, *Reason and Revelation*, pp. 153–4.

remarkable, because the truest, was that "the monks to-day are not missionaries", in other words, the evangelistic spirit was dead. The passage is as follows, and reads strangely after the passage quoted above in which he used miracles as the main evidence for the truth of Christianity:

And if thou sayest, Why do not the monks to-day do signs and wonders and strange things like those that the apostles used to do when they went out into the lands, we answer thee and say, when they went into the lands to preach and to draw the people to acknowledge the lordship of Christ, for that purpose they needed an abundance of signs and a succession of wonders to establish the truth of their preaching, that those to whom they preached might know the truth of their assertions. But the monks to-day are not missionaries, although there are a certain number of them who undertake to do that [i.e. to perform miracles] in special cases secretly so that it may be known that that blessing is permanently established amongst them....But if the monks had undertaken to raise every dead man and to heal every sick man everywhere, no one would have died, and there would have been no hope of the resurrection and no end of the world, and this would have given the lie to the promises and threats of God about the world to come. And the monks only do those [miracles] which they do, and they take place by their hands, one by one, in order to increase their confidence in the fatigues and misfortunes that come upon them, and that they may know how far they have progressed in God's sight by their obedience night and day; and also that those who seek them with a pure heart and sincere intention, and come to them seeking help and seeking their prayers and the blessing of their petitions, may attain their desire. And moreover, if signs and wonders were shown in presence of trials as they were shown to the first [disciples], and if they continued as they were in the days of ignorance and lack of culture, then men would have no more praise for their faith and obedience than the beasts which have no merit for showing obedience or for obeying the bit and bridle and the beating of a stick. But since the nature of man, over and above the beasts, is [to possess] the grace of God and He has granted them intelligence, and the discernment which enables them to use their judgment to preserve the knowledge they have of proofs of the truth of their religion, therefore men have no need to-day of signs to establish the truth of this religion, except those who abstain from the use of their intelligence and share with the beasts their ignorance and lack of understanding.[1]

[1] *Risālat*, pp. 177–8.

In the dialogue of Ēlīyyā of Naṣībīn two contemporary miracles are recorded: one was worked by a monk who healed the Wazir by giving him pomegranate juice—the effect of which in reviving and refreshing a fever patient is well known at the present day. The other was a monk who perceived, by what we should nowadays call thought-reading, that a certain man was in danger of death or imprisonment.[1] A writer of the eleventh century, Abu 'l-Faraj 'Abdallah b. aṭ-Ṭaib, who was scribe to the Nestorian Catholicus, and died 1043, boldly rejected miracles as evidence for intelligent people. He said:

> Miracles take place in a certain place, at a certain time, among a certain people; and when that place, that time and that nation cease, the miracles cease as they cease. But argument is present in every place, at every time and with every people; therefore knowledge and argument are nobler than miracles. Thus our Lord Christ used to work miracles for the common people and the crowd, but showed proofs and arguments for the distinguished philosophers who would not be led by miracles, and did not profit thereby.[2]

The picture in the last sentence of our Lord arguing with distinguished philosophers makes us aware, with something of a shock, of the distance of this writer from the historical Jesus. To defend Christianity, as he does, on purely intellectual grounds, is not only utterly contrary to the mind of Christ, but is the bankruptcy of Christianity as a spiritual religion. Equally with those who trust in the proof from miracles, he has no idea of moral arguments or of the attractiveness of the character of Christ.

Is it fanciful to see in this loss of power by the Eastern Churches a result of their failure to know Christ as the truly incarnate Lord? They held up as an example, as we have seen, the gentle side of the character of Christ, His forbearance and so on; but all the strong side of His character, including His mighty works, was taken away from His humanity and ascribed to His divinity: we were not meant to copy that; our

[1] Cheikho, *Trois Traités*, pp. 27 and 49.
[2] Sbath, *Vingt Traités*, p. 180.

union with Christ only united us with His humility and weakness, and was not a source of spiritual strength.

At the same time, through failing to see the true power of the human Christ, they sought power in another direction, and slipped into the pagan estimate of power which is synonymous with worldly success. The pagan idea is that God's favour is shown by worldly success. Old Testament writers struggled against this view. A good example is seen in the seventy-third Psalm, in which the writer tries to grapple with the obvious fact that the wicked sometimes prosper, contrary to the accepted belief of his time. But when he came to verse 17 his faith failed him, or it may be that some later writer added these verses to the original psalm: "Until I went into the sanctuary of God, and considered their latter end. Surely thou settest them in slippery places: thou castest them down to destruction". A similar struggle is seen in the Book of Job, in which the views of the main body of the book should be compared with the view expressed in the last chapter in which Job becomes rich again. But when we come to the New Testament the victory had been won: there is not a single passage in the New Testament suggesting that the righteous necessarily have the best of this world's goods and prosperity. There seems to be a great deal of evidence that such views were commonly held in the East, both by Muslims and Christians. For instance, Abū Yūsuf said:

> There is nothing more pleasing to God than virtue, and nothing more hateful to Him than vice. And committing acts of disobedience is the denial of His benefits. And those who have shown ingratitude, and have never valued His benefits, and have not afterwards turned to repentance, have almost all had their strength taken from them, and God has caused their enemies to rule over them.[1]

Even to modern times it is an idea familiar to Muslims, for instance the late Syed Ameer 'Ali said,[2] "success is always one of the greatest criterions of truth". We have seen above[3]

[1] *Kitāb al-kharaj*, p. 6, trans. p. 5.
[2] *Spirit of Islam*, 2nd ed. p. 66. [3] P. 39.

how Michael the Syrian reflected the feeling of the Christians that God's favour was shown to the Muslims in their worldly prosperity and success. Timothy, the Nestorian Patriarch, concludes a eulogy of Muhammad as follows:

And as Abraham the friend of God did, when he left the idols and the children of his people and followed God and worshipped Him, and began teaching the unity of God to the nations, so also did Muhammad when he left the worship of the idols and those who were worshipping them of the children of his people and the other Arabs, and honoured only Him who is one alone, the true God, and worshipped Him. For this reason God Most High honoured him exceedingly, and subjected under his feet the two mighty kingdoms which were roaring like a lion and like thunder, and the cry of both of them was heard in the world, I mean the kingdom of Persia and the kingdom of Rūm, for the former were worshipping created beings instead of their Creator, and the latter were attributing sufferings and death to Him who absolutely does not suffer or die. And God most high bestowed the power of His kingdom into the hand of the Commander of the Faithful and his sons, from the east to the west and from the north to the south.[1]

The Muslim al-Hashimi writing to al-Kindi said:

So God set them up in the cities and subjected to them the necks of the nations of men, except those that hearkened to them and accepted their religion and bore witness to their faith, whereby their blood, their property and their honour were safe, and they were exempt from humbly paying *jizya*.[2]

Al-Kindi in reply explains that the campaigns of the Arabs were occasioned by their poverty, and were a punishment inflicted by God upon the Persians for their sins:

They were accustomed to eating lizards and chameleons, men of poverty and misery and wretched sustenance, in deserts and waste places; burnt up by the hot wind of summer and [frozen by] the intense cold of winter; exceedingly hungry, thirsty and naked. So when there was brandished before them the vision of rivers of wine and milk, various kinds of fruits, abundance of meat and foods, and reclining on couches, and resting on carpets of silk and

[1] Cheikho, *Trois Traités*, pp. 15–16.
[2] *Risālat*, p. 13, translated in Arnold's *Preaching of Islam*.

satin and brocade, and marriage with damsels like precious pearls, and being served by men-servants and maid-servants, and limpid water poured forth, and extended shade—like the description of the palaces of the Chosroes—this vision sunk into their minds [and some of them had already seen it in their travels and journeys to the land of Fars] and they leapt for joy, and when they heard of it they felt that they had already obtained it; and they seized it, and exerted themselves to fight against the people of Fars so as to take it from them and lay hold of it.... So they fought against an impure and filthy people who had revolted and rebelled against God, and the Most High gave them the sovereignty over them who had never paid heed to Him; so they slew them, and destroyed their houses, for that they had acted tyrannically and shed innocent blood. Thus was the command of God and His deed against a people of tyrants, and He took vengeance on some of them by the hands of others.[1]

In speaking of the poverty of the Arabs, al-Kindi touched the real reason, humanly speaking, for the Arab conquest, or at any rate the conscious motive that was uppermost in the minds of many. This fact is illustrated by the story of an early governor of ar-Rai named Kathīr b. Shihāb. One day he said to his slave, "Give me something to eat", The slave answered, "I have nothing but bread and herbs". And Kathīr exclaimed, "Did I make war upon Persia and Greece only for bread and herbs?"[2] But al-Kindi himself used the same argument from success when he compared the failure of the early Muslim raids against superior numbers with the aid given by God to Joshua: then one chased a thousand, and two put ten thousand to flight. The Captain of the Lord's Host appeared to Joshua before Jericho, and at His bidding Joshua invested the city for seven days and then took it without pact or covenant, and slew every male and female therein according to the command of the angel of the Lord. "I do not think", he concludes, "that you can find any reply to that, for you have nothing like it."[3] This passage is important because it shows that the belief in the worldly success of God's servants was accepted by a Christian writer, not

[1] *Risālat*, p. 100. [2] Balādhurī, p. 326, trans. II, 5.
[3] *Risālat*, pp. 49–51.

casually, but when he was making a reasoned defence of his faith. An interesting sidelight on this sort of mentality is given by Thomas of Marga in his account of the mission of Shūbḥāl-īshū‘ (the predecessor of Yabalāhā and Qardagh) to the people of Gīlān and Dailām:

> Mar Abraham, the Catholicus, a holy man in very truth, related to me fully concerning all this matter [of Shubḥāl-īshū‘], and he told me that he made his entrance there with exceeding great splendour, for barbarian nations need to see a little worldly pomp and show to attract them and to make them draw nigh willingly to Christianity.[1]

But our chief evidence for the prevalence of this belief in worldly success as the sign of God's power is to be found in 'Alī Ṭabarī's *Book of Religion and Empire*, which was written about A.D. 855. He himself was a convert from Christianity to Islam, and this book shows clearly the reason of his conversion. Among the evidences for Muhammad's prophet-hood is that "his victory over the nations is also by necessity and by undeniable arguments a manifest sign (of the prophetic office)".[2] Again, "Among the miracles of the Prophet is his victory, which all Muslims have used as an argument".[3] Then, just as al-Kindi had to find excuses for Muslim victories, so 'Alī Ṭabarī has to find excuses for non-Muslim victories:

> As to the victories of other nations, which they oppose to us, if they had relinquished the passions which blind and deafen, and discerned their motives, they would have known that the victory of Alexander, or Ardashir son of Babak, and of others, was not in God nor to invite people to God or to His prophets, but its aim was solely victory, power and reputation, while the victors were either Materialists or Dualists or Pagans; and this cannot be compared with the victory, dignity and sublimity of Islam.[4]

After describing how Moses commanded the Israelites to spoil the Egyptians, he goes on:

> All this was not unlawful and illicit, but was simply the right of booty and spoils; for the world belongs to the Most High God,

[1] *Book of Governors*, II, 480.

[2] *Kitāb ad-dīn wad-daulat*, p. 16, trans. p. 14.

[3] *Op. cit.* p. 50, trans. p. 57. [4] *Op. cit.* p. 52, trans. p. 58.

and its kingdom and ornaments belong to those of His servants upon whom He bestows them.... So also are to be considered the holy war against the polytheists and the attacks against the unbelievers, the injunction of which God laid upon the Prophet. Without holy war no religion could stand, no inviolable thing could be safe, no gap could be filled, and the Muslims would become the prey and possession of their enemies. Men would scarcely remain in a religion with such standing, without passing to what is higher and safer. The Christ had forbidden war, and given warning against its causes, in saying, "Whosoever shall compel thee to go a mile, go with him twain; whosoever taketh away thy coat, give him thy cloak also; whosoever shall smite thee on thy cheek, turn to him the other also". By this order the Christ left but little spiritual and temporal power[1] to His followers, and transferred their heritage to the members of another nation who stirred up war in East and West, and kindled it with spears and swords as far as the countries of the Greeks, of the Franks, of the tent-dwelling Turanians and of the Armenians. Outside these countries what Christians are to be found in the country of the Turks except a small and despicable quantity of Nestorians scattered among the nations? or what are those found among the Arabs except a sprinkling of Jacobites and Melkites? Then we have seen that the Christ gave permission ultimately to take swords; and in that He abrogated the first order. He said indeed to His disciples, "Let each one of you sell his garment and buy a sword with it for himself". And He said, "Think not that I am come to sow peace, but war".[2]

With 'Alī Ṭabarī's statement that Christ's doctrine of non-resistance "left but little spiritual and temporal power to His followers", we may compare the statement of Ibn Khaldūn[3] that the office of chief of police is a religious function based on the religious law. It is clear that there was no conception of spiritual power apart from the power of the sword. Finally, as if to leave no doubt, 'Alī Ṭabarī chose a significant title for his book:

This my book, which I have entitled *Kitāb ad-dīn wad-daulat* has decisively demonstrated the unsoundness and fallacy of Judaism, the villainy and falseness of Dualism and Materialism, and the

[1] Lit. "neither religion nor world".

[2] *Op. cit.* pp. 132–3, trans. pp. 155–6.

[3] Quoted by Guillaume, *Traditions of Islam*, p. 166.

onlooker already observes their downfall and their eclipse, and sees that resplendent light and true faith are exclusively in Islam.[1]

The word *ad-dīn* of course here refers to the religion of Islam, and the word *ad-daulat* means prosperity and dominion, so that the title of the book shows the connexion in the author's mind between the true religion and the power and success of this world. It is almost the exact opposite of our Lord's saying, "Ye cannot serve God and mammon".[2] In antiquity the titles of books were often changed, and we cannot depend on their present titles having been given by the author. But in this case the author takes the unusual step of introducing the title into the body of his work. It can scarcely be doubted that these views which he held as a Muslim he had previously held as a Christian, and that it was on account of them that he decided to pass over to a "safer" religion in which power lay.

In actual practice we have examples throughout the period of our history of the way in which Church dignitaries on every possible occasion made use of the civil power for their purposes. The idea that there was in Christ a stronger power than that of earthly might seems never to have entered their minds. This lack is the condemnation of their Christianity, and probably more than anything else the cause of its downfall.

Some readers may feel that it is unfair to charge the Eastern Churches with weaknesses which were common to the whole Church. Such a criticism would be beside the point. An individual does not escape the consequences of his deeds by the reflection that he is no worse than his fellows. Our concern is not to compare the achievements of Christianity in the East and the West, nor to conjecture how Christianity in the West might have fared if the European Christians had lived under Muslim domination; but only to trace the actual course of Christian history in Asia.

[1] *Op. cit.* p. 144, trans. p. 169.

[2] In the Urdu version of Mt. vi, 24 the word *daulat* is actually used as the translation of "mammon".

Chapter VII

CHRISTIAN MISSIONARY EXPANSION

It has been mentioned in Chapter I that by the end of the fifth century there were Christian communities among the Turks near the River Oxus. One of the means by which Christianity had reached them was through Byzantine captives who had fallen into their hands; but the Nestorian Church was quick to seize the opportunity by sending missionaries to them.[1] An Armenian bishop also shared in these labours, and these facts may explain the claim, made by the Jacobite writer of a letter attributed (no doubt falsely) to Philoxenus of Mabbūg,[2] that the Turkish Christians only became Nestorians because they were unable to repair to Antioch for the consecration of their Metropolitan. In spite of this claim there seems to be no doubt that the credit for the evangelisation of the Turks is due almost entirely to the Nestorian Church. In the middle of the sixth century a priest of the Hephthalite Huns was consecrated as bishop for his people by the Nestorian Catholicus. According to the Nestorian Monument at Si-ngan-fu Christianity was brought into China in A.D. 635 by a Syrian whose name appears in Chinese as A-lo-pên.[3] The first mention of large numbers of converts beyond the Oxus is in connexion with a missionary journey undertaken by Ēlīyyā, the Metropolitan of Merv, about A.D. 644.[4] From that time onwards Christianity was making considerable progress beyond the river Oxus. The people were heathen, and it was a race between the Manichaeans and the Christians which would convert them first. Manichaeanism was of all religions the one most hated by the Muslims, for their dualistic belief

1 Mingana, *Early Spread of Christianity*, p. 303.
2 Text and translation are given in Mingana, *op. cit.*
3 Saeki, *Nestorian Monument*, p. 165.
4 Mingana, *op. cit.* pp. 304–5.

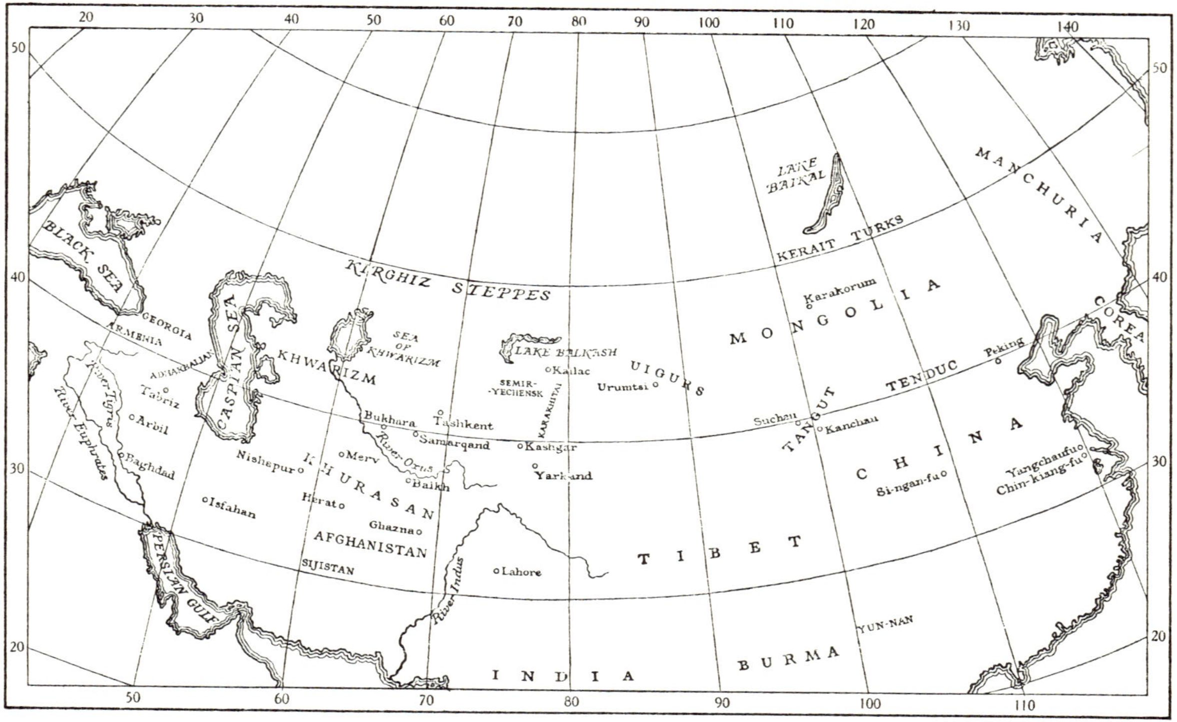
KIRGHIZ STEPPES
KERAIT TURKS
LAKE BAIKAL
MANCHURIA
COREA
MONGOLIA
Karakorum
Peking
TENDUC
TANGUT
Suchau
Kanchau
CHINA
Si-ngan-fu
Yangchaufu
Chin-kiang-fu
UIGURS
Urumtsi
Kailac
LAKE BALKASH
SEMIR-YECHENSK
KARAKHITAI
Kashgar
Yarkand
Tashkent
Samarqand
Bukhara
River Oxus
Balkh
Merv
KHURASAN
Nishapur
Herat
Ghazna
AFGHANISTAN
SIJISTAN
Isfahan
SEA OF KHWARIZM
KHWARIZM
CASPIAN SEA
ADHARBAIJAN
Tabriz
Arbil
Baghdad
GEORGIA
ARMENIA
BLACK SEA
River Tigris
River Euphrates
PERSIAN GULF
TIBET
Lahore
River Indus
INDIA
BURMA
YUN-NAN

had the inevitable result of loosening the ties of family life. Various expeditions were sent to suppress the Manichaeans who resisted the Muslim power. The last and greatest of the Manichaean revolts was that of al-Muqanna‘, "the Veiled Prophet of Khurasan". This revolt was finally and effectively suppressed by the Caliph al-Mahdī about A.D. 780.[1] The sect continued to exist and to follow their old practices, including community of wives, although they called themselves Muslims. The Muslims had begun making raids in Transoxania as early as A.D. 705, but their power was not consolidated there until well on into the ninth century, and until then Islam as a religion was not a serious rival to Christianity among the Turks.[2] In the latter half of the eighth century the number of Turkish Christians was so much increased that the Catholicus Timothy consecrated a Metropolitan for them about A.D. 781. It is also mentioned incidentally in his letters that he was about to consecrate a Metropolitan for Tibet, and that a Metropolitan had died in China. These brief references are tantalising, because they show that there must have been great missions of which we have no record. It was about this time that Shubḥāl-īshū‘ made his entry "with exceeding great splendour" into the countries of Gīlān and Dailām near the Caspian Sea.[3] Timothy had sent more than eighty monks on this mission, and some of these were sent by Shubḥāl-īshū‘ to convert the heathen of the Far East, though how far eastwards they went is not made clear. The famous Nestorian monument, which was erected at Si-ngan-fu in A.D. 779, is evidence of a considerable Christian community right in the heart of China at that time.[4] Some seventy-five names are inscribed upon the monument, all, or almost all, of which appear from their form to be the names of foreigners. One

[1] *Abu 'l-faraj*, *Ta'rīkh mukhtaṣar ad-daul*, p. 217; Muir, *Caliphate*, p. 470.

[2] Barthold, *Zur Geschichte des Christentums in Mittel-Asien*, pp. 16–21; Muir, *Caliphate*, pp. 349 ff.

[3] See above, p. 90.

[4] Saeki, *Nestorian Monument*; Moule, *Christians in China*.

was a bishop, and the rest were priests or monks. After the arrival of A-lo-pên, already referred to, Christianity seems to have spread throughout China and monasteries were built in many cities until the end of the seventh century when Buddhist opposition began to be felt. Chinese historians record that in the year A.D. 732 an embassy arrived from Persia including a monk named Chi-lieh, and that the same man had paid a previous visit to China in A.D. 713.[1] The monument also records the later visit, and connects it with a restoration of the fortunes of the Church.[2] The Emperors who reigned during the eighth century were favourable to Christianity, and one of them rebuilt some monasteries which had been destroyed, presumably by Buddhists. In A.D. 744 another Syrian missionary is mentioned by name, a monk Chi-ho. In the Chinese text of the monument, and in the Syriac inscription beneath it, there is mention of a certain I-ssŭ or Izdbuzid, who came from Balkh. He seems to have laboured for many years in China, and at the time of the erection of the monument in A.D. 781 he was "country-bishop of Khumdan" or Si-ngan-fu, and as this town was the Chinese capital at the time he was probably the chief bishop or Metropolitan of the Nestorians in China. An inscription engraved in or soon after A.D. 824 says:

> Among the different foreigners who have come there are the Mo-ni (Manichees), the Ta-ch'in (Christians), and the Hsien-shên (Zoroastrians). All the monasteries of these three sorts of foreigners in the Empire together are not enough to equal the number of our Buddhist monasteries in one small city.[3]

In A.D. 845 the Chinese Emperor issued an edict ordering that all Buddhist monasteries were to be destroyed. A few exceptions were allowed, and the number of monks in each of them was limited to thirty. Altogether 4600 Buddhist monasteries were destroyed, and 260,500 monks and nuns were secularised, i.e. an average of 56 or 57 inmates to each

[1] Saeki, *op. cit.* p. 225; Moule, *op. cit.* pp. 65–6.
[2] Saeki, *op. cit.* p. 168; Moule, *op. cit.* p. 41.
[3] Moule, *op. cit.* p. 69.

monastery. The same edict compelled the Christian and Zoroastrian monks to the number of 3000 (or 2000 according to another authority) to return to the secular life.[1] Now we are told that early in the eighth century the number of Buddhist monasteries in Ch'ang-an (Si-ngan-fu) itself was sixty-two, and of nunneries twenty-seven. As this was the capital it was probably one of the larger cities. So that we may conclude that a small city would not contain more than fifty monasteries, and if the inscription is true it means that the total number of Manichaean, Christian and Zoroastrian monasteries throughout China was not more than fifty. According to the Nestorian monument Christian monasteries were founded in every one of the departments, the Christian religion was spread over the ten provinces, and there were monasteries in every city.[2] From these facts we may conclude that the number of Christian monasteries was something between ten and forty. So small a number as fifty Christian and Zoroastrian monasteries for 3000 monks would mean an average of sixty monks in each monastery, corresponding closely to the average number in the Buddhist monasteries. At the time of its foundation the Christian monastery in Si-ngan-fu contained twenty-one monks.[3]

Whether Christianity was completely stamped out of China as a result of the edict of A.D. 845 is not certain. A Metropolitan of China is mentioned soon afterwards by the Patriarch Theodosius (A.D. 852–68) in a list of Metropolitans who could not be expected to attend the regular councils of the Church, but the mention is made in such a way as not to preclude the possibility that the see was vacant at the time.[4] A Muslim writer Abu Zaid says that a great rebellion took place in China under a certain man named Banshu (Huang Ch'ao):

> He marched first on Khanfu (very probably Canton) which is one of the cities of China and the port at which the Arab merchants

[1] Moule, *op. cit.* pp. 70–1.

[2] Moule, *op. cit.* p. 40 (but Saeki, *op. cit.* p. 167, has "in many cities").

[3] Moule, *op. cit.* p. 39.

[4] Assemani, III, pt II, CCCCXXXIX.

call. . . . The siege lasted a long time. It took place in the year of the Hijra 264 [A.D. 877–8]. Having at last made himself master of the city, he put all the inhabitants to death. Persons well informed about these affairs relate that without counting the Chinese who were massacred there perished six score thousand Mahometans, Jews, Christians and Parsis, who were living in the city and doing business there. The exact number of those who perished of these four religions could be known because the Chinese levied a tax on these foreigners according to their number.[1]

According to the historian an-Nadīm Christianity had quite died out in China a century later:

What the monk of Najrān told me who came from the land of China in the year A.H. 377 [A.D. 987]. Now this man of the people of Najrān had been dispatched some seven years before this date by the Catholicus to the land of China, there being sent with him five other men of the Christians, of those whose business it is to attend to the affairs of religion. And six years after they had thus gone forth, this monk with one other alone of all that company had returned alive [to Baghdad], whom I met in the Christian quarter of the Dār ar-Rūm behind the church, finding him to be a man in the prime of life with a fine figure, but sparing of words unless he were questioned. So I asked him what had been the cause of his remaining away so long a time, and what reason had brought him back thence, whereupon he recounted to me all the adventures that had befallen him, and what had hindered him in the journey. He said in conclusion that the Christians who had been of old in the lands of China were now disappeared, and that their possessions had perished, so that in the whole land hardly one Christian now remained alive; though in ancient times the Christians there had possessed a church, this also was now in ruins. And the monk added that when he had at length seen how none remained there of his religion, he had finally returned home, travelling back in less time than it had taken him to perform the voyage out.[2]

The statement that "the Christians there had possessed *a church*" suggests that this monk had not travelled widely in China, otherwise he would have known that there had formerly been many churches in China; but, in the absence

[1] Moule, *op. cit.* p. 76.

[2] *Fihrist*, p. 349, quoted by G. Le Strange, *Baghdad during the Abbasid Caliphate*, p. 213.

of other information, we are obliged at least to conclude that Christianity in China had greatly diminished by the end of the tenth century. Moule says:

> The mentions of Christianity in contemporary Chinese authors of the tenth, eleventh, and twelfth centuries are very few, and what there are are either extremely vague or refer definitely to an already distant past, and we believe that nothing has been found to suggest that there were Christians surviving in China during the eleventh and twelfth centuries.[1]

Among the causes of this first failure of Christianity in China must be placed the fact that it was a predominantly foreign Church. The seventy-five names on the Nestorian monument are almost without exception Syrian. This of course is not conclusive evidence that the whole ministry was Syrian, for, as we have seen, the total number of Christian monks in China probably ran into thousands. But, on the other hand, the two or three thousand Christian and Zoroastrian monks who were compelled to return to lay life were dealt with by the "Controllers of aliens". Moreover, Christianity was known as the Ta-ch'in religion, Ta-ch'in being the name for the lands near the Mediterranean Sea. Christian monasteries were at one time called Persian monasteries, but by a decree of A.D. 745 they were to be called Ta-ch'in monasteries.[2] The Chinese inscription of A.D. 824 quoted above speaks of Manichaeans, Christians and Zoroastrians as "foreigners", and the Muhammadans, Jews, Christians and Parsis mentioned by Abu Zaid were taxable as foreigners. It is scarcely likely that the number of Nestorian missionaries was great enough to staff the churches throughout China. But it may well have been the case that, while the bulk of the Christians were Turkish, the control was kept in the hands of the missionaries from Persia. Moule says:

> Analysis of these seventy names, which are quite unexplained on the monument, may suggest that they are possibly those of the staff of the diocese at the time when the stone was set up, or more

[1] Moule, *op. cit.* p. 73.
[2] Moule, *op. cit.* p. 67.

probably the names of those present at one of the annual gatherings organised by Izd-buzid.[1]

One might go further and conjecture that they were the foreign missionaries, and came together to direct the affairs of the whole Church.

Now if a Church is felt to be foreign it has not really entered the hearts of the people and made itself at home in the land. In some cases such a foreign Church can continue to exist owing to influence from the Church or the government of its home land. But in the case of the Nestorian Church in China the extreme difficulty of communicating with the Patriarchal see of Seleucia-Ctesiphon meant that they could not depend upon support from that quarter; and of course there was no support to be expected from the Caliph's government. The result was that the continued existence of the Nestorian Church in China depended on the personal favour of the Chinese Emperor. The first spread of the Church in China was due to the Emperor T'ai Tsung (A.D. 627–49) who gave special orders for its propagation. His successor Kao Tsung (A.D. 650–83) caused Christian monasteries to be founded in every one of the departments. Other Emperors cared for and restored monasteries after they had suffered from Buddhist antagonism. One passage on the monument highly extols the favour shown by the Emperor, and presents us with a picture of Christianity and the Emperor as two powers working hand in hand:

> His gracious favour was like the Southern Mountain's towering peak; his overflowing kindness was as deep as the Eastern Sea. The Way [i.e. Christianity] is almighty, what it effects it is right to name; the Sage is never idle, what he does it is right to record.[2]

No doubt if the royal favour had not been so pronounced the Christians would have attempted to secure the foundation of the Church in Chinese soil, and would not have been content that Christianity should appear as a foreign religion; but, lulled into a sense of false security by the Emperor's favour,

[1] Moule, *op. cit.* p. 52.

[2] Moule, *op. cit.* pp. 39–42; Saeki, *op. cit.* pp. 165–69.

they learnt to rely on that instead of on the might of the Spirit, and so they were found helpless when the Imperial favour was withdrawn in A.D. 845, and even more so after A.D. 907 when the T'ang dynasty fell and broke up into ten fragments ruled over by former governors of provinces.

But whatever may have been the fate of Christianity at that time in China, it had not died out in Central Asia, although no doubt many of the Christians had accepted Islam after the Muslims had completed the conquest of Transoxania. Muslim writers in the latter part of the tenth century, quoted by Barthold,[1] speak of Christians in the neighbourhood of Samarqand and of Christian immigrants on the frontier of the district of Tashkent. Saljūq, of the tribe of Ghuzz, the founder of the Saljūq Turks, had a son with the Christian name of Michael, which indicates that Christianity had made some progress by the tenth century in the Kirghiz Steppes where Saljūq lived before the southward migration of his clan into Bukhara.[2] After their migration into Bukhara the Saljūqs became zealous Muslims. Two Nestorian cemeteries have been found in the province of Semiryechensk containing over six hundred grave stones dating from the middle of the ninth to the middle of the fourteenth century.[3]

At the beginning of the eleventh century there was a remarkable mass movement towards Christianity among the Kerait Turks who lived far away to the north of Mongolia, south of Lake Baikal. It is recorded both by the Jacobite and by the Nestorian chroniclers. Barhebraeus says:

At that time [i.e. about 1007] 'Abdīshū' the Metropolitan of Merv, one of the cities of Khurāsān, wrote as follows to the Catholicus: "The king of a people called Kerait, i.e. the more distant Turks of the north-east, was hunting on one of the high mountains of his land and was overtaken by a violent snow storm, and wandered aimlessly out of the way. When he had given up all hope of safety, there appeared to him in a vision a certain saint who said to him, If thou believest in Christ I will

[1] *Zur Geschichte des Christentums in Mittel-Asien*, pp. 29–30.
[2] *Op. cit.* p. 42.
[3] Mingana, *Early Spread of Christianity*, pp. 333–4.

show thee the way that thou perish not. He promised that he would be a sheep in the Christian fold. Then he showed him the way, and led him to a safe path. Having thus returned safe to his tents, he called to him the Christian traders who were there, and asked them concerning the faith. They told him he could not be perfected except by baptism. So he received a Gospel from them which he worships daily; and now he has sent a messenger asking me to go to him or to appoint a priest to baptise him. Moreover he asked me concerning fasting, saying, Apart from meat and milk we have no other food. How then shall we fast? He asserted further that the number of those that believed with him reached 200,000". The Catholicus then wrote to the Metropolitan telling him to send two persons, a priest and a deacon, and with them the requisites of an altar, who should go there and baptise as many as believed and teach them the Christian rites. As to the Lenten fast, they should abstain from eating meat, but they should be allowed to drink milk, if indeed, as they say, Lenten food is not found in their land.[1]

The account given by the Nestorian Chronicler differs only in minor details:

A letter came from 'Abdīshū', Metropolitan of Merv, saying that...a certain king of the Turks had turned Christian, and about 200,000 men with him. And the cause of it was that when he went out hunting he wandered from his path, and as he was in a state of stupor he saw a person who promised him safety, and he asked him his name, and he said, "I am Mar Serjasān [Sergius]", and he commanded him to become a Christian, and he said to him, "Close your eyes", and he closed them, and when he opened them he saw himself in the midst of his army. And he was astonished thereat, and he asked concerning the Christian religion and the prayers and the book of the law. And he taught him "Our Father which art in heaven", and "To thee O Lord of all", and "Holy God". And the Metropolitan said that he wrote to him to come to him, and he said that it was their custom to eat milk and flesh; and this king made for himself a pavilion in place of an altar, and in it placed the cross and the Gospel, and he inscribed it with the name of Mar Serjasān. And he tied up a mare, and took some of its milk, and put it in front of the Gospel and the cross, and prayed over it what he had learnt, and crossed himself, and took a mouthful of the milk, and the rest of the company [did likewise]. And the Metropolitan asked what he

[1] *Chron. Eccles.* II, col. 279.

should do with them as they had no corn, and he [the Catholicus] commanded that he should take care to supply them with sufficient corn for the day of the Passover, and wine also; and that during the fast they were to abstain from flesh and content themselves with milk alone; and if it was their custom to take it sour they should take it sweet, so as to change the custom.[1]

From the first of these two accounts it is clear that it was Christian merchants who really brought the gospel to the Keraits. In contrast with the zeal of these merchants, the part played by the ecclesiastical authorities appears to have been altogether unworthy of the opportunity. To send one priest and one deacon to baptise 200,000 people could only mean that they were to be baptised without any instruction whatever. It is also to be noted that, while the Catholicus was careful to answer the question about the observance of Lent, he had no word of rebuke for the Kerait king's worship of the Gospel.

It may well have been, however, that the conversion of the Keraits was a stimulus to further missionary work in China. Exactly how or when that work was carried on is not recorded. Of the town of Kāshgar in Eastern Turkestan we learn that the Nestorian Catholicus Ēlīyyā III (1176–90) nominated two Metropolitans for it in succession.[2] The earliest reference to the return of Christianity to China is to be found in the *History of Yabalāhā III*.[3] Barṣauma, the senior companion of Yabalāhā, was born in Khānbāliq (Peking). As he died as an old man in 1294, he must have been born as early as 1230. At that time there was a Christian community in Khānbāliq, with a church, and a school in which theology was taught. Barṣauma himself belonged to one of the Turkish tribes, possibly the Uigurs. Khānbāliq had been in the hands of the Mongols since about 1215, so that the Christian community from which Barṣauma sprang probably came in with the Mongol conquerors. Yabalāhā

[1] Mari, fol. 218 *b*.

[2] Amr, p. 111.

[3] Budge, *The Monks of Ḳublai Khan*, pp. 124–5; Montgomery, p. 27; Moule, *op. cit.* p. 94.

also was a Turk, most probably of the tribe of Öngüt, and was born as Koshang (identified with a town in the north of Shan-hsi) in 1245. The narratives of the European travellers in the thirteenth century bring to light a large number of Christian communities which existed all over Eastern Turkestan and China. Friar William of Rubruck made a journey from 1253 to 1255 across southern Russia, north of the Caspian Sea and the Sea of Khwarizm, as far as the town of Karakorum in Mongolia where the Great Khan had his camp. He makes frequent mention of Nestorian Christians in various places on his journey. Among the Karakhitai there was a tribe called Naiman with a Christian king. Near Kailac he found a village consisting entirely of Nestorian Christians. Nestorian Christians were to be found in all the cities of the Uigurs, and there were some Christians in or near Karakorum itself. Although he did not visit Si-ngan-fu he reports that there was a Nestorian bishop there, and Nestorians in fifteen cities of Cathay. Marco Polo, following a rather more southerly route in 1278, found Nestorian Christians in Samarqand, Kashgar, Yarkand, Chichintalas (identified with Urumtsi), in the kingdom of Tangut and particularly in the towns of Suchau and Kanchau, in the province of Tenduc (i.e. the Turkish tribe of Öngüt) and the cities to the east of it, as well as in Manchuria and the countries bordering on Corea. He also refers to Christians in the province of Yun-nan which borders on Burma, and in the city of Chin-kiang-fu on the Yangtse River.[1] Fuller particulars of the Christians in Chin-kiang-fu are given in a Chinese book called the *History of Chên-chiang of the Chih-shun period.*[2] A monastery was built there in 1281 by a certain Mar Sergis, and also six other monasteries. This man's grandfather was a physician of Samarqand, and had healed a son of Chingiz Khān by the

[1] *William of Rubruck*, edited by Rockhill; *Marco Polo*, edited by Yule. The references to Christians are conveniently summarised by Yule-Cordier, *Cathay*, I, 116–19, and by Mingana, *Early Spread of Christianity*, p. 315.

[2] See Moule, *op. cit.* ch. vi.

administration of sherbet and by the prayers of the Christians, and was afterwards appointed purveyor of sherbet to the Great Khān. Mar Sergis himself held the same office under Khubilai Khān, and was some sort of assistant governor of Chin-kiang-fu. The same document gives the number of Christians in Chin-kiang-fu as 106 members of families and 109 solitary individuals. Although reckoned as foreigners, the Christians are classed as permanent residents. According to Marco Polo there were no Christians there before 1278. The existence of numerous Christians in China is explained by Marco Polo as follows:

> The Great Khān had not the rule of the province of Cathay by right, since he had taken it by force; and not trusting them he gave the rule of the province to Tartars, Saracens and Christians, who were of his own family and loyal to him, and were not of the province of Cathay.[1]

Just above Marco Polo had said that they could easily be distinguished because the Tatars, Saracens and Christians had beards, but the Cathayans had not. One manuscript of Marco Polo speaks of the Christians in several places including those of Yun-nan as Turkish Nestorians. Moule says:

> In all the long period of fifteen centuries with which we are dealing there are only two, or at most three, passages so far as I know, which show the existence of Chinese Christians.[2]

It is noteworthy that John de Monte Corvino who worked for some years in Khanbaliq before and after 1300 is said to have converted and baptised 10,000 Tatars, but there is no mention made of Chinese.[3] Friar Odoric, who was in China 1322–8, mentions Christians in Yang-chau-fu, a city close to Chin-kiang-fu.[4] The Archbishop of Sultaniyya, writing in 1330, says that there were Nestorian Christians in Khanbaliq, and estimates the number of Nestorians in Cathay as 30,000.[5] Moule gives quotations from many contemporary Chinese books and inscriptions referring to Christians in

[1] Moule, *op. cit.* p. 137.
[2] Moule, *op. cit.* p. 150 n.
[3] Moule, *op. cit.* p. 191.
[4] Yule-Cordier, *Cathay*, II, 209.
[5] Yule-Cordier, *Cathay*, III, 102.

northern and eastern China. They were sufficiently numerous to require a special government department to deal with them.[1]

But in spite of the great numerical expansion of Christianity, the quality of the Christian life appears to have been very deficient. Rubruck says of them:

> The Nestorians there know nothing. They say their offices, and have sacred books in Syrian, but they do not know the language, so they chant like those monks among us who do not know grammar, and they are absolutely depraved. In the first place they are usurers and drunkards; some even among them who live with the Tartars have several wives like them....The bishop rarely visits these parts, hardly once in fifty years. When he does, they have all their male children, even those in the cradle, ordained priests, so nearly all the males among them are priests.[2]

Yule, referring to this report, says:

> He gives an unfavourable account of the literature and morals of their clergy, which deserves more weight than such statements regarding those looked on as schismatics generally do; for the narrative of Rubruquis gives one the impression of being written by a thoroughly honest and intelligent person.[3]

Rubruck also accuses the Nestorian priests of condoning sorcery, and even practising it.[4] The intolerance of the Nestorians towards other Christians, which is reported by John de Monte Corvino, is only what we have grown accustomed to finding in the Asiatic Churches. He says:

> I proceeded on my further journey and made my way to Cathay [about 1293], the realm of the Emperor of the Tartars who is called the Grand Cham....The Nestorians, a certain body who profess to bear the Christian name, but who deviate sadly from the Christian religion, have grown so powerful in those parts that they will not allow a Christian of another ritual to have ever so small a chapel, or to publish any doctrine different from their own.[5]

[1] Moule, ch. VIII.

[2] Rockhill's *Rubruck*, p. 158, also quoted by Yule-Courdier, I, 116–17.

[3] Yule, *Cathay*, I, p. xcviii; Yule-Cordier, I, 116.

[4] Rockhill's *Rubruck*, pp. 195, 212.

[5] Yule, *Cathay*, I, 197; Yule-Cordier, III, 45.

Among the missionary work of the Nestorian Church must be reckoned the Christians of Malabar in South India. Whatever the origin of that Christian community may have been, there is no doubt that their geographical position brought them into touch with the Metropolitans of Revardashir and the Nestorian Catholici, and that their continued existence was due to their connexion with the Nestorian Church.[1]

Such is an outline of the missionary expansion of the Nestorian Church from the time of Muhammad to the Mongol invasion. Even in the rough outline that we can make out from the scattered historical notices, it is clear that it was an amazing achievement. In the extent of land covered, in the difficulties of travel at great altitudes, and in the number of the converts, it stands unique in missionary annals. But these things alone, remarkable as they are, scarcely justify the claim that the Nestorian Church is the greatest missionary Church there has ever been. In the conversion of the Keraits we have one of the worst examples of a mass movement in which converts were received into the Church without due preparation or teaching. That such methods were fairly general may be gathered from the missionary method of Shubḥāl-īshūʿ already referred to, from the very unsatisfactory manner of life of the Christians as observed by William of Rubruck, and from the rapidity with which they fell away from Christianity, first (as we have seen was probably the case) in the tenth century, and then again, as we shall see, in the fourteenth century. How can we account for the zeal and energy of the missionary work side by side with the serious defects of their methods? To the monk trained in extreme ascetic practices, the privations of travel would be but little greater than the physical discomforts to which he was already inured. Certainly their missionary undertakings needed zeal, but it would scarcely be unfair to apply to them the words St Paul wrote of the Jews,[2] "I bear

[1] Mingana, *Early Spread of Christianity in India*; Farquhar, *The Apostle Thomas in South India.* [2] Rom. x, 2.

them witness that they have a zeal for God, but not according to knowledge". The parallel is not merely verbal, for when Thomas of Marga describes the Christian message as a call "to bow their necks to the submission of the yoke of fasting and of prayer, of vigil by nights, and of abstinence from every kind of food on the stated fasts and holy festivals",[1] is it not more reminiscent of the burden of the Mosaic law than of the liberty of the glory of the children of God? On the other hand, the failure to hold up the whole Christ as the example of righteousness, and the failure to experience the power of the working of the Holy Spirit, allowed these missionaries to accept converts without making sure that Christianity was a spiritual reality in their lives; and the reliance on the secular arm, of which we have spoken, encouraged them to seek large numbers of converts. It is possible that, if we had fuller details of the lives and labours of these missionaries, we should have reason to modify this stern judgment; but with the information available, we can only suppose that the failure of Christianity in Central and Eastern Asia was due to the missionary methods employed, and that those methods were the natural outcome of the life and thought of the Church.

[1] Quoted above, p. 83.

Chapter VIII

POLEMIC

From the very commencement of Islam Christians were called upon to give an account of their faith. Of the vast amount of polemical literature that once existed, or even still exists in manuscripts in the great libraries of the world,[1] a sufficient amount has been published to give us a fair idea of the methods of approach employed by Christians on the one hand and by Muslims on the other. In Chapter VI numerous quotations are given from this literature to show the religious and theological ideas of the Christians. It only remains therefore to consider their methods of presentation of their faith, and the effect of their apologies on the minds of Muslims.

The first recorded apology is a conversation that took place in A.D. 639 between John I, the Jacobite Patriarch of Antioch, and ʿAmr b. al-ʿĀṣ, the conqueror of Egypt.[2] Under the circumstances, in which the Patriarch was summoned to appear before the great Muslim general, it was natural that the colloquy should take the form of questions put by ʿAmr and answers given by the Patriarch. It was the Muslim who chose the subjects of discussion, and the Christian who was on the defensive. Throughout the whole of the literature that we are considering the Christian writers adopted the same attitude. It was as though they were hypnotised by the power of the Muslims, and allowed their opponents to choose the field of discussion instead of striking out boldly and delivering the gospel message.

Often we find Christians using arguments which are

[1] Steinschneider, *Abhandlungen f. d. Kunde des Morgenlandes*, Bd. VI, No. 3, 1877, "Polemische und apologetische Literatur in arabischer Sprache zwischen Muslimen, Christen und Juden".

[2] Edited by Nau, *Journal Asiatique*, série xi, tome v (1915).

obviously intended, not to convert the Muslim, but only to get rid of his unwelcome attentions. This aim is fairly obvious in the following examples of dialogues between a Christian and a Muslim prepared by John of Damascus, or more probably by his pupil Theodore Abucara, as an aid to Christians when they had to meet Muslims in argument:

Saracen asks: If a Christian does the will of God Himself, do you call him good or evil?

Christian, recognising his craftiness, replies: I know what is in your mind.

Saracen: Then tell me.

Chr.: You mean to say to me, Did Christ suffer willingly or not? Because if I should say to you, He suffered willingly, you would reply to me, Then go and reverence the Jews because they did the will of God.

Sar.: That is exactly what I intended to say to you, and if you are able to say a word in reply, do so.

Chr.: You used the expression "will", but I prefer to say "tolerance" or "long-suffering".

Sar.: How can you show that?

Chr. (replying by means of an illustration): When you or I are sitting or standing, can either of us rise or move without the power and will of God?

Sar.: No.

Chr.: Since God said, Thou shalt not steal, thou shalt not commit fornication, thou shalt not kill, He obviously does not wish us to steal, commit fornication or kill.

Sar.: That is true, for had He wished it He would not have said, Do not steal, commit fornication or kill.

Chr.: Praise be to God, that in so saying you agree with what I am about to say. Verily you agree with me that neither of us can rise or move apart from God, and that God does not wish us to steal or commit fornication. So if now I rise and go off and steal or commit fornication, what do you call it? Do you call it God's will, or His indulgence, His tolerance and His long-suffering?

Sar. (convicted and astonished): Verily it is even so.

If a Saracen asks you saying, Who do you say Christ is? reply to him, The Word of God. I do not think you are erring in this, because in Scripture He is called Word, and Wisdom, and Branch, and Power of God, and many other things of this kind; for He has many names. Then you ask him in your turn, What is Christ called in your Scripture? It may be that the Saracen will want to ask you about something else, but do not answer him until he has replied to your question. When he is absolutely compelled he will reply to you, In my Scripture Christ is called the Spirit and the Word of God. Then you say to him, Are the Spirit and the Word said in your Scripture to be uncreated or created? And if he should say, Uncreated, [say to him, Then you agree with me, for everything that is not created but uncreated is God. But if he should say, Created],[1] say to him, Who created the Spirit of God and the Word? When, under pressure, he replies, God created them, reply: If I had said anything like that you would immediately have said, "You are suppressing your evidence, and in future no one will believe what you say". Nevertheless I will ask you this, Before God had created the Word and the Spirit, had He no Spirit nor Word? And the Saracen will turn away from you having nothing to answer, for those among the Saracens who say this are heretics and most abominable and infamous. And if you wish to repeat this to other Saracens he will fear thee greatly.[2]

The importance for our own time of studying the ancient polemic lies in the fact that similar methods, and even some of the very same arguments, have been employed by Christian missionaries right down to the present day, in spite of the proved failure of these arguments to convert the Muslim. But, in addition to that lesson for our own time, the study of this literature throws a flood of light on the historical problem of the cause of Christian failure in the face of Islam. Allowing the Muslims to take the initiative in debate, and arguing against the man instead of preaching the gospel, were signs of a loss of evangelical fervour. Two centuries after Muhammad, al-Kindi confessed, "the monks to-day are not missionaries",[3] and that statement was true in spite of the fact that vigorous missionary work was going on outside the Caliph's dominions as has been described in the last chapter; for a Christianity that felt that it could convert Turks, or Tibetans, or Chinese, but not Muslims, had *ipso facto* confessed that it was not the

[1] The sentence in square brackets is wanting in the Greek text, and is supplied from a text, in Latin only, which is printed in *P.G.* xciv, col. 1586.

[2] Migne, *P.G.* xcvi, col. 1339.

[3] Quoted above, p. 85.

universal religion for mankind. The fact is that the Christians of the East felt that in Islam they were up against a problem that they could not solve, up against a mighty wall they could not scale.

For the most part they spoke respectfully of Islam. Al-Kindi was bold enough to draw attention to moral weaknesses in Muhammad, saying for instance:

> So judge in these cases, for you are the people to do this, whether your master was a prophet as you claim. For what have prophets to do with sending out forays, with shooting arrows, with traps and enterprises for seizing men's goods? Why did not your master leave this to robbers and highwaymen?[1]

Such language was about as strong as was possible in a Muslim land, and it speaks well for the freedom of speech of the time that even so much was permitted. It was only possible for one living outside the Caliph's dominions to use the really violent language of Nicetas of Byzantium who spoke of Muhammad as an ignorant and shameless liar, a false prophet, a tempter, son of Satan, devoid of any divine or human wisdom, and so on, and of the Quran as full of lies, deceptions, fables and contradictions.[2] This man was commissioned by the Byzantine Emperor to write a treatise against Islam somewhere about A.D. 880, but he understood very little of Islam, and only knew the Quran through Greek translations. On the other hand, occasionally a desire to win the friendship of Muslim rulers prompted Christian writers to eulogise Islam, as in the following example from the Nestorian Patriarch Timothy:

> Muhammad deserves the praise of all the Arabs, and that because his manner of life among them was in the way of the prophets and the lovers of God, for the rest of the prophets taught concerning the unity of God, and Muhammad taught concerning that, so that he also walked in the way of the prophets. Then, as all the prophets turned men away from wickedness and sins, and led them to integrity and virtue, so Muhammad turned the

[1] *Risālat*, p. 53.

[2] Güterbock, *Der Islam im Lichte der byzantinischen Polemik*, pp. 26–7.

children of his people away from wickedness and led them to integrity and virtue, so he also walked among them in the way of the prophets.

And after a good deal more in that style, he says:

> And who will not praise and honour and venerate him who fought for the sake of God not with word only but also with the sword, most evident in his zeal for the Most High Creator?[1]

It must be admitted that the eulogy in this case goes to the extent of blurring the distinction between Muslim and Christian morality. The fact is that none of the Christian writers had a real grasp of the fundamental difference between Christianity and Islam. Some of them had a fair knowledge of Islam itself, but none seem to have been able to search below the surface differences of the two religions to find the underlying presuppositions which caused those differences. This statement of course applies equally well to the Muslims in their polemic against Christianity. It is worth while quoting a sentence from Illingworth, written in another connexion, which may be applied to the controversy between Christianity and Islam:

> The controversies that gather round the Gospels, then, are controversies between rival presuppositions; and it is of great importance that this fact should be clearly apprehended, for its recognition removes at once much irrelevant argument from our discussions, and enables us to concentrate attention upon the real points at issue.[2]

It is for this reason that practically all the arguments used in the ancient Christian polemic against Islam are valueless at the present day.

As an example of the way in which the Muslims chose the field of controversy we may notice first how the Christian Scriptures were made the centre of controversy. From Muhammad's term "the people of the Book" for Jews and Christians, and his belief that the Torah was sent down to

[1] Cheikho, *Trois Traités*, p. 15.
[2] *Reason and Revelation*, p. 98.

Moses, and that the Gospel was sent down to Jesus, it is clear that he overestimated the importance of the Scriptures in Christianity. The result was that, though Christians never wished to make such extravagant claims for the Bible as the Muslims made for the Quran—for instance that it was the eternal Word that had from all time existed with God—yet the centre of Muslim polemic was the attack on the Christian Scriptures, and the centre of Christian polemic was the proof of Christianity from the prophecies concerning Christ in the Old Testament, and the miracles related of Him in the New Testament. Thus, while one side drew its arguments from the Bible, the other side refused to accept the Bible as the Christians quoted it, a procedure which obviously could never lead to conviction on either side. Yet this unprofitable bandying of words—it can scarcely be called argument—went on for centuries. It began with the colloquy to which reference has been made between John of Antioch and 'Amr b. al-'Āṣ in A.D. 639. The means by which 'Amr brought the argument round to the integrity of the Scriptures was exceedingly skilful. First he asked whether the Gospel was the same everywhere, and, receiving a reply in the affirmative, asked why different Christian sects held different opinions. The Patriarch parried this attack by pointing out that Christians, Muslims, Jews and Samaritans all accepted the Torah, but were not of one mind. Then 'Amr asked what was the religion of Abraham and Moses. The Patriarch fell into the trap, and claimed Abraham, Isaac, Jacob, Moses and all the prophets as Christians. Thereupon 'Amr asked why these Old Testament writers did not speak clearly about the divinity of Christ. John obviously found it difficult to reply, but asserted that these writers knew all about Christ and the Trinity but expressed their belief mysteriously instead of openly so as not to give occasion of error to a people who were inclined towards polytheism and idolatry. 'Amr asked for proof of this, and John in reply asserted that:

not only Moses, but all the holy prophets as well, prophesied beforehand and wrote these things concerning Christ. One wrote about His birth of a virgin, another that He would be born in Bethlehem, another about His baptism; and all, so to speak, wrote about His saving passion and His life-giving death and His glorious resurrection from the tomb after three days; and he proceeded to prove this from all the prophets and also from Moses. The illustrious emir did not accept the words of the prophets, and demanded that he should show from Moses that Christ is God. The blessed patriarch cited, among many other passages, this one from Moses: "The Lord caused fire and brimstone to descend on Sodom and Gomorrha from before the Lord".

The Patriarch had fallen entirely into the trap set for him. Instead of declaring that the evidence of Christ's divinity was to be found in His words and deeds, and in His influence seen in Christian lives, he attempted to prove it from the Old Testament. 'Amr refused to accept the evidence of the prophets, and left John with nothing but an exceedingly feeble proof from the Torah. If the Patriarch had remembered the words of Christ Himself:

> The witness which I receive is not from man...but the witness which I have is greater than that of John; for the works which the Father hath given me to accomplish, the very works that I do, bear witness of me, that the Father hath sent me,[1]

he would have saved himself from his discomfiture. It may well be that this first false step of John of Antioch originated the unending attempts of later apologists to prove the Christian faith in Christ by external proofs instead of by Himself, proofs which were invariably set aside by the Muslim counter-attack that the Christians had perverted the Scriptures. The Muslims themselves were on much firmer ground when they asserted that the Quran needed no external witness, for it bore its witness in itself in its incomparableness. In regard to another matter the Patriarch John showed greater wisdom: the emir asked him either to show that the laws of the Christians were written in the Gospel, and to conduct his life accordingly, or to accept the Muslim law. John replied:

> We Christians have laws which are just and right, which are in accordance with the teaching and precepts of the Gospel and the canons of the apostles and the laws of the Church.

[1] St John v, 34–6.

This answer was so perfectly true that the Christians were never again troubled on the matter, but were allowed to live under their own laws. Had the Patriarch claimed that all the Christian laws could be proved from the Bible, it is probable that later Christians would have been continually subject to interference from the Muslims, who, whenever it suited them, would have demanded that a Christian legal decision should be revised in the light of the Bible as interpreted by the Muslims.

The extent to which Christian writers came to rely upon Old Testament prophecies of Christ is seen in the *Apology of Timothy* (about A.D. 781), not merely by his quotations from the Old Testament concerning Christ, but by the definite statement that the Old Testament contains the whole of Christian teaching,[1] "Since all the teaching of Christ is embraced in the Torah and the Prophets, for what reason should we have altered it?" Further, Timothy argued against the truth of Muhammad's prophethood by the absence of Biblical prophecies concerning him:

> So these verses and many others bear witness clearly to Jesus Christ; but I never saw a single verse in the Gospel or the Prophets or elsewhere bearing witness to Muhammad or his works or his name.[2]

Finally he went to the length of saying:

> But I say the truth, if I had found a single prophecy in the Gospel concerning the coming of Muhammad I would have left the Gospel and have followed the Quran, and I would have gone over from the one to the other, just as I have gone over from the Torah and the Prophets to the Gospel.[3]

[1] *Trois Traités*, p. 24. Here is a clear instance of the inferiority of the Syriac to the Arabic text of the dialogue. The Syriac text (*Woodbrooke Studies*, II, 56) says, "While all the corpus of the Christian doctrine is embodied in the Torah and the Gospel", although the context consists of quotations from the Old Testament only. The reference to the Gospel is out of place and spoils the argument, and is evidently due to the desire of the Syriac translator or reviser to defend the New Testament Scriptures as well as the Old against the charge of corruption. See *The Moslem World*, January, 1931.

[2] *Trois Traités*, p. 10. [3] *Op. cit.* p. 12.

The serious implications of this statement must not be overlooked: if he had found in the Gospels a prophecy of Muhammad—and we have to remember that his critical powers would not have been sufficient to discover if it was an interpolation, or a copyist's error—he would have paid no attention to the different moral standards of Christianity and Islam, but would straightway have become a Muslim. At any rate that is what he said. Actually he was probably much more firmly established in the Christian faith than he made out. He and other Christian apologists did not give of their best in presenting the faith to the Muslims, because, as we have said, they allowed the Muslims to choose the field of discussion. As a matter of fact, when the Muslims took the hint and pretended to find not one but dozens of prophecies of Muhammad both in the Old Testament and in the New, it does not seem to have hastened the apostasy of Christians to Islam. Within three-quarters of a century from the time when Timothy threw down this challenge to find prophecies of Muhammad in the Bible, 'Alī Ṭabarī wrote his great apology for Islam. The problem of getting Christians to accept Muhammad presented itself to this writer as follows:

> If we were to ask the Christians in particular why they disbelieve in the Prophet, they would say, Because of three reasons, first because we do not find that any one of the prophets prophesied about him before his coming, secondly because we do not find in the Quran any mention of a miracle nor any prophecy ascribed to the man who brought it, and thirdly because Christ prophesied to us that there would be no prophet after Him. These are their strongest arguments, and I will refute them by the help of God. If I am able to prove that the contrary of what they assert is true, and that for our belief in prophets there is no such necessary condition as they mention, they will have no more excuse before God and their conscience, and those who adduce such pleas and cling to them are in the path of unbelief and perdition.[1]

While he thus did not admit that a prophet must necessarily be foretold by previous prophecies, he was quite prepared to find any number of prophecies of Muhammad in the Old Testament, which he was able to do, thanks to the knowledge

[1] *Kitāb ad-dīn wad-daulat*, p. 17, trans. p. 15.

of the Bible he had had as a Christian. His method was to translate from the Syriac version of the Bible, and to emphasise every place where words from the root *hmd* occur. One example out of the many will suffice:

> The prophet David said in the forty-fifth psalm, "Therefore God hath blessed thee for ever; gird on then thy sword, O giant, because thy majesty and thy *ḥamd* are the conquering majesty and *ḥamd*. Ride thou on the word of truth and on the course of piety, because thy law and thy prescriptions are associated with the majesty of thy right hand; and thy arrows are sharp, and the people fall under thee". We do not know anyone to whom the features of girding on a sword, sharpness of arrows, majesty of the right hand, and falling down of people under him, are due, except the Prophet who rode on the word of truth, humbled himself before God in devotion, and fought the idolaters until the faith prevailed. And David said in the forty-eighth psalm, "Great is our Lord, and He is greatly *maḥmūd*; and in the city of our God and in His mountain there is a Holy One and a *Muḥammad*; and the joy hath come to the whole earth".[1]

A yet more daring attempt to find prophecies of Muhammad in the Old Testament was made early in the fourteenth century by a convert from Judaism named Saʿīd b. Ḥasan. One can only suppose that he traded upon his readers' ignorance of Hebrew, for he not only gave fanciful meanings to words, but did not hesitate to alter the text, e.g.[2]

> Another indication of his prophetic office is that when Moses battled with the Amalekites, and the children of Israel were routed, Moses made entreaty to God asking for help through Muhammad, saying in the Hebrew language זְכֹר לַעֲבָדֶיךָ לְאַבְרָהָם וּלְיִשְׁמָעֵאל.[3] This is the interpretation: Remember the covenant with Abraham in which thou didst promise to him that

[1] Text, p. 75, trans. p. 88.

[2] *Kitāb masālik an-naẓar*, edited and translated by S. A. Weston, *Journal of the American Oriental Society*, XXIV (2nd half), 1903, pp. 363, 375.

[3] I.e. "Remember thy servants Abraham and Ishmael". The Hebrew really runs, "Remember thy servants Abraham, Isaac and Jacob".

of the offspring of Ishmael thou wouldst render victorious the armies of the believers. So God answered his prayer, and made the children of Israel victorious over the Amalekites through the blessing of Muhammad.

Another indication of his prophetic office is that his name in the Torah is מְאֹד מְאֹד[1] and in the books of the Prophets יֹאשִׁיָּהוּ.[2] Now the wise men of the children of Israel who comment on the Torah explain this. Some say, "very, very"; others say, "Aḥmad, Aḥmad"; still others say, "great, great". And as for him who says, "very, very", it is an homonymous expression, i.e. it signifies "great, great". But there has not appeared of the offspring of Ishmael one mightier than Muhammad. His name in the books of the Prophets is יֹאשִׁיָּהוּ. This name is one of the names of God almighty, and it is not applied to anyone else but Muhammad.

The idea that the prophets of God are to be accepted, not on the grounds of the truth of their message, but on external witness, thus forced its way into Islam, and is expressed by al-Baghdādi (who died 1037) in these words:

The proof of the prophets does not rest upon faith, for if the proof of them rested upon it, then the establishing of their truth and the knowledge of what they brought would all be of faith.[3]

On the other hand the controversial writer Ibn Taimīyya, who died 1328, threw aside as worthless all the Christian arguments both from the Old Testament prophecies of Christ and from miracles:

It must be known that the causes of the error of the Christians, and their likeness to those who go beyond the bounds, as for instance the 'Ibād and the Shī'a etc., are three. The first of them consists of uncertain, embellished and doubtful words which they have received from the prophets. They have turned aside from the pure, sound words, and grasped hold of those. And whenever they hear a word which is uncertain to them, they grasp hold of it, and carry it away to their religion, even though there is no

[1] "Exceedingly."

[2] "Josiah."

[3] *Al-farq bain al-firaq*, ed. Hitti, pp. 122–3. The text of this passage is corrupt, and the translation given here follows Hitti's restoration which necessitates some small changes.

proof for it.... And the second consists of marvels which they imagine to be signs, and they are the works of satans, and this is the means whereby most of the polytheists etc. are deceived, as when satans enter into idols and talk to men, and as when satans give information about secret things to the priests, and inevitably they tell lies, and as the wily tricks wrought by satans. And the third is information handed down to them, which they suppose to be true, but is in reality error.[1]

Like 'Alī Ṭabarī before him, Ibn Taimīyya said: "It is not one of the conditions of a prophet that he should be foretold by one who preceded him".[2]

The question whether Muslims would or would not use the Christian Scriptures depended upon whether they regarded the corruption of the Scriptures as affecting the text itself or only the interpretation of it. A tradition as recorded by al-Bukhārī speaks of the corruption in quite general terms as follows:

O congregation of Muslims! How can you ask questions of the people of the book, when your book, which God revealed to His prophet, brings the best news from God. Ye read it unfalsified, and God has told you that the people of the book have altered what God wrote, and have falsified the book with their hands, and said, This is from God, that they may get some wretched reward for it. Has He not forbidden you to ask those people about what you have received in the way of knowledge? By God! We have never seen any one of them asking you about what has been revealed to you.[3]

As the Muslims gained a fuller knowledge of the contents of the Bible they stated more precisely what was meant by the corruption of the Scriptures. Some like Ibn Ḥazm supposed that the actual text had been altered, but this view, though held by many uneducated Muslims to the present day, has never been generally accepted by the learned. The view of the theologians was merely that the Jews and Christians had deliberately misinterpreted the passages of the Scriptures referring to Muhammad. Goldziher devoted an important

1 *Al-jawāb aṣ-ṣaḥīḥ*, I, 328.
2 *Op. cit.* I, 182.
3 *Ṣaḥīḥ, Kitāb ash-shahādāt*, No. 29 (Cairo ed. Book II, p. 68).

article[1] to a discussion of this subject, and quoted the following opinion from Ibn Qayyīm al-Jauzīyya:

> It is an entirely false idea when it is asserted that Jews and Christians have agreed together to expunge this name out of their Scriptures in all the ends of the world wherever they live. No one amongst learned Muslims asserts this, and God said nothing of this in the Quran, nor did any of the Companions or Imams or the Quranic scholars after them express themselves in this way. It is indeed possible that the common folk think that they can help Islam by such an interpretation, but herein is the proverb true which says, "The clever opponent can wish nothing better than that an ignorant friend should help the enemy". They misunderstood in fact the sense of the word in the Quran vii. 156, and think that the name that comes in the Taurat and the Injil is the actual Arabic name, which really never comes once in those books. What is mentioned is the description of his characteristics and the time of his appearing,

as it was of course unthinkable that there should be no mention in the writings of the prophets of events of such great importance

> the like of which the world since its beginning has never seen, and till the resurrection day will not see.

At the same time that the Muslims were discovering prophecies of Muhammad in the Old Testament to meet the Christian argument from prophecy, they were inventing miracles of Muhammad to match those of the Gospels so as to counter the Christian argument from the miracles of Christ. Guillaume notes[2] that al-Kindi only knew of four miracles that were attributed to Muhammad, yet within a very short time al-Bukhārī made his collection of *Traditions* in which many miracles of Muhammad are mentioned. These facts enable us to date the invention of Muhammad's miracles in the middle of the ninth century. The miracles recorded by Bukhārī include feeding large numbers of people with a few loaves, evidently based on the feeding of the five thousand in the Gospels, providing many people with water in the

[1] *Z.D.M.G.* xxxii, 1878, "Über muhammedanische Polemik gegen Ahl al-kitāb".

[2] *Traditions of Islam*, p. 134.

desert, and healing the sick. Besides these, miracles of all sorts were attributed to him, such as his causing rain to fall, trees bowing down before him, and animals speaking to him, which have their parallels in non-Biblical literature. The works which give in fullest detail the miracles of Muhammad are called *dalā'il an-nubuwwa*, i.e. proofs of the prophethood, and were written with the express purpose of showing that in the matter of miracles Muhammad did not fall short of Jesus. The chief of such works was a book written by Abu Nu'aim, who introduces his account of the miracles of Muhammad's infancy with these words:

> If anyone should say that Jesus was distinguished above other prophets by the fact that the Holy Spirit announced Him to His mother, and that He spoke of His prophethood in the cradle, we reply that similar signs took place also in the case of our Prophet.[1]

Tor Andrae, who has made a careful study of the various possible sources of the miracles attributed to Muhammad, says:

> It follows that the unknown inventors of the Muhammad-legend drew freely from the store of myths and legends of the lands where Hellenistic culture had extended. The borrowings appear almost exclusively to have come through the medium of Judaism and Christianity. Even the Buddhistic elements only came to Islam through this medium. In fact, a number of features from the Buddha-legend were received into the extra-canonical Gospels of the Infancy which we do not find either in the canonical Gospels or in the legendary biographies of Muhammad.[2]

This carefully weighed conclusion is an indication of the extent of the effect of Christian emphasis on the miracles of Christ.

As an example of the failure of Christians to get down to the underlying presuppositions of the Christian and Muslim faiths, we may notice the attempts to present the doctrine of the Trinity. The complete failure to give an intelligible explanation of this doctrine is sufficiently shown by the fact that to this day Muslims think that Christians worship three

[1] Tor Andrae, *Die Person Muhammads*, p. 61.

[2] *Op. cit.* p. 52.

Gods. Perhaps Asiatic Christians should not be blamed too much for this, for no statement of the doctrine of the Trinity has ever done more than touch the fringe of the mystery. But all the same, the Asiatics seem to have been strangely forgetful of the vital truths that the doctrine of the Trinity was intended to teach, namely that the character and works of Christ are the character and works of the heavenly Father, and that the indwelling Spirit inspires and enables men to do the same sort of works. The Oriental Christians used the technical language of the West without understanding its underlying significance. For them the doctrine had become little more than a kind of mathematical puzzle, as the following example will show.[1] The Caliph al-Mahdi, arguing with the Nestorian Patriarch, said,

> The fact that they are three precludes the statement that they are one, and the fact that they are one precludes the statement that they are three,

to which the Patriarch gave the following reply:

> One is the cause of three, O our king, because this number one is the cause of number two, and the number two that of the number three.... On the other hand, the number three is also the cause of number one, because since the number three is caused by the number two, and this number two by the number one, the number three is therefore the cause of number one.

In this perfectly fatuous reply one is struck, not so much by the weakness of the mathematical reasoning, as by the complete absence of anything that has any moral or spiritual interest whatever. In the eleventh century Ēlīyyā of Naṣībīn attempted to prove the Trinity philosophically. The following extracts from a dialogue with a certain wazir, though not doing him full justice as being only parts of his argument, are a sufficient indication of his method:

> One of the results of the proof that God is living by life and speaking by speech is that our expression "self-existent" signifies

[1] Part 2 of the Dialogue between Timothy and al-Mahdi, in the Syriac version only, *Woodbrooke Studies*, II, 63.

to us something other than our expression "speaking" and than our expression "living". So our expressions "self-existent", "living", "speaking" signify to us three things, viz. essence, speech and life. And we call the speaking "Word" [*kalima*], since there is no speech without a word, and no word without speech; and we call the life "Spirit" since there is no life without spirit, and no spirit without life....And since it is absurd to say that the Essence and the Word and the Spirit are three accidents or three essences in general, it is established that they are three "persons" [*aqānīm*] in particular. And since the Essence is the cause of the generation of the Word, and the cause of the procession of the Spirit; and since the Word is begotten of the Essence as speech is begotten of the soul and brilliance is begotten of the sun; and since the Spirit proceeds from the Essence as life proceeds from the soul and heat from the sun; therefore the Essence is called Father, and the Word is called Son, and the Life is called Holy Spirit.[1]

Even philosophically the argument is weak, because it could be applied to any characteristics or activities of God, so that He would have any number of "persons". In another treatise Ēlīyyā tried unsuccessfully to meet this obvious objection by dogmatically asserting[2] that there is a difference between "self-existent", "wise" and "living" on the one hand, and all other qualities on the other, the former being essential qualities and others being active. But even apart from the weakness of the actual argument, what was the result of his philosophical method of approach? In his own words the result was,[3] "There is no difference between our saying 'one nature, three persons', and our saying 'self-existent possessor of life and wisdom'", in which it is hard to see any resemblance to the Christian doctrine of the Trinity. The more serious result is given in the words of the wazir, after Ēlīyyā had presented a carefully worded statement of his philosophy of God:

The matter is as thou hast said, and I confess that every one who is of this opinion and of this religion is a monotheist, and there is

1 *Trois Traités*, p. 33.
2 Cheikho, *Vingt Traités*, pp. 126–7.
3 *Op. cit.* p. 126.

no difference between him and the Muslims except concerning the prophethood of Muhammad b.'Abdallah.[1]

Ēlīyyā's statement of the Trinity was so far removed from anything related to Christian experience that it had ceased to be distinctively Christian. He probably was not intentionally whittling down his faith, but was trying to meet his opponent on common ground.

[1] *Trois Traités*, p. 52. Compare also a similar statement by the Qāḍi Abu Bakr Muḥammad b. aṭ-Ṭayyib, known as Ibn al-Bāqillānī, quoted by Ēlīyyā, *Vingt Traités*, p. 128.

Chapter IX

THE MUSLIM REACTION TO CHRISTIAN LIFE AND TEACHING

The reaction of the Muslims to Christian life and teaching may be treated under three headings—the impression of Christian morality upon Islamic thought, the attribution to Muhammad and to the Quran of the qualities of Christ, and the appreciation of the person of Christ.

That Christian morality should have made a great impression on Islam is not surprising in view of the large number of Christians who became Muslims and of the close relations which existed between Christians and Muslims. It was mainly under Christian influence that Islam as a religion underwent a great development in the first two centuries of its existence. This development has largely been obscured from view by the fact that the newly accepted elements of Christian morality were put in the form of traditions going back to Muhammad himself, so that it is only the critical studies of recent times which have demonstrated the later origin of these traditions. Characteristic of these is the tradition which occupies the first place in Bukhārī's *Ṣaḥīḥ*, "Deeds are judged according to intentions, and reckoning will be made to every man according to the measure of his intention". Muslim asceticism and mysticism grew up as a borrowing from the corresponding elements in Oriental Christianity. It would take us too far from our subject to trace the growth of Islamic mysticism or Sufism; and it is sufficient to state the well-known fact that the early Muslim ascetics, the precursors of the Sufis, modelled their lives on those of Christian monks, and that Christian mysticism played the greatest part in influencing the development of Sufism. It is not difficult to see Christian influence in the following mystical tradition preserved by an-Nawawī,

My servant's drawing near to me is dearer to me than the

prescriptions I have laid upon him. And my servant continues to draw near to me by free-will works of piety till I love him. And when I love him I am his ear by which he hears, and his eye by which he sees, and his hand by which he holds, and his foot by which he walks. If he asks of me I will surely grant his request. If he seeks refuge in me I will surely grant him protection.[1]

We have already seen how, as a result of Christian polemic, miracles were attributed to Muhammad, and prophecies of him were found in the Old Testament. But further than this, sayings similar to those of Christ were attributed to him. For instance in the Ḥadith he is made to promise a blessing to "the man who does good and keeps it secret, so that his left hand does not know what his right hand has done", and to have said, "My companions in relationship to my community are like salt in food, for food without salt is of no use", and "He who wastes knowledge on the unworthy is like him who binds pearls on swine".[2] According to ʿAlī Ṭabarī he said[3], "I stood by the gate of paradise, and behold the most part of those who entered in were the poor, while the rich were imprisoned, though in the world riches had been their portion". Perhaps the most instructive of these borrowings is a parody of the Lord's Prayer: Muhammad is reported to have said:

If any man suffers, or a brother of his suffers, let him say, Our Lord God, who art in heaven, hallowed be thy name, thy power is in heaven and on earth; as thy mercy is in heaven, so practise thy mercy upon earth; forgive us our fault and our sins, thou art the Lord of the good men; send down mercy from thy mercy, and healing from thy healing, on this pain, that it may be healed again.[4]

This parody is striking as showing certain elements of Christianity which the Muslims could not accept: they could

[1] *Arbaʿūn*, No. 38, p. 57.

[2] Goldziher, *Muhammadanische Studien*, II, 384, 391, 392.

[3] *Kitāb ad-dīn wad-daulat*, p. 26, trans. p. 27.

[4] *Abū Dā'ūd, kitāb aṭ-ṭibb, bāb kaif ar-ruqā* (Delhi ed. II, 187), quoted by Goldziher, *op. cit.* II, 386. It is interesting that this tradition is placed, not under the heading "Prayer", but under "Incantations" or "Sorcery".

not speak of God as Father; they could not speak of the coming of the kingdom as future, because the only kingdom known to Islam was the earthly realm of the Caliphs; they could not make God's forgiveness of men dependent upon their forgiveness of their enemies, because the mere fact of being a Muslim was sufficient to earn the favour of God. The most daring falsification of history was the attempt to make Muhammad an ascetic. 'Alī Ṭabarī said:

I will mention some points relating to the asceticism of the Prophet, his austerity, and his disregard of the allurements and deceitfulness of this world, by which it will be seen that no one would imagine deceit and falsehood in a man of his devotion and temperance. It is said that he never satisfied himself with bread till he had suffered intense pains of hunger [lit. "except with pain and severity"].[1]

A further development of the legend of Muhammad, taken from the Christian doctrine of the pre-existent Christ, was the doctrine of the pre-existent *Nūr Muhammad*, or Light of Muhammad, which was the first thing to be created.

But it was the Quran which was made to occupy the chief place in Muslim thought as the equivalent of the eternal Logos. The orthodox doctrine was

that speech is an eternal attribute of God, which as such had no beginning and is never discontinued any more than His knowledge, His might, or the other characteristics of His endless being. What then is recognised as the activity of the speaking God, namely His revelation, did not originate in time by a special creative act of God's will, but from eternity has existed, and of course for a Muslim "revelation" meant *par excellence* the Quran.[2]

This doctrine was attacked by the Mu'tazilites on the ground that it made the Word of God a being by the side of God from all eternity, and so infringed His unity; and for this reason the Mu'tazilites said that the Quran was created.

[1] *Op. cit.* p. 25, trans. p. 25.
[2] Goldziher, *Vorlesungen*, p. 113 (2nd ed. p. 109).

St John of Damascus also forcibly took up the same argument, saying:

> They call us Associaters because they say we have introduced a companion for God when we call Christ Son of God and God.... But since you say that Christ is the Word of God and Spirit, how can you revile us as Associaters? For the Word and the Spirit are inseparable from Him in whom they came into being. If therefore the Word is in God it is clear that it is God. But if it is outside of God, then, according to you, God is without word and without mind. Therefore, while you avoid giving God a partner, you divide Him. It were better for you to say that He has a partner than to divide Him and to treat Him as if He were stone or wood or some other inanimate object. Therefore you speak falsely when you call us Associaters, but we call you Dividers of God.[1]

This was a sound argument, worthy of a great theologian, for Muslim theology had never, like Christian theology, faced the question how the Word of God can have existed from all time with God without impairing His unity; though St John of Damascus seems not to have noticed the verbal distinction made by Muslims between Christ as the Word of God, and the eternal Word of God, by calling the former *kalimat Allah*, and reserving for the latter the synonym *kalām Allah*. But no Christian ever thought of expressing the real difficulty about the Muslim belief in the Quran as the eternal Word of God that, whereas God might be revealed in a moral being, He could not be fully revealed in, or united with, the lifeless words of a book. If the Christians had brought the argument on to this moral plane there might have been more effect; but the philosophical arguments, whether of the Muʿtazilites or of St John of Damascus, made no impression, and orthodox Islam continued to believe in the eternal and uncreated Quran.

It will have been noticed that the elements of Christianity borrowed by Muslims were not those stressed in the Christian polemic, and that the only effect of those doctrines which filled the Christian polemical works was to find some parallel

[1] "De Haeresibus", Migne, *P.G.* XCIV, col. 768.

to them—without the moral implications—in the case of Muhammad. Nothing could be a greater condemnation of the Christian methods of polemic than this result.

When we come to consider the Muslim ideas of Christ, we notice first of all an attempt on the part of certain Mu'tazilites to give Christ something approaching the place He holds in Christian doctrine. Thus the author of the *Kitāb al-intiṣār* said:

> As for his saying [i.e. of the Mu'tazilite al-Jāḥiẓ] "Among you there are some who say that 'Alī is God", we say, "Among you there are some who say that Christ is He who created the world, and He is the Lord of the first and the last things, and He will be the reckoner for the people on the resurrection day, and He will be revealed to them; and it is He to whom the Prophet referred when he said, 'Ye shall see your Lord as ye see the moon, ye shall not be gathered together to see Him'".[1]

On the same page it says that "he then described the saying of Faḍal and Ibn Ḥāyiṭ concerning the superiority of Christ over Muhammad". Further information about these two men is given by ash-Shahrastānī:

> The Ḥāyiṭīyya are the followers of Aḥmad b. Ḥāyiṭ, and similarly the Ḥadathīyya are the followers of Faḍal b. al-Ḥadathī. They were the followers of an-Naẓẓām and also read the books of the philosophers. And to the teaching of an-Naẓẓām they added three heresies. The first was their acceptance of a certain doctrine of divinity with regard to Christ, as the Christians do, according to their belief that Christ is He who will make reckoning with the Christians at the last day...and Aḥmad b. Ḥāyiṭ said that Christ clothed Himself with a material body, and He was the eternal Word who became incarnate as the Christians said.[2]

Al-Baghdādi gives even more precise details of their belief:

> The Ḥāyiṭīyya are the followers of Aḥmad b. Ḥāyiṭ al-Qadari, and he was one of the companions of an-Naẓẓām in the I'tizāl.... And Ibn Ḥāyiṭ and Faḍal al-Ḥadathī said that the creation had two lords and two creators. One of them was from eternity, and He is Allah, and the other is created, and He is 'Isa b. Maryam. And

[1] P. 148.
[2] *Kitāb al-milal wan-niḥal*, p. 42, Haarbrücker's trans. p. 62.

they two said that Christ was the Son of God in the sense of adoption and not of birth. And they also said that the Christ is He who will judge creation at the last day, and it is He to whom God referred when He said [Sura lxxxix. 23] "and thy Lord comes and the angels in ranks", and it is He who will come [ii. 206] "with the covering of clouds"; and it is He who created Adam after His own likeness—and that is the explanation of the saying that God created [the creatures][1] after His likeness.[2]

Ash-Shahrastānī also speaks[3] of a certain Manṣūr al-'Ijlī who lived in the days of Hishām b. 'Abd al-Malik (A.D. 724–43), who, among other heresies, said "that the first thing God created was 'Isa b. Maryam and then 'Ali b. Abi Talib". Al-Hallāj, who was executed as a heretic in A.D. 921, uttered a verse at the moment before his death in which he spoke of himself as about to drink the cup of suffering that Christ had drunk before him:

He who invites me, so as not to wrong me,
Has given me to drink of the cup that He drank of, as a host treats his guest.
Then, when the cup had passed from hand to hand, He brought the executioner's leather and the sword.
Thus it befell from Him who drank the wine, with Leo in the height of summer.[4]

Such views as these were not, however, of any permanent importance in Islam, and their authors were definitely regarded as heretics. It is noteworthy that those who gave an eternal significance to Christ were Mu'tazilites, the rationalists of Islam. They, the Muslim intellectuals, had accepted from Christianity ideas which among the Christians themselves belonged rather to the intellect than to the heart. Orthodox Islam, while refusing to accept any such views as these, which savoured too much of the philosophical doctrines of Christianity, was influenced by the popular Christian conception of Christ to think of Him as the great ascetic and saint.

1 Emended text. The text as printed by Badr has "a God".
2 *Al-farq bain al-firaq*, ed. Badr, p. 260, ed. Hitti, p. 166.
3 *Kitāb al-milal wan-niḥal*, p. 136, Haarbrücker's trans. p. 206.
4 Massignon, *La Passion d'al-Hallaj*, tome I, p. 301.

A poem, on the face of it pre-Islamic, but in all probability a Muslim product of a later age, said,[1] "The monks in every church praise the monk of monks, the Messiah, the son of Mary". Al-Ghazzālī (1059–1111) in his book *The Precious Pearl* tells the story of how departed souls went from one prophet to another seeking an intercessor. When they came to Moses he sent them on to Jesus, saying:

> But go to Jesus, for He is of all the apostles the one who offers most guarantees for certainty, the one who knows God best, the most ascetic and the wisest of them. Perhaps He will intercede for you.... Then they went to Jesus and said to Him, Thou art the Spirit of God and the Word of God. To thee God has given the highest title in the world below and in the world to come. Intercede therefore for us with God to pronounce the judgment. Jesus replied to them, Men have taken me and my mother as Gods in the place of God Most High. How dare I intercede for you with Him by the side of whom they adore me, and of whom they say that I am His Son and He is my Father?[2]

This passage carefully excludes the Christian doctrine of Christ, and at the same time gives Him a peculiar dignity. The story also comes in Ghazzālī's great book, the *Iḥyā*,[3] but instead of the eulogy of Jesus it only has, "Thou art the apostle of God and His Word which came to Mary, and a Spirit from Him, and thou didst speak to men in the cradle". It also says that God was angry with Him, but does not specify the reason. The asceticism of Christ is also brought out in the following passage of *The Precious Pearl*:[4]

> Then one cried, "Where are the poor?" They were led in in various groups, and were asked, "Who has turned you away from living according to the will of God Most High?" They replied, "God proved us in the world below by wretched poverty which turned us away from living according to His will". Some one said to them, "Who is the poorest, you or Jesus?" They replied, "Certainly Jesus". It was said to them, "That did not turn Him away from living according to the will of God Most

[1] Horovitz, *Koranische Untersuchungen*, p. 129, and see the references given there.

[2] *La Perle Précieuse*, p. 62 (text) and p. 53 (trans.).

[3] *Iḥyā*, IV, 378.

[4] P. 90 (text), p. 76 (trans.).

High and from consecrating Himself to remember Him"....O reader, take Christ as your model, for it is said that He had no purse. For twenty years He wore the same shirt of wool [*ṣūf*]; on His journeys [*siyāḥāt*][1] He carried nothing but a mug and a comb. One day He saw a man drinking out of the hollow of his hand. Immediately He threw away His mug and used it no more. Then He passed by a man combing his beard with his fingers. Immediately He threw away His comb and used it no more.

The great Sufi, Ibn al-ʻArabī (who died 1165), went so far as to say,[2] "Surely the seal of the saints is an apostle; and in the world He has no equal. He is the Spirit and the Son of the Spirit, and Mary is His mother". Those who praised Jesus for His asceticism did not, however, have it all their own way; for the anti-ascetic spirit in Islam was responsible for a tradition that

Jesus son of Mary will descend to the earth, marry, and beget children. He will stay on the earth forty-five years, and then die and be buried in my grave. He and I shall arise in one grave between Abu Bakr and ʻUmar.[3]

Jalāl ad-dīn ar-Rūmī mocked at the idea of Christians seeking help from the crucified Christ:

See the ignorance of the Christian appealing for protection to the Lord who was suspended [on the cross]! Since according to his [the Christian's] belief He was crucified by the Jews, how then can He protect him?[4]

But he also thought of Jesus as the great ascetic, showing by asceticism the path of life. After telling the story of a parrot which escaped from its cage by feigning death, he said:

The meaning of dying [as conveyed] by the parrot was supplication [self-abasement]: make thyself dead in supplication and poverty [of spirit], that the breath of Jesus may revive thee and make thee fair and blessed as itself.[5]

[1] Incidentally the words for "wool" and "journeys" stamp Christ as a Sufi.

[2] *Futūḥāt al-makkīyya*, IV, 195.

[3] Quoted from Mishkāt al-masābih by Guillaume, *Traditions*, p. 158.

[4] *Mathnavi*, Nicholson's translation, Book II, line 1401.

[5] Book I, lines 1547–1909.

Hasluck[1] has produced archaeological evidence that there was in Konia (Iconium) in the days of Jalāl ad-dīn and Shams ad-dīn of Tabriz (the co-founder of the Mevlevi order) an organised *rapprochement* between Christianity and Islam: (1) There is a church of St Amphilochius at Konia in which there is a tomb, which is reverenced by the Christians under the name of the tomb of St Amphilochius, and by the Muslims under the name of Plato the divine philosopher. (2) The monastery of St Chariton, an hour north of Konia, contains three churches and a mosque hewn out of the rock. The place is connected by various traditions with Jalāl ad-dīn, and in Mevlevi tradition is called the monastery of Plato. (3) The great convent of the Mevlevi order at Konia contains the tomb of Jalāl ad-dīn, and by its side another tomb about which there are various traditions which all attribute it to a Christian ecclesiastic connected in some way with Jalāl ad-dīn. (4) The mausoleum of Shams ad-dīn, also in Konia, contains only his tomb. But the Christians were also able to reverence the same tomb, because they had a tradition that he was secretly converted before his death, and received "the body of God" in an apple from an Armenian priest. It is possible that there may have been a tendency to a similar *rapprochement* between the two religions in other places. In the patriarchate of Gabriel of Alexandria (1136–50) the superintendent of the monastery of St John in Cairo "treacherously allowed the Muslims to attend the liturgies".[2] Abū Ṣāliḥ also tells us of visits paid by the Egyptian ruler Khamārawaih (A.D. 883–95) to the Melkite monastery of al-Quṣair on the Muqaṭṭam hills near Cairo. In the monastery was

> the Church of the Apostles or disciples, in which there was a picture of the Lady, carrying the Lord, with angels on the right and on the left, and pictures of all the twelve disciples, the whole being composed of tesserae of glass, and skilfully executed, as at Bethelehem; and some of these glass tesserae were gilded and

[1] *Christianity and Islam under the Sultans*, II, pp. 370 ff.
[2] *Abū Ṣāliḥ*, ed. Evetts, p. 127.

some were coloured. Kharmarawaih, son of Aḥmad b. Ṭūlūn, used to stand before these pictures and admire the beauty of their execution, and was much delighted with them, especially with the picture of the Lady; so that he even built a *manẓarah* for himself at this monastery, that he might come there for recreation.[1]

Speaking of the district of Isnā (Esneh) Abū Ṣāliḥ says:

> At the weddings and other rejoicings of the Muslims the Christians are present, and chant in the Sahidic dialect of Coptic, and walk before the bridegroom through the market places and streets, and this has become a recognised custom with them, [and has continued] up to our own day [i.e. the beginning of the thirteenth century]. And on the night of the feast of the holy Nativity every year the Muslims, as well as the Christians, burn candles and lamps and logs of wood in great numbers.[2]

In Shirāz in the eleventh century the markets were decorated for the feasts of unbelievers,[3] and in the same town in the thirteenth century Yāqūt says that non-Muslim rites were openly celebrated: he speaks of festivals in connexion with several monasteries as if they were familiar spectacles, and of the inhabitants of the villages gathering to the show.[4]

The result of this brief survey of the Muslim reaction to Christian life and teaching is very instructive. The arguments and doctrines of the learned Christians had no effect whatever. The Muslims were not even convinced of manifest errors, such as their denial of the death of Christ on the cross or their assertion that the Bible had been corrupted. On the other hand Christian life had made a great impression. Many elements of Christian morality had been accepted, and especially morality with that ascetic colouring which it had developed in the East. But strangest of all, there was a wistful looking towards Jesus to supply something that was not to be found in Islam. It was not the Christ of the theologians, but the Jesus of the common people to whom they looked.

[1] *Op. cit.* p. 148. Also *Yāqūt*, II, 685.

[2] *Op. cit.* p. 278.

[3] Tritton, *The Caliphs and their non-Muslim subjects*, p. 107, quoting Mukaddasi, 429.

[4] Tritton, *op. cit.* p. 110, quoting *Yāqūt*, II, 641, 643, 658.

The few instances we have been able to quote of Muslims and Christians joining in each other's festivals are probably significant of a great deal of daily contact. It is true that in some places there was strong communal feeling against the Christians on economic grounds, wherever they continued to hold important offices under government; and from time to time this feeling showed itself in open riots. But apart from this communal feeling, which does not appear to have been universal, Christians and Muslims probably lived on fairly friendly terms up to the time of the Turkish invasion of the eleventh century, and even on into the thirteenth century. It was these normally friendly relationships which accounted for the influence of popular Christianity on Islam. One cannot read the history of this time without real regret; for the wistful longing of Muslims towards Christ strongly suggests that they might have responded if Christ had been more truly presented to them. In that sense it was a day of opportunity missed by the Church. If only at the end of the eleventh century there had been a revival of true Christianity in the East, or such a missionary movement from the West as could have presented Islam with a vision of the living Christ, Islam might at that time have accepted Him as Lord, and so have entered on to that stage of development which alone will save it. The next chapter tells of the two movements, the one from beyond the Oxus, and the other from Europe, which held up the possibility of such an understanding of Christ, and delayed the true development of Islam until another day of opportunity should dawn in the twentieth century.

Chapter X

THE TURKS AND THE FRANKS

For a period of four centuries from the time of the Arab invasion the various cultural elements of Western Asia were being brought together, and from their interaction there was emerging the distinctively Muslim type of civilisation. On account of the common language of Arabic, and the original stimulus to the Islamic movement which came from Arabia, this Muslim civilisation is frequently spoken of as Arab civilisation. But it must be remembered that the main cultural elements which combined to bring about this result were Syriac Christianity and Persian Zoroastrianism, Arabia only contributing the religious system which cemented together the various elements, and the rulers whose firm sway ensured sufficient peace for the pursuit of intellectual studies. The intermingling of cultures followed on the intermingling of races. Although men in later times might call themselves Arabs, and proudly trace their genealogy in the male line to Arab tribes, there had been so much intermarriage with non-Arab women that racially as well as culturally the Muslims of the eleventh century were heirs to a variety of strains. At the same time the Christian community was also of mixed Syrian and Persian origin. On the cultural side, by reason of their religion, the Christians were also the inheritors of a great deal of Greek and Hebrew thought; and most of this inheritance they had passed over to the Muslims. Thus, whereas in the seventh century the Christian and Muslim communities were widely separated in culture, by the eleventh century they were practically equal shareholders of the same culture.

Within the ranks of Islam there had gradually developed the distinction between the Sunnis and the Shī'a. The Shī'a had started in 'Irāq as a purely political party which resisted the domination of Syria, and so came to set their hopes on 'Alī and his descendants. The peculiar views which in course of time separated the Shī'a from the Sunnis were probably due in the first instance to an inheritance from 'Irāqian heathenism. Although thus the Shī'ites had a freedom of thought which allowed them to tolerate some ideas about Christ which were unacceptable to the Sunnis, yet owing to its origin their religion really had less affinity with Christianity than had orthodox Islam. The Shī'a owed its political importance to the fact that by origin they were rebels against the constituted order of the Caliphate, so that, when the power of the Caliphate weakened and rebel governors in various parts declared themselves independent of the Caliph, a good proportion of the petty dynasties that arose were Shī'ite. Among these Shī'ite dynasties one of the most important was that of the Buwaihids, for they were in the extraordinary position of being the rulers of Baghdad (from A.D. 945) professing the Shī'ite faith, while the Caliph, who was of course a Sunni, was allowed to retain the title but none of the power of his office. These Buwaihids were a clan from the highlands of Dailām near the Caspian Sea, and their presence at the capital of the Caliphate was a foretaste of the less cultured elements which were shortly to overrun the sphere of Arab civilisation.

Before speaking of the Turkish invasion a few words are necessary about their previous history. From ancient times there had been warlike nomads in Central Asia who caused trouble to the Chinese Empire. The name of Turk as applied to some of these nomads occurs first in the sixth century of our era, and so powerful had they become during that century that they even sent an embassy to the Roman Emperor Justin II with a view to a commercial alliance to prevent the Persians from holding a monopoly of the silk trade and diverting it all to the Persian Gulf. In the lifetime of Muhammad the Turks were helping Heraclius in his campaign against Persia. The first part that Turks played in Muslim life was when Hārūn ar-Rashīd (A.D. 786–809) employed

Turkish officers in his army. His son Mu'tasim employed a bodyguard of three thousand Turks. This unwise precedent was followed, and the bodyguards of Turks often wielded great power. But the rise of an independent Turkish dynasty was long delayed by the rise of the Persian Sāmānids, who ruled over most of the territory of the Western Turks from A.D. 874 to 999. The centre of their realm was Transoxania; and the two towns of Bukhārā and Samarqand became the chief centres of Muslim learning in the world. It was under this dynasty that Islam began to make serious headway among the Turks. Many Turks were employed as slaves in the royal palace, and some rose to considerable power, learning from their masters not only the religion of Islam but also the thirst for empire. Eventually at the end of the tenth century these Turks seized the power from the hands of their Persian rulers and two Turkish dynasties arose. One of these was the dynasty of the Īlak Khāns who held the lands north of the Oxus. The other was that of the Ghaznavids who ruled, from their capital of Ghazna in Afghanistan, over a great stretch of country from Lahore to Ispahan, and at one time held Samarqand and Bukhārā beyond the Oxus. Maḥmūd of Ghazna, Turk though he was, was a great patron of learning, so that Ghazna as an intellectual centre became the successor of Bukhārā and Samarqand.

But Western Asia was now to suffer something more than mere changes of rulers, namely an invasion of nomad Turks. Tribal movements in Central Asia caused the Saljūq clan to migrate southwards from the Kirghiz Steppes into Transoxania. There they became converted to Islam, but remained what they had been before, uncultured and predatory nomads, a great contrast to the Ghaznavids who had absorbed Islamic culture under the Samanid sovereigns. Wars with the Īlak Khāns and the Ghaznavids resulted in the Saljūqs crossing the Oxus. In 1037 Chagar Beg became the master of Merv, and his brother Tughril Beg master of Nīshāpūr. From that time their advance was rapid. Swarms of Turkish tribes joined in the invasion, and in 1055 Ṭughril Beg was proclaimed Sultan in Baghdad. All the petty dynasties of Persia fell before the onslaught, and the Ghaznavids were driven eastwards into India. The whole of Western Asia from Afghanistan to the borders of Asia Minor and Egypt was united in the great empire of the Saljūqs. Once more the whole of this area was under Sunni rule, and all the Shīʿa rulers had disappeared. But more significant than this change was the interruption of the cultural life by the inroads of the uncivilised Turks. Even two centuries later the contrast between the Muslims of older standing and the recent invaders was very marked, as is shown by Ricoldus de Monte Crucis (who died about 1309).

> From his own experiences in personal relationship, both with prominent Arabs and with sons of the desert, he praises them for their gentleness and hospitality even towards non-Muslims, their moral earnestness and their reverence for the name of God. He even set them forth as examples worth copying by Christians. But this favourable judgment of his only applied to the Saracens, i.e. the Arabs and related tribes: our traveller depicts with startling colours the character of the Turks and Mongols [whom he calls Tatars] and their evil manners and cruelty.[1]

The effect of the Turkish invasion was greatest in Palestine and Syria; and it is necessary to go back and observe the relations that existed between Christians and Muslims before the Turkish invasion.

Palestine, with its holy places connected with our Lord's life on earth, had been from the beginning of special interest to a wider circle of Christians than those who inhabited it; and the practice grew up, especially amongst the Christians of Europe, of making pilgrimage to the holy places. The practice of pilgrimage was greatly stimulated by the victory of Christianity and was increased by the influence of St Jerome towards the end of the fourth century and the development of monasticism. The Muslim invasion of the seventh century checked the pilgrimages somewhat, but they did not cease altogether. We have seen how the early Muslim rulers did not

[1] Güterbock, *Der Islam im Lichte der byzantinischen Polemik*, p. 42.

favour one Christian sect above another. While in 'Irāq it was only the heads of the Nestorian Church who received diplomas from the Caliphs, we have seen that in A.D. 744 a diploma was given to the Jacobite Patriarch of Antioch. Although it is not expressly stated, it may safely be assumed that this diploma recognised the Jacobite Patriarch of Antioch as head of all the Jacobites in Syria and Palestine. It was natural therefore that the Melkites in the same land should seek for the recognition of someone as their head and representative. It was probably with this purpose in view that ambassadors were sent to Baghdad in A.D. 762 by Pepin the Short. We are not told whether anything came of this embassy, but a later embassy sent to Hārūn ar-Rashīd by Charlemagne in A.D. 797 attained its object. The chronicler who records this event is far from explicit, but he says that the Caliph allowed their request, and also granted Charlemagne proprietary rights over the Church of the Holy Sepulchre in Jerusalem.[1] The authority given to Charlemagne is frequently spoken of as the Frankish Protection of the Holy Land. Obviously there can have been no question of his having any political power except such as naturally inhered to the head of a *melet* or religious community. It was probably a matter of indifference to the Caliph whether this responsibility for the Melkites in Palestine rested with the Pope of Rome or some other person; and the part played by Charlemagne in Europe marked him out specially as the protector of Christians. The system appears to have worked well, for Europeans were able in considerable numbers to make the pilgrimage to Jerusalem in safety, and the taxes to which they were subject, though heavy, were fixed and regularised. The long persecution of al-Ḥākim of course put an end to pilgrimages for the time being. After the persecution was over, it was the Byzantine Emperor who entered into negotiations for the rights of the Palestinian Christians, and took steps for the rebuilding of the churches that had been destroyed. This is an indication that the Western

[1] Bréhier, *Les Croisades*, p. 24.

Emperors had now lost whatever powers of protection they had formerly held over the Christians of Palestine. Pilgrimages soon recommenced, and the conversion of the Hungarians to Christianity early in the eleventh century opened up the trans-continental route to the Holy Land. The result was that the number of pilgrims became greater than ever. But the Fāṭimid government was losing power in Palestine, and was too weak to control marauding Bedouins, for fear of whom the pilgrims came in large parties carrying arms.

In 1054, the year before the Saljūqs captured Baghdad, the long rivalry between Rome and Constantinople reached its climax: the Pope excommunicated the Oecumenical Patriarch, and the Patriarch excommunicated the Pope. The following year a French Archbishop was prevented by an Orthodox governor of Cyprus from setting foot in Palestine on the pretext of the unsettled state of the country. This was the beginning of difficulties put in the way of pilgrims from the West who wished to pass through Orthodox territory. The Saljūq invasion which had reached Baghdad in 1055 proceeded westwards again after fifteen years. In 1070 Jerusalem was taken, and the following year a huge Byzantine army was utterly defeated at Manzikart. This victory opened Asia Minor to the Saljūqs, who by 1092 had not only occupied the mainland but even seized the chief of the islands of the Archipelago. The Saljūq conquests alarmed the Byzantine Emperors for the safety of Constantinople. In 1073, two years after the battle of Manzikart, the Byzantine Emperor Michael VII wrote to the Pope begging assistance against the Turks, and promising in return a reunion of the Orthodox Church with the Church of Rome. Although this appeal was received favourably, and the Pope recognised the danger to Christian Europe of a Turkish invasion, internal affairs of Europe prevented any immediate response. Later appeals of the same kind seem to have been made by the Emperor Alexius, and it is probable that these appeals first suggested to the Westerners the idea of intervention in the East.

The actual call to the first crusade was made by Pope

Urban II in 1095, but it was a call to deliver the Holy Land from the hands of the Turks, and not to assist the Byzantine Emperor. In fact from the beginning of the Crusades there was not merely lack of sympathy, but even open hostility towards the Byzantines. The call of Pope Urban was received with enthusiasm in Western Europe. The main motive behind the movement was the religious ideal of the time, an ideal which had already been expressing itself in the increasing number of pilgrimages to Palestine. It seemed in those days that the only certain way of attaining salvation was to leave the world and adopt the monastic life. The majority of men were unwilling to do this, and the call to the Crusades seemed to offer them salvation by a way more congenial to their spirit. To fight in the way of the Lord seemed worthy of their mettle; and the individual hoped also for the benefits he would receive from visiting the holy sites. "Deeds are judged by their intentions, and reward will be made to every man according to the measure of his intention", is a Muslim tradition breathing the spirit of Christianity. By that rule the Crusades must be judged. These were no wars to defend Europe from invasion—though they did serve that purpose, and delayed the capture of Constantinople for three and a half centuries—nor were they ordinary wars of aggression and annexation. The first intention in the minds of the Crusaders was to win for Christ a kingdom by the sword. This was the very method which had been presented to our Lord in the temptation, "All these things will I give thee if thou wilt fall down and worship me", and our Lord had definitely rejected it. We need not stay over other motives that lay behind the Crusades, or which urged on the individuals who took part in them—the desire of princes to found kingdoms for themselves in the East, the enterprise of discovery, and so forth—for it is undoubted that Urban's call was to fight with the sword to win a kingdom of this world for Christ, and as such the call was accepted by the people when they shouted "Deus le volt! Deus le volt!" Never had Christ been so completely misunderstood by His followers. Nor need we stay to consider the undoubted advantages that followed from the Crusades, particularly the spread of culture which resulted from the meeting of East and West, and the opening of the eyes of Westerners to future fields for exploration. For, however great these advantages were, even if they could have been obtained in no other way, they were bought at too high a price. The price was the denial by Christians of the Saviour who bought them, a denial in which was involved the whole of Western Christendom, with the exception of a few such clear spirits as St Francis of Assisi, Raymon Lull, and William of Rubruck. One cannot help regarding the Crusades as the greatest tragedy in the history of Christianity, and the greatest set-back to the progress of Christ's kingdom on earth. It must not be supposed that the Crusaders were mere hypocrites. Many of them were sincerely trying to follow the highest religion they knew. It was for Christ's honour that they fought, but they were ignorant of what sort of deeds would do honour to Christ. Those among the Crusaders who were evil livers, breaking the commandments of Christianity and the laws of the Church, we can ignore; for the Church itself would have condemned their deeds. The real tragedy lies in the approval by the Church of an undertaking that was a complete denial of Christ.

Of the four invasions of Western Asia which fall within the period of this book, those of the Arabs, the Turks, the Franks and the Mongols, the Frankish invasion was the least successful. The only measure of success they had was due to their arrival some five or six years after the break-up of the Saljūq Empire. The rise of the Saljūq Sultanate of Rūm soon after the battle of Manzikart was the first sign that the empire could not hold together; and when the Great Saljūq Mālik Shāh died in 1092 civil war broke out, and the Saljūq Empire was thrown into confusion. The first Crusaders reached Syria in 1097, and, profiting by the disunion of the Muslim forces, were able to get a firm foothold. The actual course of the Crusades was decided, not by those who held the highest ideals of the Church, but by those who wished to use the Crusades for their own advantage and build up for themselves new kingdoms in the East. The different nationalities each went their own way, with no Commander-in-Chief, and no common policy. The men of Burgundy founded kingdoms in Jerusalem and Edessa; the men of Provence in Tripoli; and the Normans in Antioch. Their divided counsels, and the great distance from their home bases, made it exceedingly difficult for them to advance or even to hold their own. Once or twice every year new contingents came out, sometimes in larger, and sometimes in smaller numbers, thus enabling the Frankish kingdoms to carry on more or less continuous warfare with the surrounding Muslim powers for two centuries. Sometimes the Frankish kingdoms were fighting against one another, and did not even disdain occasionally to make alliance with Muslim powers in their petty warfare. After the first victories of the Franks, the Muslims gradually consolidated their power, and before the end of the twelfth century had regained control over the greater part of Syria. W. B. Stevenson describes how, before the middle of the twelfth century, the "spirit of the second generation" took possession of the Latins of Jerusalem.

> The men of the first generation regarded all Moslem Syria as an unoccupied promised land. Their successors viewed the Moslems as joint occupants with themselves. The country which was theirs "by divine right" was practically co-extensive with the land they now occupied. They discovered that their neighbours had much in common with themselves. They adopted Eastern dress and Eastern habits and ceased to be "exiles" in a foreign land. The purpose of the first crusade was accomplished and its force was spent.[1]

In the thirteenth century the Frankish towns were little more than colonial trading centres, existing only by the favour of the Muslims. Interest in the venture gradually waned in the West. It had lost its glamour as a religious duty; and the material advantages were not great enough to justify the

[1] *The Crusaders in the East*, p. 146.

expense and labour of the expeditions. Consequently the reinforcements became smaller and less frequent; so that when, towards the end of the thirteenth century, the Muslims determined to drive the Franks out from their last strongholds, the latter had no power to resist.

Thus ended the episode of the Crusades. Looked at from the point of view of the West they appear as a great adventure. But from the point of view of the country in which the wars were fought they were nothing but a distressing disturbance in the ordered life of the day. Both Turks and Franks were unwelcome visitors, who had little in common with the former inhabitants, whether Muslim or Christian, and nothing in common with one another. Turks and Franks met as enemies, and two centuries later parted as enemies; and the enmity extended from them to the indigenous Muslims and Christians, who from this time onwards showed a mutual hostility far more marked than ever before.

Chapter XI

CHRISTIANITY UNDER THE MONGOLS

The conquests of Chingiz Khān, the great founder of the Mongol power, extended from one end of Asia to the other. Crossing the River Oxus he laid waste Khurāsān and Afghanistan, and came in touch with the Khwarizmian Shahs. The Shahs of this dynasty had extended their borders from the province of Khwarizm, East of the Caspian Sea, until they ruled over the same wide area as the Saljūq Turks before them. Chingiz Khān did not consolidate his conquests south of the Oxus. But his son Ogotai, who succeeded him, invaded Mesopotamia, slew the last of the Shahs of Khwarizm in 1231, and ravaged the whole of Mesopotamia and the districts of Armenia, Adharbaijān, Arrān and Georgia, on the west of the Caspian Sea. These conquered districts contained large numbers of Christians, and they must have suffered severely from the plundering and murderous Mongols. We hear of churches being cast down and of crosses being trodden under foot. It is perhaps surprising that the Christians did not suffer more than they did. An Armenian chronicler

> Guiragos tells us that at this time a Syrian doctor named Simeon. . . gained great influence over Ogotai. He asked the great Khakan to issue an order exempting the innocent people who did not resist the Mongol arms from massacre. Ogotai assented to this, and sent him westwards, amidst great pomp, and bearing a note for the Mongol commander, ordering him in these matters to conform to the wishes of the Syrian doctor. On his return he greatly eased the condition of the Christians. He built Christian churches in the Mussalman towns, where hitherto no one dared pronounce the name of Christ, notably in Tabriz and Nakhchivan [both in Adharbaijān]. In these two towns their condition had been particularly humiliating, and they dared not show themselves even. He built churches and raised crosses there, while the

[board used for a bell] was heard by night as well as by day. Christian funerals accompanied by the cross and Gospel, and the surroundings of the liturgy, openly paraded the streets. All who opposed were liable to be put to death. The Mongol troops treated him with great deference.... He baptised numbers of the Mongols.[1]

In the years which followed, in which the Mongols were attacking the Saljūq Sultans of Rūm, we find Armenians and Georgians allied with the Mongols and fighting on their side.

At this time efforts began to be made to bring about an alliance between the Mongols and the Christian nations of Europe. The first European embassy to the Persian Mongols, consisting of Dominican monks, reached the Mongol camp in 1247. The object of this embassy was twofold, to convert the Mongols to Christianity, and also to induce them to be less cruel to the Christians. The bearing of the ambassadors towards the Mongols, and their praise of the Pope, greatly incensed the Mongols, and the monks barely escaped with their lives.[2] In the following year, 1248, the first year of the Great Khan Kuyuk, two Tatar envoys had an audience of the Pope. In the same year envoys were sent by a Mongol general to St Louis who was then in Cyprus. They presented a letter, the genuineness of which has, however, been disputed, which included the following sentences:

We strongly wish and command that all Christians should be free from slavery and tribute and vexations and tolls and such like; and that they should be honoured and revered, and no one should touch their possessions; and that destroyed churches should be rebuilt; and that the boards should be struck, and that no one should dare to prevent them, that they may pray with a quiet and free heart for our kingdom.... The king of the earth thus orders that in the law of God there should be no difference between Latins, Greeks, Armenians, Nestorians, Jacobites, and all who adore the cross; for all are one in our sight.[3]

When Mangū became Great Khan in 1251 it was decided to extend the Mongol conquests in China and in the West. To

[1] Howorth, *History of the Mongols*, Part III, *The Mongols of Persia*, p. 34.

[2] Howorth, pp. 72–76.

[3] Assemani, III, pt II, CV.

this end two expeditions were entrusted to brothers of Mangū, the Chinese expedition to Khubilai, who afterwards succeeded Mangū as Great Khān in 1257, and the Western expedition to Hūlāgū. Of Mangū it is reported by the Armenian historian Haithon that

> he wished to receive the sacrament of baptism, and so was baptised by the hands of a certain bishop who was chancellor of the kingdom of Armenia; and all those of his house were also baptised, and many others of both sexes, nobles and magnates.[1]

Hūlāgū was the founder of the dynasty of the Īl-Khans of Persia, who, though paying nominal allegiance to the Great Khān, were practically independent. Hūlāgū's first work was to crush the Ismailians or Assassins, and having accomplished that, he set about to destroy the caliphate. In 1258 he took Baghdad, and sacked the city with terrible slaughter. Nearly the whole population was slain, numbering at the lowest estimate 800,000.[2] The last of the Abbasid Caliphs was slain. The Christians of Baghdad, however, suffered no harm. They were all gathered together into a certain church, and their lives were spared, for Hūlāgū professed himself a Christian. There seems to be some doubt whether he was actually a baptised Christian, but his wife was certainly a zealous Christian, and influenced him in favour of the Christians. He also had Armenian and Georgian Christians as allies, and the latter took a prominent part in the capture of Baghdad.[3] It now seemed to the Christians that their day of prosperity had come. What could be more significant of the changed status of the Christians than the fact that one of the palaces belonging to the Caliphs, the Dār al-Dawīdār or Secretariat, was granted to the Nestorian Catholicus to live in, and he was allowed to build a new church in it?[4] For the first time in the whole history of the Eastern Churches the civil ruler called himself a Christian. For centuries the Christians had been a subject *melet*, and it was a severe moral

[1] Assemani, III, pt II, CVI.
[2] Howorth, p. 127. [3] Howorth, p. 126.
[4] Assemani, III, pt II, CI, Amr, p. 120.

test for them whether they would have learnt from their centuries of subjection to behave with consideration and justice when the power was in their own hands. The story of the next few years shows not only that Christianity had failed to redeem the Mongols who called themselves by the name of Christ, but that the Christians of older standing were as lacking in tolerance as the Muslims had been. The Muslim historian Maqrīzī tells us that after the capture of Damascus by the Mongols the Christians there

> began to be in the ascendant. They produced a diploma of Hūlāgū guaranteeing them express protection and the free exercise of their religion. They drank wine freely in the month of Ramadān, and spilt it in the open streets, on the clothes of the Mussalmans and the doors of the mosques. When they traversed the streets, bearing the cross, they compelled the merchants to rise, and ill-treated those who refused. They carried the cross in the streets, and went to the Church of St Mary, where they preached sermons in praise of their faith, and said openly, "The true faith, the faith of the Messiah, is to-day triumphant". When the Mussalmans complained they were treated with indignity by the governor appointed by Hūlāgū, and several of them were by his orders bastinadoed. He visited the Christian churches, and paid deference to their clergy. The governor here meant was no doubt Kitubuka, who was a Kerait and a Christian.[1]

In two places the intolerance of the Christians towards the Muslims caused them to forfeit the favour which they generally received from the Mongols in the days of Hūlāgū. In Takrīt they took the opportunity of the Muslim invasion to slay many of the Muslims and plunder their goods. Complaint was made by a Muslim to the Mongolian prefect, and the matter was reported to Hūlāgū, by whose orders the Christians of Takrīt were slain, except the aged who were spared, and the boys and girls who were taken captive. Their cathedral also was handed over to the Muslims.[2] The Crusaders of Sidon also brought trouble upon themselves by plundering some Muslims, and then killing a nephew of

[1] Howorth, p. 150. For the conversion of the Keraits see p. 101.
[2] Howorth, pp. 140–1.

Kitubuka who had been sent to get the plunder restored.[1] With these two exceptions the Christians seem to have been much better treated in the days of Hūlāgū than under the Caliphs. The Armenian Christian chronicler Haithon relates of the wife of Hūlāgū,

> This devoted Christian lady at once sought permission to destroy the Saracens' temples, and to prohibit the performance of solemnities in the name of Muhammad, and caused the temples of the Saracens to be utterly destroyed, and put the Saracens into such slavery that they dared not show themselves any more.

Thus the Christian historian applauded intolerance towards the Muslims, and in so doing reflected the opinion of the Christians at large, for the Jacobite historian Barhebraeus says of Hūlāgū and his wife, "There was great sorrow through the whole world at the death of those two great luminaries and zealous combatants of the Christian religion".[2] It is terrible to read such a verdict, from a Christian writer, of a man of the barbarous character of Hūlāgū.

Some of the Mongol rulers seem deliberately to have deceived the European sovereigns and the Pope by pretending that they were Christian or wished to be Christian; and the Europeans in reply seem to have promised help which they were scarcely in a position to give, in order to win them over to Christianity. There is a letter which is said to have been written by Pope Alexander IV to Hūlāgū in 1261 when it had been reported to the Pope that Hūlāgū was thinking of being baptised as a Catholic. The Pope urges him not to delay his baptism, and proceeds:

> See how it would enlarge your power in your contests with the Saracens if the Christian soldiery were to assist you openly and strongly, as it could, with the grace of God. You would thus increase your temporal power, and inevitably also secure eternal glory.[3]

We must not, however, suppose that the Mongols were altogether insincere in their enquiries about Christianity.

[1] Howorth, p. 164. [2] Assemani, III, pt II, CVIII–CIX.
[3] Howorth, p. 210.

They could have understood little of the faith of Christ, and they were seeking the religion that would give them most success. It was therefore not mere hypocrisy when they asked for European aid against the Turks, and in the same breath said that they were thinking of becoming Christians. We must remember that in the days of Khubilai Khān and Hūlāgū the greater number of the Mongols were still heathen, though some like Hūlāgū professed Christianity and others professed Islam. We have a most interesting story from Marco Polo, from which we may picture how the mass of the Mongols were watching the success of those rulers who professed Christianity or Islam. There was a certain Tatar chief named Nayan who was lord over many lands and owed allegiance to the great Khubilai Khān. This man Nayan rebelled against the Great Khan, but after being defeated in battle he was captured and slain. Marco Polo says:

> Now you must know that Nayan was a baptised Christian, and bore the cross on his banner; but this nought availed him, seeing how grievously he had done amiss in rebelling against his lord. For he was the Great Kaan's liegeman, and was bound to hold his lands of him like all his ancestors before him.[1]

The story proceeds:

> And after the great Kaan had conquered Nayan, as you have heard, it came to pass that the different kinds of people who were present, Saracens and Idolaters and Jews, and many others that believed not in God, did gibe those that were Christians because of the cross that Nayan had borne on his standard, and that so grievously that there was no bearing it. Thus they would say to the Christians: "See now what precious help this God's cross of yours hath rendered Nayan, who was a Christian and a worshipper thereof". And such a din arose about the matter that it reached the Great Kaan's own ears. When it did so, he sharply rebuked those who cast gibes at the Christians; and he also bade the Christians be of good heart, "for if the cross had rendered no help to Nayan, in that it had done right well; nor could that which was good, as it was, have done otherwise; for Nayan was a disloyal and traitorous rebel against his lord, and well deserved that which had befallen him. Wherefore the cross of your God did well

[1] Edited by Yule, I, 331.

in that it gave him no help against the right". And this he said so loud that everybody heard him. The Christians then replied to the Great Kaan: "Great King, you say the truth indeed, for our cross can render no one help in wrong-doing; and therefore it was that it aided not Nayan, who was guilty of crime and disloyalty, for it would take no part in his evil deeds."[1]

Khubilai Khān professed himself favourable to all religions, but especially towards Christianity. But when asked why he did not become a Christian he is said to have replied:

How would you have me to become a Christian? You see that the Christians of these parts are so ignorant that they achieve nothing, whilst you see the idolaters can do anything they please, insomuch that when I sit at table the cups from the middle of the hall come to me full of wine or other liquor without being touched by anybody, and I drink from them. They control storms, causing them to pass in whatever direction they please, and do many other marvels; whilst, as you know, their idols speak, and give them predictions on whatever subjects they choose. But if I were to turn to the faith of Christ and become a Christian, then my barons and others who are not converted would say, "What has moved you to be baptised and to take up the faith of Christ? What powers or miracles have you witnessed on His part?" (You know that the idolaters here say that their wonders are performed by the sanctity and power of their idols.) Well, I should not know what answer to make; so they would only be confirmed in their errors, and the idolaters, who are adepts at such surprising arts, would easily compass my death. But now you shall go to your Pope, and pray him on my part to send hither an hundred men skilled in your law, who shall be capable of rebuking the practices of the idolaters to their faces, and of telling them that they too know how to do such things but will not, because they are done by the help of the devil and other evil spirits, and shall so control the idolaters that these shall have no power to perform such things in their presence. When we shall witness this we will denounce the idolaters and their religion, and then I will receive baptism; and when I shall have been baptised, then all my barons and chiefs shall be baptised also, and their followers shall do the like, and thus in the end there will be more Christians here than exist in your part of the world![2]

[1] P. 335.

[2] According to Ramusio, the biographer of Marco Polo. Yule, *op. cit.* I, 339.

The desire for an Italian mission seems on a par with the desire of so many of the Mongol rulers for a European alliance. Yule adds:

> He may have been quite sincere in saying what is here ascribed to him in *this* sense, viz., that if the Latin Church, with its superiority of character and acquirement, had come to his aid as he had once requested, he would gladly have used *its* missionaries as his civilising instruments instead of the lamas and their trumpery.[1]

The eagerness with which the Mongols sought a European alliance against the Muslims is easily understood when we realise that they received at Muslim hands the first check to their victorious advance. After the capture of Damascus it was clear that the Mongols were threatening Egypt. The Mamluk Sultan of Egypt made a desperate effort. With great difficulty he persuaded his people to follow him, and then met the Mongols in battle at 'Ain Jālūt between Nablus and Baissan. There in 1260 a fierce battle was fought, which ended in the complete defeat of the Mongols. Of this victory Howorth says:

> The victory of the Egyptians was a turning point in the world's history. It was the first time for a long while that the Mongols had been fairly beaten, and although the defeat was probably largely due to the smallness of their numbers, Kitubuka having apparently only 10,000 men with him, it was none the less decisive. It stopped the tide of Mongol aggression and probably saved Egypt, and in saving Egypt saved the last refuge where the arts and culture of the Mussalman world had taken shelter; where, under the famous Mamluk dynasties, and under the new line of Khalifs, it blossomed over in wonderful luxuriance.[2]

It is possible that this victory had another effect of world-wide importance; for it may have been as a result of it that the Mongols first began to think seriously whether Islam might not be the most powerful religion. The Christians of Damascus now suffered the fruits of the arrogant behaviour they had shown to the Muslims during the few months of the Mongol occupation of the city. Many Christians were slain,

[1] P. 340. [2] Pp. 169–70.

and others enslaved. Jews were similarly treated, and also those Muslims who had supported the Mongol invaders.[1] The incident is of interest as showing how the attitude of the Christians enraged the Muslims, but it must not be allowed to distract our attention from the really vital question of the attitude of the Mongols towards the Christians. The same may be said of the slaughter of Christians in Mosul, and the forcible conversion of many of them to Islam in 1262 during a temporary set-back to the Mongols and an occupation of the city by Muslims.[2] For some time yet the Christians enjoyed the favour of the Mongols.

Hūlāgū was succeeded in 1265 by Abāgā, who was favourable to the Christians, though not one himself. He confirmed the Nestorian Catholicus Dēnhā I in his possession of the Dār al-Dawīdār, which Hūlāgū had granted to his predecessor. The spirit of the Christians now they wielded power is exemplified by the behaviour of this Catholicus Dēnhā who, in 1268, "ordered a certain man whose home was Takrīt, who many years before had abjured the Christian religion and had embraced the religion of the Hagarenes, to be taken and drowned in the Tigris". The people of Baghdad were so angry at this high-handed action that they tried to burn the house of the Catholicus, and to slay him, and would have done so had he not been rescued by Alai ad-din, the chief of the Mongol Council.[3] The unpopularity of Dēnhā resulting from this incident had a repercussion three years later.

In 1271 some Ishmaelites [i.e. Bedouins] tried to assassinate Alai ad-din. They failed, and were cut in pieces. The Muhammadans declared the attempt had been made by some Christians, emissaries of Mar Dēnhā. This sufficed to cause a general imprisonment of the bishops and the heads of the regular and secular clergy at Baghdad. At the same time Kutbuka, the governor of Irbil [Arbil], imprisoned the Catholicus and his bishops, and they were only released after some weeks, and by order of the court. Thereupon the Nestorian patriarchs fixed their residence at Ashnu in Adharbaijān.[4]

[1] Howorth, p. 170.
[2] Howorth, p. 180.
[3] Assemani, III, pt II, CXII.
[4] Howorth, p. 247.

Three years later the Muslims of Arbil again had an opportunity of attacking the Christians. The Christians were carrying out a Palm Sunday procession under the military protection of the Mongols, when they were set upon by Muslims and dispersed, and for some time afterwards were afraid even to come out of their houses.[1]

In 1280 there was another decisive defeat of the Mongols by the Egyptians, and this must have furthered the belief in the strength of Islam and the weakness of Christianity; for 5000 Georgian Christians, and a contingent of Armenians, and some Franks, were fighting on the side of the Mongols. The battle was fought in Syria, between Hamath and Hims. The Mongols seemed to have secured a complete victory when, for some reason not fully explained, their leader fled; and the Mongol victory was turned into a disastrous defeat. The Muslim historian Maqrīzī says,

> It was a wonderful proof of the divine protection afforded to the Mussalmans, for if it had pleased Him that the enemy should return, the troops of Islam were not in a position to resist.[2]

But the general feeling of the Mongols had not yet gone so far as to tolerate a Muslim ruler. In 1280 Abāgā was succeeded by Aḥmad, who, although brought up as a Christian, was converted to Islam. According to Haithon his conversion to Islam was followed by that of many of his people, and also by a persecution of the Christians.[3] *The History of Yabalāhā III* says:

> He lacked education and knowledge, and he persecuted the Christians greatly because of his association with the Hagarenes, towards whose religion he leaned, and because of the two envious old men [i.e. bishops] who found the opportunity to fulfil their desire.[4]

The author goes on to recount the persecution that befell Yabalāhā on account of the false accusations levelled against him by the two bishops who had plotted to supplant him.

[1] Howorth, p. 247. [2] Howorth, pp. 270–3. [3] Howorth, p. 287.

[4] Edited by Sir Wallis Budge under the title *The Monks of Ḳublai Khan*, p. 158, and by J. A. Montgomery, p. 47.

Eventually the accusations were disproved, and the Catholicus was released; and it is pleasing to read that the Catholicus would not agree to the Khān's suggestion that the wicked bishops should be killed, but had them excommunicated and degraded from their office. Barhebraeus, who was still alive, denies the persecution of Christians, so it can scarcely have been at all general. He says:

> He showed himself towards all people clement and just, and especially to the Christian leaders, whom, together with the churches, monasteries, priests and monks dwelling everywhere among the nations, he freed from tribute and taxes.

This account further states that the Maphrianus, i.e. the head of the Eastern part of the Jacobite Church, arrived at Tazacum at the time of Aḥmad's coronation,

> and when the Maphrianus arrived there, the illustrious Aḥmad was placed on the throne of the kingdom, the Maphrianus was introduced into his presence by the nobles, and, according to custom, prayed for his welfare. The king in turn granted an admirable diploma for the building of the churches of Adharbaijān, Assyria and Mesopotamia.[1]

Whether he actually persecuted the Christians or not, it is evident that his conversion to Islam was in advance of the public opinion of the Mongols, for a revolt against him was successfully carried through which placed Arghūn on the throne in 1284. A fragment of a letter sent by Arghūn to the Pope and the Christian princes of Europe says:

> Since Aḥmad had turned away from the law of our fathers, and entered the way of the Arabs, which our fathers knew not, all the sons of the kings with one consent cast him from the kingdom, and appealed to the Great Khān our father that he should be judged by him, and that they might put me on the throne of the kingdom.[2]

Haithon also reports that the conversion of Aḥmad to Muhammadanism, and his efforts to convert the Mongols, were reported to Khubilai Khān, who was much irritated by the news, and sent to reprove him.[3]

[1] Assemani, III, pt II, CXIV.
[2] Assemani, III, pt II, CXVI. [3] Howorth, p. 310.

The new king Arghūn was very friendly to the Christians, and to the Nestorian Catholicus Yabalāhā in particular. He had a church tent erected next to the royal tent in the camp, and ordered the regular recitation of the Eucharist and the daily offices.[1] *The History of Yabalāhā* says:

> Arghūn loved the Christians with his whole heart. And Arghūn intended to go into the countries of Palestine and Syria, and to subjugate them, and take possession of them, but he said to himself, "If the Western kings who are Christians will not help me I shall not be able to fulfil my desire".[2]

Thereupon he sent Barṣauma on the famous embassy to Europe in 1287 which is described in such interesting detail in *The History of Yabalāhā*. Previously to this, in 1285, the year after his accession, he had sent an embassy to Pope Honorius IV and various European sovereigns. The passage quoted above is from a fragment of one of the letters sent on that occasion. Two later embassies were sent by Arghūn to the West. In a letter sent with one of them he said that he would become a Christian if God vouchsafed to him to take Jerusalem.[3]

In 1291 Gaikhātu succeeded to the throne, a king noted for his friendship to the Christians and for his prodigal liberality.

> He established in his position every one of those who followed [divers] cults, he paid honour to the leaders of all religions, whether Christians, or Arabs, or Jews, or Pagans. He considered the face of no man [i.e. he was strictly impartial], and he neither turned aside nor swerved from justice, gold being accounted as dross in his sight. His alms were boundless, and there was no end to his gifts in charity.
>
> And the glory of the Holy Catholic Church became as great, nay greater, than it was before. And the hearts of the Christians gained courage and waxed strong, when they knew the mind of the victorious king and heard his words, for his good qualities and his gracious acts could be felt with hands [or, as otherwise translated, "attaining with their hands his gifts and favours"]. And from day to day their glory increased, and the splendour of

[1] Budge, *op. cit.* p. 198; Montgomery, p. 74.

[2] Budge, p. 165; Montgomery, p. 51.

[3] Montgomery, pp. 8–9.

their Church grew apace, and this took place through the great care and foresight and the wise rule of Mar Catholicus, [in which] he used his understanding for the glorification of the children of the kingdom [i.e. the royal family], [or "his skill in adulation of the royal household"].[1]

But while the Christians were thus basking in the sunshine of Gaikhātu's favour, an event was taking place which sealed their fate. For in the very year 1291 in which Gaikhātu began to reign, the Muslims captured 'Akka, the last stronghold of the Crusaders. This must have seemed to the Mongol onlookers the final proof of the weakness, not only of the European powers, but of the religion they professed. In the following year a blow was struck at another Christian power. The Sultan of Egypt attacked and captured Qal'at ar-Rūm, where the Armenian Patriarch had his see. The garrison of Mongols and Armenians was put to the sword, the Patriarch's palace and church were burnt down, and he was led away as a prisoner.[2] But of course the capture of a single town was not in itself a significant matter, and the fall of 'Akka owed its significance to the fact that it was the end of the Crusades, the final failure of the Christian powers in their two centuries of war against Islam.

For once and all there were dashed to the ground any hopes that may have been entertained by the Oriental Christians that the Western powers would be the means of delivering them from the hands of the Muslims. Less than seventy years before, a Nestorian bishop Shelēmōn of Baṣra (consecrated about 1222) had written a kind of apocalyptic vision of the destruction of the Muslims by the powers of the West:[3]

When men are oppressed and beaten, and hunger and thirst, and are tormented by that bitter chastisement; while the tyrants

[1] Budge, pp. 201–3; Montgomery, pp. 75–6.

[2] Howorth, p. 362.

[3] *Book of the Bee*, p. 126. In true apocalyptic style he uses archaic names such as Yathrib, Cush, Ishmael; so when he says "king of the Greeks" we may take it as referring indefinitely to Western powers, and not necessarily to the Byzantine Emperor.

shall live luxuriously and enjoy themselves, and eat and drink, and boast in the victory they have won, having destroyed nations and peoples, and shall adorn themselves like brides, saying, "The Christians have neither a God nor a deliverer"; then all of a sudden there shall be raised up against them pains like those of a woman in childbirth; and the king of the Greeks shall go forth against them in great wrath, and he shall rouse himself like a man who has shaken off his wine. He shall go forth against them from the sea of the Cushites, and shall cast the sword and destruction into the wilderness of Yathrib and into the dwelling-place of their fathers. They shall carry off captive their wives and sons and daughters into the service of slavery, and fear of all those round about them shall fall upon them, and they shall all be delivered into the hand of the king of the Greeks, and shall be given over to the sword and to captivity and to slaughter, and their latter subjection shall be one hundred times more severe than their [former] yoke. They shall be in sore tribulation from hunger and thirst and anxiety; they shall be slaves unto those who served them, and bitter shall their slavery be. Then shall the earth which has become desolate of its inhabitants find peace, and the remnant that is left shall return every man to his own land and to the inheritance of his fathers; and men shall increase like locusts upon the earth which was laid waste. Egypt shall be ravaged, Arabia shall be burnt with fire, the land of Hebron shall be laid waste, and the tongue of the sea shall be at peace. All the wrath and anger of the king of the Greeks shall have full course upon those who have denied Christ. And there shall be great peace upon the earth, the like of which has not been from the creation of the world until its end; for it is the last peace. And there shall be great joy on earth, and men shall dwell in peace and quiet; convents and churches shall be restored, cities shall be built, the priests shall be freed from taxes, and men shall rest from labour and anxiety of heart.

The final failure of the Crusades put an end to any hopes or fears such as these, and it is not surprising to find a Muslim author, writing within a few years of the fall of 'Akka, speaking of the defeat of the Christians in these contemptuous terms:

Even as it [Islam] has blotted out their strong and well-defended kingdoms, and their lofty and towering fortifications, and has turned them into refugees in hiding.[1]

[1] "Ghāzī b. al-Wāsiṭī, Kitāb radd 'alā ahl adh-dhimma", fol. 2*a* (*Journal of the American Oriental Society*, XLI, 1921).

The year of the fall of 'Akka may be regarded as the turning point of Mongol history. From that moment the feeling of the Mongols grew more and more against Christianity and in favour of Islam. In 1295, on the death of Gaikhātu, there were rival claimants for the throne, Baidū and Ghāzān. The former was at heart a Christian, though he outwardly professed Islam. Haithon says of him,

This Baidū was such a good Christian that he rebuilt the churches of the Christians, and ordered that no one should dare to preach the doctrines of Muhammad among the Tatars. And because those who followed the sect of the false Muhammad were greatly increased, they were annoyed at the command of Baidū, and went so far as to send messengers secretly to Ghāzān, who was the son of Arghūn, and promised to give him the kingdom which Baidū held, and make him lord over them, if he would renounce the Christian faith. Now Ghāzān cared little for the faith, and greatly desired the kingdom, so he promised to do what they wished; and so Ghāzān became a rebel. But Baidū gathered his people together intending to seize and hold Ghāzān, for he was ignorant of the treachery which his people were working against him. And when they came to the battle-field, behold all who adhered to the sect of Muhammad left Baidū and fled to Ghāzān. And Baidū, seeing himself deserted by all, took to flight hoping to escape; but he was followed in his flight by enemies, and he died.[1]

The Continuator of the Syriac Chronicle of Barhebraeus, though not quite agreeing with Haithon as to the history of the struggle between the two claimants for the throne, makes it equally clear that the matter was regarded by the people as a religious issue between Christianity and Islam. He says:

But since for many years he [Baidū] had been familiar with the Despina of the Greeks, the Emperor's daughter, the wife of Abāgā, he was very favourably inclined towards the Christians, so that he even allowed a church to be consecrated in his camp, and bells to be struck; but publicly and openly he never dared be called a Christian. But because at this time all the Mongols, people and nobility, women and boys, old and young, had embraced the religion of the Hagarenes, and everywhere were observing circumcision and washings, and had learnt correctly the special prayers of the Muslims and were using them, Baidū

[1] Assemani, III, pt II, CXIX.

himself, in order to please them, accommodated himself to the manners of the Hagarenes, by which means he greatly conciliated all the leaders of the kingdom to himself. However, he could not be torn away from familiarity with Christians, nor persuaded to commit the affairs of the kingdom to any but Christians. Thus he began to halt between the two opinions. To the Christians he said he was a Christian, and he used to wear a cross hung round his neck; but to the Saracens he professed that he was a Muhammadan, though he did not go so far as to observe the fast or learn the washings. And whenever the priests of the Saracenic religion came together for the solemn prayers, Baidū bade his son go with them to the place of prayer, thinking by this artifice to pacify their minds and allay their indignation: but in vain, for it could not be concealed from the Saracens that Baidū was much more favourably inclined towards the Christians.[1]

The History of Yabalāhā also shows that it was a movement in favour of Islam that set Ghāzān on the throne:

> The peoples of the Arabs roused themselves to take vengeance on the Church and its children for the destruction which the father of these kings [i.e. Hūlāgū] had inflicted upon them.[2]

On October 5th, 1295, Baidū was slain, and Ghāzān came to the throne. The event which brought all the people to the side of Ghāzān was his public profession of Islam on the previous June 16th. He had been urged to take this step by the general Naurūz who was chiefly instrumental in putting him on the throne, and who said to him,

> The Mussalmans, raised by you from the degradation they have suffered at the hands of the pagan Tatars, will be devoted to your cause, while God, recognising that you have saved the true faith from extinction, will bless your arms.[3]

His example was followed by his officers and soldiers; and couriers were sent with the news of his conversion to 'Irāq and Khurāsān. It is important to recognise that the change of attitude now adopted towards the Christians was not imposed by the new Khan on his people, but was imposed

[1] Assemani, III, pt II, CXXI.
[2] Budge, p. 209; Montgomery, p. 80.
[3] Howorth, pp. 383–4.

by the people on the Khan. We have already seen that he only accepted Islam to please the people; and now that he was on the throne it was popular pressure which compelled him to favour Islam and persecute the Christians. According to *The History of Yabalāhā* an edict was put out by Naurūz as follows:

> The churches shall be uprooted, and the altars overturned, and the celebrations of the Eucharist shall cease, and the hymns of praise, and the sounds of calls to prayer shall be abolished; and the heads [or chiefs] of the Christians, and the heads of the congregations [i.e. synagogues] of the Jews, and the great men among them, shall be killed.[1]

The Continuator of the Syriac Chronicle of Barhebraeus relates that Ghāzān himself initiated the persecution:

> He put forth an edict and commanded that the churches [of Christians], and the temples of idols, and the synagogues of the Jews, should be destroyed, and that capital punishment should be inflicted on the priests of the ethnic superstition; he dishonoured the priests of the Christian religion, and wished also to increase their tribute and exactions; and he gave warning that no Christian henceforth should go out without a waistbelt, and that all Jews should wear a conspicuous mark on their heads.[2]

The same author thus recounts the persecution:

> At the same time the citizens of Tabriz razed all the churches in that city to the ground, and great sorrow was caused to the Christians in the whole world.... But when the writings were put forth, and the Mongol legates were sent to every place and city to destroy the churches and break down the monasteries, if they found any Christian who came to them and showed any sort of submission, and was willing to offer presents, they were turned to pity; for they were more zealous to collect money than to destroy churches, as happened in the city of Arbīl. For the leaders that were sent there waited twenty days, expecting some one of the Christians to be willing to redeem the churches of that place with gold and gifts. But no one came forward, and even the Metropolitan of the city himself did not take up the care of his own churches, but they were all looking after their own affairs. Wherefore authority was immediately given to the people to rage against

[1] Budge, p 210. [2] Assemani, III, pt II, CXXII.

the sacred things of the Christians at their pleasure. So they attacked the two churches of that place, once magnificent structures, one our church of the Jacobites, and the other that of the Nestorians, and demolished them. These things took place on Wednesday 28th Tishri II [November] of that year. But afterwards the people of Nineveh heard the sighing and groaning of the people of Arbīl, and were greatly afraid. And when the magnates and leaders came to Mosul, immediately men famous for piety, fearing the ruin of their holy churches, in order to avert this, offered a vast sum of money as an indemnity for them; and since they possessed none of the wealth of this world they collected all the instruments and vessels of their own churches. Wherefore they left neither cross, nor ikon, nor censer, nor book of the Gospels covered with gold or silver. But since it by no means reached the required sum, they were obliged to have recourse to the Christians who dwelt in the neighbouring towns and places. In this way, by begging on all sides, they paid 15,000 denarii of money as tribute for the immunity of the churches and Christians. By this way God helped those faithful ones, and no church received any injury, although this involved the sacrifice of their possessions for the vast number of Christians. But the persecution, contumely, trials and ignominies, which the Christians endured at that time, especially in the city of Baghdad, who is able to describe? They say that a Christian man dared not appear in the market, but the women went forth in public and bought and sold, since they could not be distinguished from Saracen women; and if they were recognised they were burdened at once with trials and contumely, and even received blows and beating. And behold, the Christians of those regions were punished with attacks of this kind, and were tossed about most wretchedly by storms and tempests. Meanwhile the enemies of justice insulted them, saying, "Where is your God? Let us see if you have a helper, or who it is who will save and free you". Moreover that persecution and shame in those days pressed not only on our own people, but also on the Jews and idolaters and their priests, and indeed more grievously, after the great honour with which the Mongol kings had been wont to treat them, so much so that half the taxes which were brought into the royal treasury used to be spent in making images of gold and silver.[1]

The attack on the Christians in Baghdad took place in March 1296, i.e. about five months after Ghāzān's accession, for 'Amr gives us the date of the transfer of the remains of

[1] Assemani, III, pt II, CXXIII–CXXV.

Dēnhā I from their original resting place to another church when the Dār al-Dawīdār was seized by the Muslims.[1] *The History of Yabalāhā*[2] records fighting in Arbīl between Christians on the one hand, and Arabs and Kurds on the other, in the course of 1297, so that presumably the destruction of the two churches mentioned in the Syriac Chronicle took place in November 1296. An Armenian writer, Stephen the Orphelian, gives a general account of the persecution.

He says many churches were destroyed and priests killed, and those who escaped were plundered, while their wives and children were made slaves of. At Baghdad, Mosul, Hamian, Thavrej,[3] and Marāghā the persecution had most dire results. In Armenia the churches and monasteries of Nakhchivan were plundered, their doors broken, and the altars overturned, but out of respect for their Georgian allies the churches were not destroyed. The metropolitan church of Sinnia, of which the chronicler was then bishop, paid a ransom for its safety. The Nestorian Catholicus of Marāghā was captured and put to great indignities. Ter Tiratsu, Bishop of the Church of the Apostles [probably that of Dadi Vank or Kutha Vank, dedicated to St Thaddaeus] was tortured and robbed, while his monastery, in which reposed the remains of St Thaddaeus, was ruined.[4]

The persecution in Marāghā is described fully in *The History of Yabalāhā*,[5] because it included the imprisonment and torture of the Catholicus Yabalāhā. It began on September 25th, 1295, that is, actually a few days before Ghāzān's accession, and lasted till Easter 1296. Enormous sums of money were paid in the hopes of ransoming the Catholicus. The Armenian king Haithon also came and expended large sums of money to save the great church which Barṣauma had built in Marāghā; and then went and interceded with Ghāzān for the Catholicus, and gained for him a temporary

[1] P. 122.

[2] Budge, pp. 231–9.

[3] That is, Hamadān and Tabriz, from the reference to the destruction of these two towns in *The History of Yabalāhā*, Budge, p. 223.

[4] Howorth, p. 397.

[5] Budge, pp. 210–19.

respite. The Khan then granted an interview to a monk sent by the Catholicus, and

he gave to the Catholicus a *pukdānā* [i.e. a royal edict], according to custom, in which it was laid down that poll-tax should not be exacted from the Christians; that none of them shall abandon his faith; that the Catholicus shall live in the state to which he hath been accustomed; that he shall be treated with the respect due to his rank; that he shall rule over his throne; and shall hold the staff of strength over his dominion. And he promulgated an edict throughout all countries, and addressed it to all the amirs by their names, and to the soldiers, ordering them to give back everything which they had taken from the Catholicus or from the holy old men by force, and to give back to him what those men of Baghdad and their envoys, whom we have mentioned above, had taken. Moreover, he allotted and despatched to the Catholicus 5000 dinars for his expenses, saying, "These will serve him as a supply until he cometh to us".[1]

When the edict was received it was read publicly, and much of the plunder was restored. Thereupon in July 1296 the Catholicus set out to visit the Khān who received him well,

and from that time he began to treat him with affection. And in proportion as the king, little by little, was increasing the honour which he paid to the Catholicus, the hatred which was in the hearts of the enemies [of the Catholicus] increased, and they forged evil plots, and they sent information about everything which took place to that son of perdition, that accursed man Naurūz.[2]

The part played by king Haithon in inducing Ghāzān to treat the Christians better is made much more of by his namesake and relative the Armenian chronicler:

When the pious, just and faithful Haithon king of Cilicia [i.e. Little Armenia] heard that Baidū had overcome and obtained the kingdom of the Mongols, and loved the Christians and was more disposed towards them than towards other sects, he desired to see the king and make obeisance, and with great zeal to transact much business with him. With that plan therefore he set out from his place, and spent about two months on the journey. When he arrived near Ṣiāhkū he learnt that the great leader Naurūz with

[1] Budge, pp. 221–2. [2] Budge, p. 225.

his armies was about to fight with Baidū, and that the latter was expecting to be overthrown. Then Baidū sent a legate to Haithon king of the Armenians, telling him to proceed to Marāghā, and there wait quietly awhile, till, when matters had been settled, and he had returned to his camp, he should summon him to him. Wherefore the king set out for Marāghā, and stayed there about ten days. Meanwhile Baidū, being conquered by the great warrior Naurūz, had taken to flight, and Ghāzān the king of kings had come to the castle Tel Ūkamā near Diahkūrkān. Immediately Haithon humbly approached him and offered him magnificent gifts. The king of kings said to him, "But you have not come to us but to Baidū". The king replied, "Yes, but I am bound to the whole family of Chingiz Khān, and I ought to hasten in obedience to him, whoever he may be, of that family, who ascends the throne". Therefore the king of kings received him kindly, and clothed him in royal garments, and moreover commanded that a diploma should be written, and that his wishes should be satisfied. And since he had previously published an edict that the churches should be destroyed, the king Haithon begged that the churches should not be demolished because they were temples of God and houses of prayer; and he obtained a revocation of the former edict, and a new one in favour of the king was promulgated, by which the destruction of churches was forbidden, and at the same time it was commanded that only the temples of idols should be converted into houses of prayer and schools for the Saracens. Thus by the work of this Christian king most of the churches escaped that ruin. Wherefore the king went forth from the camp full of joy and gladness, on Sunday 9th Tishri I [October] of that year, i.e. at the beginning of the year 1607 of the Greeks [1296].[1]

Thus, whatever Ghāzān may have done at the time of his accession, within a year he was doing his best to stay the persecution of the Christians. But evidently it was beyond his control. For we have already seen that the troubles in Arbīl went on through 1297; and in the same year an edict was issued in Marāghā without the Khān's authority that everyone who did not abandon Christianity and deny his faith should be killed, and much damage was done before it could be stopped.[2] In 1299, after conquering the Egyptian

[1] Assemani, III, pt II, CXXVI–CXXVII.

[2] Budge, pp. 226–30.

army, Ghāzān issued an edict in Damascus in the course of which he said:

> Among the crowds of our warriors some have been found who, notwithstanding our prohibition, have dared to pillage and to reduce the people to slavery. We have had them put to death as an example to the rest of what they may expect; and as a proof that we mean this to be carried out rigidly, we also forbid them to molest those of other faiths—Jews, Christians or Sabaeans, "For they pay tribute, so that their goods may be as our goods, their blood like our blood". Rulers owe protection to their tributaries as they do to their Mussalman subjects, as the Prophet says. The Imam placed over men is in the position of a shepherd; and a shepherd has to give account for his sheep.[1]

His conquest of Syria brought him a letter of congratulation from James II, King of Arragon, with renewed proposals for alliance with the Mongols, in reply to which Ghāzān sent envoys to Europe stating his willingness to become a Christian.[2] For the remainder of Ghāzān's reign Yabalāhā enjoyed his favour, and was able in peace and security to build a magnificent monastery at Marāghā.

Uljāitū succeeded to the throne in 1304. He had been brought up as a Christian, but became a Sunni Muslim under the name Khudābanda, and afterwards left the Sunnis and joined the Shī'a. The Sunnis thereupon changed his name from Khudābanda "Servant of God" to Kharbanda "Muleteer". He appears to have been personally kindly disposed towards the Christians, and treated the Catholicus well. *The History of Yabalāhā* says of him:

> The king showed great mercy in the favourable edicts which he issued, and he allotted to the Catholicus the whole of the poll-tax of Arbīl, and commanded that the poll-tax should never again be levied on the Christians.[3]

In 1305 he sent an embassy to the King of France, and apparently it also went to England, as there are two replies

[1] Howorth, p. 442.
[2] Howorth, pp. 488–9.
[3] Budge, p. 260.

written from Northampton in 1307 from Edward II. The second letter,

> as D'Ohsson says, shows that the Khan's envoy had not only concealed the fact that Uljāitū was a Mussalman, but had even imposed on him so far as to persuade him that he would aid in extirpating the abominable sect of Muhammad.[1]

In spite of such professions Uljāitū was so weak that in 1307 he allowed himself to be seduced by certain Muslims to order the king and people of Georgia to apostatise and their churches to be destroyed. One Georgian authority says that he was so much impressed by the bravery of the king and his companions who said they were ready for death, that he spared them. Another Georgian authority says the king was put to death with cruel tortures.[2] There is a notice of a somewhat similar persecution, stirred up by Muslims, which is said to have taken place in 1306. Our authority in this case is the *Book of the Histories of Johannes of Dzar*, so it may be that the persecution particularly affected Armenia. The passage runs as follows:

> Kharbanda Khān, autocrat of the nation of the Archers, a wicked man, who hated the Christians, led away by sorcerers and heretical sheikhs, and inspired by the wicked counsels of their assistant, Satan, began the struggle against the invincible rock of Christ. A decree was published in all the universe, referring to the Christians under his domination, that they should adopt the stupid religion of Muhammad, or that each person should pay a *kharāj* tax of eight dahecans; that they should be smitten in the face, their beards plucked out, and should have on their right shoulders a black mark—all on account of his hatred to Christ. The wicked ones thereupon spread themselves over the towns and villages, and convents, sowing terror everywhere; for the fatal decree forbade the performing of mass, the entering of a church, and the baptism of infants. It was determined to overwhelm the Christian religion by one blow. Meanwhile the Christians remained faithful. They paid the exactions, and bore the torments joyfully. Kharbanda Khān, seeing that these means were insufficient, ordered them all to be made eunuchs, and to be

[1] Howorth, p. 576. [2] Howorth, p. 543.

deprived of one eye, unless they became Muhammadans. Many perished in this persecution.[1]

The weakness of Uljāitū is seen at its worst in the terrible massacre at Arbīl in 1310. From the account given in *The History of Yabalāhā*[2] of the events in Arbīl it is perfectly clear that there was plenty of time and opportunity for the Khan to interfere. At one moment he believed lying reports against the Christians without making any enquiries; at another moment he issued edicts for the protection of the Christians without taking any measures for the enforcement of the edicts. His culpable weakness gave full rein to the passions of Arabs, Kurds and Mongols to wreak their vengeance on the hated Christians. The Catholicus, who had been present all the time in Arbīl, and who had barely escaped with his life, reached the royal camp; and we are given a pathetic picture of the last meeting of these two men, the truly great Yabalāhā and the feeble Uljāitū:

> He [Yabalāhā] went to the victorious king, and blessed him according to custom, and placed the cup in his hands, and the king likewise gave him the cup, but neither of them spoke a word with the other. And sorely afflicted, the Catholicus went forth from the presence, for he had intended, if the king had questioned him, to make known to him all that had happened to himself and to his flock. At this treatment his heart was broken grievously, and he sat down there for a month of days, hoping that peradventure some new thing might happen, or that someone would ask him about what had happened....And he made up his mind that he would never again go to the Camp, saying, "I am wearied with the service of the Mongols".[3]

Yabalāhā lived till 1317, having survived long enough to hear of another terrible calamity which befell the Christians of Āmid (Diyārbakr) in the year of his death. The following account we owe to the appendix to the Syriac Chronicle of Barhebraeus:

> In the year of the Greeks 1628 [1317] on the 20th of June at dawn on Monday, Aliaddin, known as the son of Degiaga, occupied Āmid, leading a strong army of Arabs from various

[1] Howorth, pp. 770–1, quoting from Brosset, *Collection d'Historiens Arméniens*, I, 568–9.

[2] Budge, pp. 261–302.

[3] Budge, pp. 303–4.

parts of Syria. And Āmid went into bitter slavery: 12,000 were captured, many Christians were slain, and Mar Gregorius the bishop of that city[1] was first beaten with blows and then slain. But also they dared to tear down the great Church of the Virgin, and then burn it. Its beautiful and wonderful buildings, ornaments and columns, succumbed to the flames, and the fire lasted for about a whole month. These things took place because the people of Āmid had revolted against the toparch Salechus the lord of Mārdīn, and he called the above-mentioned leader from Syria, who immediately came with 12,000 horsemen. Now there dwelt in the city of Āmid a certain man named ʻIlm ad-dīn, who moreover opened the gates secretly to all the enemy and led them into the city, and immediately fled to the lord of Mārdīn. But they entered in and laid waste the city.[2]

These events took place in the beginning of the reign of Abū Saʻīd, who was Khan from 1316 to 1335. We have no further record of the lot of the Nestorian or Jacobite Christians during this reign. In 1318 Pope John XXII founded an archbishopric in Sulṭaniyya, the new capital of the Mongols founded by Arghūn. As this archbishop's authority was to extend over the Catholics not only in Persia but also in Ethiopia and India, we may assume that their numbers were few, just as historians of the future might draw a similar conclusion from the fact that the first Bishop of Calcutta had jurisdiction over Australia as well as India. In 1320 Armenia was overrun, first by Egyptians and then by Turks. Pope John XXII came to their help, and also wrote a letter to Abū Saʻīd reminding him of the ancient friendship of the Mongols for the Franks and their reverence for the Apostolic See.[3] The absence of information about the Nestorians does not mean that they were unmolested. Such days of continual disaster were too unsettled for the writing or preservation of history. The Īl-Khān dynasty was breaking up, and from the death of Abū Saʻīd the power was divided, and there can be little doubt that the Muslims, unrestrained by the government, took the opportunity of persecuting the Christians that remained. ʻAmr, writing about the middle of the

[1] "Apparently the Jacobite bishop"—Assemani.
[2] Assemani, III, pt II, CXXXII–CXXXIII.
[3] Howorth, pp. 602–3.

fourteenth century, gives a list of twenty-seven metropolitan sees under the Nestorian Catholicus,[1] but it does not follow that all these posts were filled at the time as no names are given. The lists of Nestorian Catholici have a gap of nine years and nine months about 1369–78 when the see is said to have been vacant; but as the length of the reigns of the Catholici whose names are given during the latter half of the fourteenth and the whole of the fifteenth century are much more than the average—none of them less than twenty years, and one as much as thirty-nine years—we may suspect that there were other long periods when the see was unoccupied. The see of the Jacobite Maphrianus is said to have been vacant for twenty-five years from 1379–1404. By the time of Tīmūr Lang (Tamerlane) whose invasion took place in 1394 there can have been but few Nestorians left, and very few Jacobites in the Eastern provinces. Many towns were devastated during the invasion, including Baghdad, Takrīt, Āmid, Mārdīn, Arbīl, Mosul and Tūr ʿAbdīn. All these were formerly important Christian centres, and probably contained the greater number of Christians who had survived up till then. Few can have escaped the destruction of Timur. At Āmid we are told that all the inhabitants were burnt in a great fire. At Tūr ʿAbdīn, once the great centre of the Jacobites, the Christians were hunted out, and those who took refuge in underground caves were suffocated with smoke.[2]

We have seen that European travellers in the Far East in the thirteenth and fourteenth centuries reported the presence of Nestorian Christians in many parts, and that their evidence is corroborated from Chinese sources. Christianity seems to have entered China for the second time with the Mongol invasion at the beginning of the thirteenth century, but, as we have seen, it was the religion of foreigners, members of Turkish and Mongol tribes. While the Western Mongols

[1] P. 126.

[2] Assemani, III, pt II, CXXXIV–CXXXVII, quoting from an anonymous Syriac Chronicle.

hesitated between Christianity and Islam, and eventually became Muslims, the Eastern Mongols had become Buddhists. In 1368 the Mongol dynasty of China came to an end, and they were driven out of the land by a rising of the Chinese. Howorth says:

> It is quite certain that among the causes which led to the expulsion of the Mongol dynasty from China, and its supersession by a native dynasty [i.e. that of the Ming Emperors] was the general revolt against the Buddhist priesthood.[1]

With the expulsion of the Mongols, Christianity also was uprooted from China. After 1368 Christians in China are no longer mentioned in Chinese or European documents.[2] Whether Christianity survived among Eastern Turks or Mongols outside of China is uncertain. It is quite possible that the example of the Persian Mongols of persecuting Christianity as a religion of proved feebleness was copied by the Mongols of the East. The latest reference appears to be about 1440 when a messenger arrived in Europe from the Patriarch of a Nestorian kingdom which is described as being twenty days' journey from Cathay. Yule-Cordier says:

> It remains a difficult problem to say whence he did really come. It would seem as if some tribe of the Kerait or the Uighurs had maintained their Christianity till near the middle of the fifteenth century.[3]

Eventually even the memory of Christianity was wiped out of China, so that when the Jesuit missionaries went there at the end of the sixteenth century they were led at first to believe that Christianity had never existed there before their own day.[4]

The Christians of Malabar were the only part of the Nestorian Church which, as far as we know, did not suffer

1 *History of the Mongols*, Part IV, p. 131.
2 Moule, p. 271.
3 Yule-Cordier, *Cathay*, I, pp. 177–8.
4 Yule-Cordier, *Cathay*, I, p. 121.

directly as a result of the conversion of the Persian Mongols to Islam. We learn that in 1490 they sent to the Nestorian Catholicus for bishops, because for a long time they had been without bishops, and according to Burkitt this was due to a persecution by Muslims of South India.[1] Supposing this persecution to have taken place about 1450, more than a century had elapsed since the conversion of the Mongols to Islam. During that century the Malabar Christians must have been fairly prosperous, as otherwise the community would scarcely have been strong enough to survive for a long period without a ministry. The first Portuguese missionaries arrived early in the sixteenth century, and the Christian community then consisted of 30,000 families. The later changes in their fortunes were only connected with their ecclesiastical allegiance. By the Synod of Diamper in 1599 they were forcibly united to the Church of Rome; but after the expulsion of the Portuguese by the Dutch the greater number of them secured their independence from Rome and became Jacobites, receiving a bishop from the Jacobite Patriarch in 1665.[2]

While the Christians of Western Asia were being persecuted to the death, a similar fate was befalling their brethren in Egypt. The conditions leading up to the persecution of the Egyptian Christians were very much like those obtaining in Asia, only differing in the fact that the rulers were not Mongols. For a long time there had been a strong feeling of the populace against the employment of Christians in the high offices of state, but the practice had nevertheless continued. The campaigns of the Crusaders in Egypt had greatly embittered the Muslims; and in particular they were incensed by the attempts of the European powers to form alliances with the Mongols. In December 1299, as we have seen,[3] the Egyptian forces were routed and driven from

[1] Assemani, III, pt I, pp. 590–4; Mingana, *Early Spread of Christianity in India*, pp. 468–73; Burkitt, "The Old Malabar Liturgy" in the *Journal of Theological Studies*, XXIX, 155.

[2] *E.R.E.*, art. "Syrian Christians", XII, 180.

[3] P. 167.

Damascus by the Mongols, but by March of 1300 a new Egyptian army was in the field and reoccupied Damascus which had been evacuated by the Mongols. Revenge was taken by the Egyptians on those inhabitants of Damascus who had helped the Mongols, and it was probably the same feeling which prompted the order to close all the churches of Egypt in 1301, the Christians being regarded as the friends of the Mongols. Alexandria was exempted from this order, presumably so as not to offend unnecessarily the European powers.[1] We may look on this order to close the churches as the first concession of the Egyptian government to the popular clamour against the Christians. Even then the government seemed rather half-hearted in their action; for in 1305 they agreed to reopen the churches on representations by ambassadors from the King of Arragon. As in the case of the Mongols, the rulers were gradually forced by public opinion to turn against the Christians. A foolish indiscretion on the part of the ambassadors of the King of Arragon hastened the process. For just as the ambassadors were embarking at Alexandria after their successful mission, messengers came from the Sultan asking for ransom for a captive who had been freed. Not only did they refuse the ransom, but they carried off the messengers as captives. The result was a strict enforcement of the ancient restrictions against Christians.[2] The enforcement of these restrictions probably satisfied the Muslims for the time being, but gradually popular feeling against the Christians grew, encouraged by the news continually coming in of how Christianity was being stamped out by the Mongols. A fortunate chance has left us a polemical treatise written by a Jew who had become converted to Islam, named Saʿīd b. Ḥasan of Alexandria, in which he urges the destruction of pictures and images in churches, and shows how Ghāzān's conquest of the Egyptians was God's reward for his persecution of the Jews and Christians, and how the Egyptian victory over the

[1] *Encyclopedia of Islam*, art. "Ḳibt", p. 996.

[2] Muir, *The Mameluke or Slave Dynasty of Egypt*, pp. 54–60.

Mongols was the immediate result of the closing of the churches of Egypt. He says:

> God promised His servants the prophets the removal of the pictures and likenesses from the synagogues and temples. And He promised the king, by whose hand this removal should be brought about, a peaceful kingdom, long life, continuance of power, and the submission of the kings of the earth to him. The evidence of this and its proof is that at the end of the recorded periods which the books of revelation indicated, viz. at the end of the 700 lunar years from the Hijra of the Prophet, God laid waste the synagogues of the East by the hands of the king Ghāzān [1295 = A.H. 695]. So Ghāzān overcame the troops of the Muslims [1299]. But when the Muslims returned from their rout, God inspired them to close the churches; and they closed them [1301] according to the noble and pure Muslim law. Then the Muslims went forth to meet their enemies at Shakhab and God gave them the victory [1303].[1]

This treatise was composed in 1320, and illustrates well how the example of the Mongols was reacting upon popular feeling in Egypt till it broke out into open fury in the following year, 1321. Maqrīzī gives a long account of the disturbances of that year.[2] The Mamluk Sultan An-Nāṣir Muhammad wished to build an embankment to the Nile, and in order to provide earth they began digging round the church of az-Zuhrī. They dug round till the church stood as an island, the intention being that the church should fall of its own accord. But during prayers on Friday 9th Rabīʿ II, A.H. 721 (1321), when the excavators were away, a mob of common people attacked the church and destroyed and looted it. Other churches in Cairo were destroyed at the same time, so that when the Muslims came out of prayers the destruction

[1] *Kitāb masālik an-naẓar*, edited and translated by S. A. Weston in the *Journal of the American Oriental Society*, XXIV (2nd half), 1903, p. 381.

[2] In the concluding sections of the *Khiṭaṭ* (pp. 409–end) dealing with the monasteries and churches of Egypt, translated by Evetts as an appendix to Abū Ṣāliḥ's *Churches and Monasteries of Egypt*, pp. 329 *sqq*.

was already done. Gradually news came in that the same thing had happened in all parts of Egypt. A curious feature of these attacks, showing that they were prearranged, was that in several places a fakir rose in the mosque and shouted "Down with the churches!" but afterwards disappeared. This led the people to think that the destruction was due to a divine intervention. The Sultan was furiously angry and completely lost his head, ordering general massacres of the Muslims which it was impossible to carry out. About a month later a series of fires broke out in Cairo, the first being on the 10th of Jumādā I. All the water-carriers were mobilised, but it was scarcely possible to cope with the recurrent outbreaks. Several Christians were caught apparently red-handed in acts of incendiarism, and some confessed under torture that they had plotted to commit this arson out of revenge for the destruction of the churches. The Sultan and his Keeper of the Privy Purse incurred great hatred for trying to protect the Christians who were innocent. Someone said to the Sultan, "All this comes from the Christian secretaries, for the people hate them, and my advice is that the Sultan should take no step against the people, but should remove the Christians from the Divan". This advice displeased the Sultan, who again ordered indiscriminate massacre of the Muslims in the streets. Actually not more than two hundred were captured, some of whom were tortured and slain. Meanwhile another fire broke out, and when the Sultan rode forth he was met by a crowd of 20,000 shouting slogans in favour of Islam and against the Christians. Thereupon the Sultan gave way to their clamour, and had a proclamation made that anyone who should find a Christian should be at liberty to kill him and seize his goods. An order was issued dismissing all Christians who held government office. The attacks of Muslims on Christians increased so greatly that Christians dared not appear in the streets except in disguise. Many Christians adopted Islam. We are told that in the small town of Qalyūb 450 Christians became converts to Islam in one day, and that this was typical of the whole country.[1] The long process of attrition, by which the Copts had gradually gone over to Islam, thus ended in a bitter persecution to the death, in which the Coptic Church was reduced to the meagre numbers of the present day. The cause of this catastrophe was the hatred incurred by the Crusades, and the success in arms of those who fought against the Christians. Again, as in the case of Asiatic Christianity, the determining factor was the belief that worldly success is the criterion of the divine favour.

[1] *Encyclopedia of Islam*, art. "Egypt" by C. H. Becker, p. 8.

Chapter XII

THE EMPTY TRIUMPH OF ISLAM

It is not the purpose of this book to set forth the stages of the decline of Islam, the decay of its culture, and the failure of its worldly might. But lest any should suppose that the eclipse of Christianity was in any sense a real triumph for Islam, it is well to remember that this very period marks the turn of the tide for Islam. Ibn Baṭūṭṭa began his travels in 1325, that is, almost directly after the events related in the last chapter. It is striking to note the number of towns which he found in ruins. In Syria, which he visited in 1326, he reports as follows:

I journeyed thereafter from Jerusalem to the fortress of Askalon, which is a total ruin.

I went on from here to Sūr [Tyre], which is a ruin, though there is outside it an inhabited village, most of whose population belong to the sect called Rāfiḍīs [i.e. Shi'ites].

Next I went to the town of Tabarīya [Tiberias]. It was formerly a large and important city, of which nothing now remains but vestiges witnessing to its former greatness.[1]

As these three cities had been occupied by Crusaders, one might suppose that their desolation was merely caused by their capture and the departure of the Crusaders. But a similar explanation will not account for the ruin of famous towns in 'Irāq which he visited in 1327. In not one of these cases does he attribute the cause of decay to destruction by the Mongol invaders which we might have expected. The ruin of two he attributes to feuds between Muslims, and of one to attacks by nomad Arabs. The ruin of Baṣra and Kūfa is eloquent to the failure of Islamic culture, and that of

[1] Ibn Baṭṭūṭa, *Travels in Asia and Africa*, translated and selected by H. A. R. Gibb, pp. 57–8.

Ubullah to the failure of commerce with the East. He says:

Baṣra was in former times a city so vast that this mosque stood in the centre of the town, whereas it is now two miles outside it.

This Baṣra, in whose people the mastery of grammar reached its height, from whose soil sprang its trunk and its branches, amongst whose inhabitants is numbered the leader whose primacy is undisputed—the preacher in this town cannot deliver a discourse without breaking its rules.

Ubullah was formerly a large town, frequented by merchants from India and Fārs, but it fell into decay, and is now a village.

Isfahān is one of the largest and fairest of cities, but the greater part of it is now in ruins as a result of the feud between Sunnis and Shī'ites which is still raging there.

Though Kūfa was once the abode of the Companions of the Prophet, and of scholars and theologians, and the capital of 'Alī the Commander of the Faithful, it has now fallen into ruins, as a result of the attacks which it has suffered from the nomad Arab brigands in the neighbourhood.

In [Karbalā] too the inhabitants form two factions between whom there is constant fighting, although they are all Shī'ites and descended from the same family, and as a result of their feuds the town is in ruins.

This town [Surra-man-rā'a or Sāmarrā] is a total ruin and only a very small part of it remains. It has an equable climate and is exceedingly beautiful in spite of its disasters and the ruins of its noble buildings.

From Mosul we journeyed to Jazīrat ibn 'Umar, a large town surrounded by the river, which is the reason why it is called Jazira (island). The greater part of it is in ruins.... Two stages from Jazīrat ibn 'Umar we reached the town of Naṣībīn, an ancient town of moderate size, for the most part in ruins, lying in a wide and fertile plain.

We went on next to the town of Dārā, a large, ancient and glistering town, with an imposing fortress, but now in ruins and totally uninhabited.[1]

Ibn Baṭṭūṭa visited Khurāsān and Māwara-n-Nahr (Transoxania) in 1332–3, and reports the ruins of three great towns as due to the Mongol invasion. Of Bukhārā he says:

[1] Pp. 86–104.

This city was formerly the capital of the lands beyond the Oxus. It was destroyed by the accursed Tinkīz the Tatar (Chingiz Khān), the ancestor of the kings of 'Irāq, and all but a few of its mosques, academies and bazaars are now lying in ruins. Its inhabitants are looked down upon, and their evidence [in legal cases] is not accepted in Khwārizm or elsewhere, because of their reputation for fanaticism, falsehood and denial of the truth. There is not one of its inhabitants to-day who possesses any theological learning or makes any attempt to acquire it.

[Balkh] is an utter ruin and uninhabited, but anyone seeing it would think it inhabited on account of the solidity of its construction. The accursed Tinkīz destroyed this city, and demolished about a third of its mosque on account of a treasure which he was told lay under one of its columns. He pulled down a third of them, and found nothing, and left the rest as it was.

There are four large cities in this province [Khurāsān], two of them, Herāt and Naysabur (Nīshāpūr) inhabited, and two, Balkh and Merv, in ruins.[1]

To this mention of Merv must be added a notice taken from Yāqūt:

At the approach of the Mongol hordes in 1220 Yāqūt sought safety at Mosul in Mesopotamia, and all the glories of the Merv libraries fell a prey to the flames, which followed in the wake of the Mongol sack of this great city, when nine million corpses are said to have remained unburied among the ruins.[2]

It should be noticed that none of the towns referred to above owed its ruin to the Black Death which did not begin till 1348. That plague added greatly to the devastation of the lands of Islam. Islamic culture was not, however, wiped out in a day. As late as 1437 important astronomical tables were published in Samarqand.

We are now in a position to form some conclusions about the causes of the failure of Christianity in Asia, and the rise and fall of Islam. Perhaps it may sound premature to speak of the fall of Islam when there are still many millions of Muslims in the world; but culturally Islam was a spent force by the fifteenth century. Carra de Vaux concludes his chapter

[1] Pp. 171–5.
[2] Guy Le Strange, *Lands of the Eastern Caliphate*, p. 402.

on Astronomy and Mathematics in *The Legacy of Islam* with these words:

> Such then in its broad outlines was the scientific work of the Arabs. It came to an end when that of the Western genius began, that is to say in the fifteenth century. It is sometimes asked what were the causes of this cessation of intellectual activity in the Muslim world. Whence came this torpor after a period of such prolific activity? This, however, is a question which raises very obscure problems of general psychology about which no one has yet put forward any very definite theory, and, as I have none to propound myself, I do not think I ought to attempt to discuss it.[1]

What Carra de Vaux says of the cessation of intellectual activity is equally true of religious activity. From the fifteenth century Islam had no religious contribution to give to the world, unless one includes its effect in modern times on the primitive races of Africa which have indeed been raised somewhat by the influence of Islam, but then hindered from further advance. Whether we are speaking of intellectual or of religious activities, the cause of their rise and fall is to be sought, not only nor chiefly in the realm of mind, but in the realm of spirit. It is perfectly obvious that Islam contained in itself the weaknesses that led to its failure, and prevented it from being of permanent service to mankind. The imperfections of its moral standard at the commencement would not necessarily have brought about this result, had it not been for the stereotyping of the *shari'a* in the early centuries of Islam, by which further moral progress was stayed. It is unthinkable that Islam could progress beyond a certain stage, either in religion or in secular learning, when it was once tied to an infallible Quran and an infallible Hadith.

The problem of the rise of Islam is more difficult than the problem of its fall. That it brought a real gift to the heathen of Arabia, to the Gnostics of 'Irāq, and to a lesser extent to the Zoroastrians of Persia may readily be acknowledged. As far as they are concerned there is no difficulty in regarding Islam as a movement blessed by God to bring to them truths

[1] Edited by Arnold and Guillaume, p. 397.

which they had not known. But the real difficulty comes when we think of how Islam checked the advance of Christianity in Asia and eventually practically extinguished it. Following the Biblical doctrine of God's control of history, and in particular Second Isaiah's claim that God had raised up Cyrus from the East for the punishment of the Babylonians and the deliverance of Israel, it was natural for some Christians of those days to say that God had raised up the Arabs from the South, like a swarm of locusts, to punish the Christians for their evil deeds. That was the rough and ready way in which the ancients tried to understand history. It was unsatisfactory because it failed to suggest any positive beneficent purpose on the part of God, but it contained a vital element of truth that God the Creator had not left His creatures untended, but still guides and controls them. We must not suppose that God is responsible for the course of history in the sense that everything that happens is of His ordaining. The truth rather is that He is ever willing to reveal Himself to men, to impart His grace to them, and to give them opportunities of service; and this benevolent attitude is continued even when they have sinned and come short of what was expected of them. Looking at events in this way it is possible to believe that Muhammad was the recipient of divine gifts, without making God responsible for the whole of his extraordinary career. In the same way it is possible to believe that God found means of conferring divine gifts to men through the agency of Islam, without making God responsible for the whole course of the Islamic movement. In other words, and more generally, history as we see it is the resultant of man's use and abuse of divine opportunities.

The history that we have tried to unfold in this book shows that Islam was not forced upon the Christians of Asia at the point of the sword, at any rate until the days of bitter persecution under the Mongols. Nor, on the other hand, was Islam spread among Christians by preaching. There were indeed elements of truth in Islam, such as the belief that God could be served by men living a normal human life in the midst of their families, which had almost been lost sight of by the Christians of the day. But Christians were not attracted to Islam by this truth, for had that been the case they would have found the same truth more ready to hand on almost every page of the Gospels. The thing that turned Christians to Islam was, as we have seen, the common acceptance by Muslim and Christian alike of the error that the favour of God is shown by worldly success. It needed no preaching of Islam, or threat of the sword, to turn the allegiance of the Christians. The vision of the might of the Muslim Empire had the same overawing effect as the colossal golden image set up on the plain of Dura. They fell down and worshipped. Now this exaltation of worldly might on the part of the Christians was as much a denial of Christ as it would have been a denial of Judaism for Shadrach, Meshach and Abednego to worship Nebuchadnezzar's image. We have no reason to suppose that this error of the Christians began in the days of Islam. It was probably there before, only Islam came as a touchstone and revealed it. Here then we can trace the hand of God, but only if we look at history in long perspective. The people who called themselves Christians had accepted the false idea of the supremacy of worldly might—an idea closely akin to what in our own day we call secularism—in other words, the denial of the supremacy of the spirit. So they were allowed to join themselves to a system in which religion and worldly empire were one, until the time should come when its empire would fail and worldly might would be seen to be no criterion of the divine favour. The benevolent activity of God did not cease towards those Christians who had apostatised to Islam. Within Islam they were allowed such measure of truth as they could appreciate, for, as we have seen, many elements of truth were taken over from Christianity into Islam. True, they no longer worshipped Christ as Lord, but they had already denied Him in life, if not in word, before they became Muslims. They had denied the Sun of Righteousness, but God in His mercy, rather than leave them in total darkness, gave them the light of a narrow crescent moon. Within Islam opportunities were given which might have led on to the fuller truth in Christ, for the Muslims knew that He was the Seal of the Saints and the Word of God. But they would not face the consequences of that belief, and allow it to come to fruition. So they failed; and when they had handed on their inheritance of learning to the awakening Christian nations of the West their work was done. It is easier for us to gain the perspective in which these events must be seen, for we can include in our view the new chapter of history now opening in our own days in which Christianity is returning to Asia. At the moment it seems that the return of Christianity to Asia is a task depending entirely on the missionary activities of the Churches of the West. But it may be that the faithful remnants of the Churches of the East, who, through centuries of oppression such as we have not known, have refused to deny Christ, strengthened now with fresh outpourings of the Holy Spirit, will play their part in the new evangelisation of Asia.

BIBLIOGRAPHY

Histoires d'Ahoudemmeh et de Marouta. Edited and translated by F. Nau, *Patrologia Orientalis.* Paris.

Tor Andrae: (1) "Der Ursprung des Islams und das Christentum" in *Kyrkohistorisk Årsskrift*, 1923, 1924, 1925. These articles were afterwards published in book form. References are here given to the journal, quoting year and page.

—— (2) *Die Person Muhammeds in Lehre und Glauben seiner Gemeinde.* Stockholm, 1918.

Ibn al-'Arabī: *Futūḥāt al-makkīyya.* Cairo.

Sir Thomas Arnold: *The Preaching of Islam.* Westminster, 1896.

Sir Thomas Arnold and A. Guillaume (editors): *The Legacy of Islam.* Oxford, 1931.

J. S. Assemani: *Bibliotheca Orientalis*, vols. I, II, III, pt I and III, pt II. Rome, 1719–28.

Baedeker: *Palestine and Syria.* Leipzig, 1912.

Al-Baghdādī: (1) *Kitāb al-farq bain al-firaq.* Edited by Muhammad Badr. Cairo, 1910.

—— (2) *Mukhtaṣar kitāb al-farq bain al-firaq.* Edited by Philip K. Ḥitti. Cairo, 1924.

Al-Baiḍāwī: *Tafsīr al-Qur'ān.* Edited by Fleischer. Leipzig, 1846.

Al-Balādhurī: *Kitāb futūḥ al-buldān.* (1) Arabic text. Cairo, A.H. 1319.

—— (2) Translated by P. K. Ḥitti (vol. I) and F. C. Murgotten (vol. II), *The Origins of the Islamic State.* New York, 1916 and 1924.

W. Barthold: *Zur Geschichte des Christentums in Mittel-Asien bis zur mongolischen Eroberung.* Herausgegeben von Rudolph Stübe. Tübingen and Leipzig, 1901.

Ibn Baṭṭūṭa: *Travels in Asia and Africa*, 1325–1354. Translated and selected by H. A. R. Gibb. London, 1929.

R. Bell: (1) *The Origin of Islam in its Christian Environment.* London, 1926.

—— (2) "Who were the Hanifs?" in *The Moslem World*, April, 1930.

L. Bréhier: *L'Église et l'Orient au moyen âge, Les Croisades.* Paris, 1928.

L. E. Browne: "The Patriarch Timothy and the Caliph al-Mahdī" in *The Moslem World*, January, 1931.

Sir Wallis Budge: (1) *The Book of the Bee.* Oxford, 1886.
—— (2) *The Book of Governors, the Monastic History of Thomas of Marga.* London, 1893.
—— (3) *The Monks of Kublai Khan.* London, 1928.
F. C. Burkitt: (1) *Early Eastern Christianity.* London, 1904.
—— (2) "The Old Malabar Liturgy" in the *Journal of Theological Studies*, vol. XXIX, p. 155.
A. J. Butler: *The Arab Conquest of Egypt.* Oxford, 1902.
L. Cheikho: (1) *Le Christianisme et la littérature chrétienne en arabe avant l'Islam* (in Arabic). Beyrouth, 1912–23.
—— (2) *Vingt Traités théologiques d'auteurs arabes chrétiens* (in Arabic). Beyrouth, 1920.
—— (3) *Trois Traités anciens de polémique et de théologie chrétiennes* (in Arabic). Beyrouth, 1923.
Abū Dā'ūd: *Sunan.* Delhi, A.H. 1346.
R. Duval: "Histoire politique, religieuse et littéraire d'Édesse jusqu'à la première croisade" in *Journal Asiatique*, série 8, tome XIX, 1892.
Encyclopedia of Islam. Leiden and London, 1915–.
Encyclopedia of Religion and Ethics. Edinburgh, 1908–26.
Eutychius Patriarcha Alexandrini: *Annales* (in Arabic). Edited by L. Cheikho and B. Carra de Vaux, *Corpus Scriptorum Christianorum Orientalium.* Beyrouth, 1906–9.
J. N. Farquhar: "The Apostle Thomas in South India" in the *Bulletin of the John Rylands Library*, Manchester, January, 1927.
George Finlay: *History of the Byzantine Empire from* A.D. 716 *to* 1507. Everyman's Library. (First published in 1854.)
E. Fritsch: *Islam und Christentum im Mittelalter.* Breslau, 1930.
Alice Gardner: *Theodore of Studium.* London, 1905.
Ghazi b. al-Wāṣitī: *Kitāb radd 'alā ahl adh-dhimma.* Edited and translated by R. Gottheil, "An Answer to the Dhimmis", in the *Journal of the American Oriental Society*, vol. XLI, 1921.
Al-Ghazzālī: (1) *Ad-durra al-fākhira.* Edited and translated by Massignon, *La Perle précieuse.* Leipzig, 1925. (Original edition Geneva, 1878.)
—— (2) *Iḥyā 'ulūm ad-dīn.* Cairo, A.H. 1306.
Ignaz Goldziher: (1) *Muhammedanische Studien.* Halle, 1889.
—— (2) "Über muhammedanische Polemik gegen Ahl al-kitab" in *Zeitschrift der deutschen morgenländischen Gesellschaft*, Band XXXII, 1878.
—— (3) *Vorlesungen über den Islam.* Heidelberg, 1st edition 1910, 2nd edition 1925.

Gregory Barhebraeus Abu 'l-faraj: (1) *Chronicon Ecclesiasticum.* Edited by Abbeloos and Lamy. Louvain, 1872.
—— (2) *Ta'rīkh mukhtaṣar ad-daul.* Beyrouth, 1890.
C. Güterbock: *Der Islam im Lichte der byzantinischen Polemik.* Berlin, 1912.
A. Guillaume: *Traditions of Islam.* Oxford, 1924.
Hasluck: *Christianity and Islam under the Sultans.* Oxford, 1929.
Ibn Ḥazm: *Al-faṣl fi 'l-milal wa 'l-ahwā wa 'n-niḥal.* Cairo, A.H. 1347.
Ibn Hishām: *Sīrat an-nabī.* Cairo, A.H. 1329.
Horovitz: *Koranische Untersuchungen.* Berlin and Leipzig, 1926.
H. H. Howorth: *History of the Mongols*, chiefly Part III, *The Mongols of Persia.* London, 1888.
Abu 'l-Ḥusain 'Abd ar-Raḥīm b. Muḥammad b. 'Uthmān al-Khayyāt al-Mu'tazilī: *Kitāb al-intiṣār.* Edited by H. S. Nyberg. Cairo, 1925.
J. R. Illingworth: *Reason and Revelation.* London, 1928.
E. L. Iselin: *Der Untergang der christlichen Kirche in Nordafrika.* Basel, 1918.
Commentaries of Isho'dad of Merv. Edited by Mrs Gibson. Cambridge, 1911.
Al-Jāḥiẓ: *Three Essays.* Edited by J. Finkel. Cairo, 1926.
Jalāl ad-dīn ar-Rūmī: *Mathnawī.* Edited by R. Nicholson. Books I and II (text 1925, translation 1926). Gibb Memorial Series. Leiden.
M. R. James: *Apocryphal New Testament.* Oxford, 1924.
St John of Damascus: (1) "De Haeresibus". Migne, *Patrologia Graeca*, XCIV.
—— (2) "Disputatio Saraceni et Christiani". Migne, *Patrologia Graeca*, XCVI and XCIV.
Chronicle of John, Bishop of Nikiu. Edited by R. H. Charles. London, 1916.
Kidd: *Churches of Eastern Christendom.* London, 1927.
Risālat 'Abdallah b. Isma'īl al-Hāshimī ilā 'Abd al-Masīḥ b. Ishāq al-Kindī, warisālat al-Kindī ila 'l-Hāshimī. Published by the Bible Lands Missions Aid Society, 7, Adam Street, Strand, London, 1912.
J. Labourt: (1) *Le Christianisme dans l'Empire perse.* Paris, 1904.
—— (2) *De Timotheo I Nestorianorum Patriarcha.* Paris, 1904.
H. Lammens: "Le Chantre des Omiades, notes sur le poète arabe chrétien Akhṭal", in *Journal Asiatique*, série 9, tome IV, 1894.
S. Lane-Poole: (1) *A History of Egypt in the Middle Ages.* London, 4th edition, 1925.
—— (2) *The Mohammedan Dynasties.* Paris, 1925.

C. J. Lyall: *Translations of Ancient Arabic Poetry*. London, 1885.

Al-Maqrīzī: *Al-khitat*. Cairo, A.H. 1324–26.

D. S. Margoliouth: "The Origins of Arabic Poetry" in the *Journal of the Royal Asiatic Society*, July, 1925.

Maris, Amri et Slibae Commentaria. Edited by Gismondi. Rome, 1896–9.

G. L. Marriott: "The Homilies of Macarius" in the *Journal of Theological Studies*, vol. XXII, p. 259.

L. Massignon: *La Passion d'al-Hosayn ibn Mansour al-Hallāj*. Paris, 1922.

Al-Mas'ūdī: *Kitāb murūj adh-dhahab*. Edited and translated by B. de Meynard and P. de Courteille, *Les Prairies d'Or*. Paris, 1863.

Al-Māwardī: *Al-aḥkām as-sulṭānīyya*. Text and translation by E. Fagnan, *Les Statuts gouvernmentaux*. Alger, 1915.

A. Mez: *Die Renaissance des Islams*. Heidelberg, 1922.

Chronique de Michel le Syrien. Edited by J. B. Chabot. Paris, 1901.

A. Mingana: (1) "The Early Spread of Christianity in Central Asia and the Far East" in the *Bulletin of the John Rylands Library*, Manchester, July, 1925.

—— (2) "The Early Spread of Christianity in India" in the *Bulletin of the John Rylands Library*, Manchester, July, 1926.

A. Moberg: *The Book of the Himyarites*. Lund, 1924.

J. A. Montgomery: *The History of Yabalāhā III*. New York, 1927.

A. C. Moule: *Christians in China before the year 1550*. London, 1930.

Sir William Muir: (1) *The Apology of al-Kindy*. London, 1882.

—— (2) *The Caliphate, its rise, decline and fall*. Revised edition by T. H. Weir. Edinburgh, 1915.

—— (3) *The Mameluke or Slave Dynasty of Egypt*. London, 1896.

An-Nadīm: *Kitāb al-fihrist*. Edited by Flügel. Leipzig, 1871.

F. Nau: (1) "Le Colloque du Patriarche Jean I et d'Amrou (9 Mai, A.D. 639)" in *Journal Asiatique*, série 11, tome v, 1915.

—— (2) *Les Récits inédits du moine Anastase*. Paris, 1902.

An-Nawawī: *Matn al-arba'īn*. Cairo, A.H. 1344.

De L. O'Leary: (1) *Arabia before Muhammad*. London, 1927.

—— (2) *Arabic thought and its place in history*. London, 1922.

—— (3) *A short history of the Fatimid Khalifate*. London, 1923.

E. Power: (1) "Umayya ibn abi 'ṣ-Ṣalt" in *Mélanges de la faculté orientale*. Beyrouth, 1906.

—— (2) "The Poems of Umayya b. abi 'ṣ-Ṣalt" in *Mélanges de la faculté orientale*. Beyrouth, 1912.

William of Rubruck. Edited by W. W. Rockhill. London, 1900.
E. Sachau: "Zur Ausbreitung des Christentums in Asien" in *Abhandlungen der preussischen Akademie der Wissenschaften* (Phil.-hist. Klasse), 1919.
S. de Sacy: *Exposé de la Religion des Druzes.* Paris, 1838.
Saeki: *The Nestorian Monument in China.* London, 1916.
Sa'īd b. Ḥasan: *Kitāb masālik an-naẓar.* Edited and translated by S. A. Weston in the *Journal of the American Oriental Society*, vol. XXIV (2nd half), 1903.
Abū Ṣāliḥ: *The Churches and Monasteries of Egypt.* Edited by B. T. A. Evetts. Oxford, 1895.
Paul Sbath: *Vingt Traités philosophiques et apologétiques d'auteurs arabes chrétiens* (in Arabic). Cairo, 1929.
F. Schulthess: "Umayya ibn abi 'ṣ-Ṣalt" in *Beiträge zur Assyriologie und semitischen Wissenschaften*, VIII, 3. Leipzig, 1911.
Chronique de Séert. Edited by Addai Scher, *Patrologia Orientalis.* Paris, 1907–18.
Ash-Shahrastānī: *Kitāb al-milal wan-niḥal.* (1) Text edited by Cureton, *Book of Religious and Philosophical Sects.* Leipzig, 1923. (Reprint of the London edition, 1846.)
—— (2) Translation by Haarbrücker, *Religionspartheien und Philosophen-Schulen.* Halle, 1850.
G. Simon: *Der Islam und die christliche Verkündigung.* Gütersloh, 1920.
Steinschneider: "Polemische und apologetische Literatur in arabischer Sprache zwischen Muslimen, Christen und Juden" in *Abhandlungen für die Kunde des Morgenlandes*, VI, Band III.
W. B. Stevenson: *The Crusaders in the East.* Cambridge, 1907.
Guy Le Strange: *Lands of the Eastern Caliphate.* Cambridge, 1905.
Aṭ-Ṭabarī: *Ta'rīkh ar-rusul wal-mulūk.* Edited by De Goeje, *Annales.* Leiden, 1881–1901.
'Alī b. Rabban aṭ-Ṭabarī: *Kitāb ad-dīn wad-daulat.* (1) Text edited by Mingana. Manchester, 1923.
—— (2) Translation by Mingana, *The Book of Religion and Empire.* Manchester, 1922.
Ibn Taimīyya: *Al-jawāb aṣ-ṣaḥīḥ liman baddala dīn al-Masīḥ.* Cairo, 1905/1322.
Theodore Abucara. See St John of Damascus, *Disputatio Saraceni et Christiani.*
L. S. Thornton: *The Incarnate Lord.* London, 1928.
Apology of Timothy I. (1) Syriac text and translation by A. Mingana, *Woodbrooke Studies*, vol. II, 1928.
—— (2) Arabic text, see Cheikho, *Trois Traités.*

J. Tixeront: *Histoire des Dogmes*. Paris, 1922.

A. S. Tritton: *The Caliphs and their non-Muslim subjects*. Oxford, 1930.

W. A. Wigram: *An Introduction to the History of the Assyrian Church*. London, 1910.

Yaḥyā b. Ādam: *Kitāb al-kharāj*. Edited by Th. W. Juynboll. Leiden, 1896.

Yāqūt: *Kitāb mu'jam al-buldān*. Edited by Wüstenfeld, *Geographisches Wörterbuch*. Leipzig, 1866–73.

Henry Yule: (1) *Cathay and the Way Thither*. London, 1866, 2 vols.

—— (2) The same, revised by Cordier. London, 1913–16, 4 vols.

—— (3) *Travels of Marco Polo*. 2nd edition, London, 1875.

Abū Yūsuf: *Kitāb al-kharāj*. (1) Arabic text. Cairo, A.H. 1346.

—— (2) Translated with notes by E. Fagnan, *Le Livre de l'impôt foncier*. Paris, 1921.

INDEX

Aba, Mar, 8, 46
Abāgā, 155
'Abdīshū', Catholicus, 41
'Abdīshū' of Merv, 101
'Abdīshū' of Naṣībīn, 79n.
Abraham III, 57
Abrashahr, 9
Abū Bakr, 31
Abū Ḥanīfa, 30
Abu 'l-Faraj 'Abdallah b. aṭ-Ṭaib, 86
Abū Nu'aim, 122
Abū Sa'īd, 171
Abū Ṣāliḥ, 40
Abū Yūsuf, 29, 38, 87
Abū Zaid, 97
Abyssinia, 12
Abyssinian Church, 10, 21
Adharbaijān, 147
Adiabene, 9
Africa, North, 43n.
Aḥmad b. Ḥāyiṭ, 130
Aḥmad, Mongol Emperor, 156
Aḥmad b. Ṭūlūn, 81
Aḥūdemmeh, 67
'Ain Jālūt, 154
'Akka, 159ff.
Aleppo, 53
Alexander IV, 151
Alexius, 142
'Alī, 41
A-lo-pên, 93, 96
Ameer 'Ali, Syed, 87
Āmid, 170ff.
'Amr b. al-'Āṣ, 42, 109, 114
'Amr b. Mattai, 78, 171
Anastasius, 38
Anbār, 32
Antioch, 145
Apocryphal Literature, 19
Apostasy, death penalty for, 63
'Arabī, Ibn al-, 133
Arbīl, 155f., 163ff., 170, 172
Arghūn, 157f.
Armenia, 147, 165, 171
Armenians, 10, 49, 93, 148f., 156, 159
Arrān, 147
Asceticism, 66f.
Ashnu, 155
Askelon ('Asqalān), 55, 179
Assassins, 149
Assemani, J. S., 53
Athanasius of Antioch, 27

Bābak, 50
Babylonia, 8
Bactria, 9
Baghdad, 47, 56f., 140, 149, 164f., 172
Baghdādī, al-, 119
Bahrā, Banū, 13
Baḥrain, 9
Bahram V, 2
Bahram, General, 24
Baidu, 161f.
Balkh, 181
Barṣauma, companion of Yabalāhā, 103, 158, 165
Barṣauma of Naṣībīn, 9
Basil, 50
Baṣra, 9, 53, 179f.
Baṭṭūṭa, Ibn, 179ff.
Benjamin, 27
Bēth 'Arbāyē, 9
Bēth Garmai, 9
Bēth Lāpāṭ, 8
Bēth Mādhāyē, 9

Bēth Rāzīkāyē, 9
Bible, 7, 14, 113ff., 120ff., 135
Black Death, 181
Bokhtīshū', 54
Borborians, 20, 55
Buddhism and Buddhists, 96, 122, 153, 173
Bukhārā, 139, 180f.
Bukhārī, al-, 120, 121, 126
Burkitt, F. C., 4
Butler, A. J., 27
Buwaihids, 138

Caesarea, 55
Cairo, 176ff.
Carra de Vaux, 181f.
Catholicus, 4, 45, 51, 53, 172
Chalcedon, Council of, 8, 50, 64
Ch'ang-an (*see* Si-ngan-fu)
Charlemagne, 51, 141
Cheikho, L., 8
Chichintalas, 104
Chi-ho, 96
Chi-lieh, 96
China, 10, 49, 95ff., 172f.
Chinese Christians, 105
Chingiz Khān, 104, 147, 181
Chin-kiang-fu, 104
Chosroes I, 2, 45
Chosroes II, 2, 24
Christ, death on the cross, 20, 135
Christ the great ascetic, 131ff.
Christ, imitation of, 64
Christ in Muslim thought, 130ff., 185
Churches, 25, 32, 38f., 45f., 54ff., 147, 161ff., 175ff.
Collyridians, 20
Communicatio idiomatum, 72
Constantine Copronymus, 74
Constantinople, 25
Copts, 10, 27, 174ff.
Cross, 7, 26, 78f., 147f., 152
Crusades, 143ff., 159f., 174, 179
Culture, 1, 3, 137, 139f., 179, 181f.
Cyriacus, 73
Cyrus, 27

Dailām, 83, 90, 95, 138
Damascus, 55, 150, 154, 168 175
Dārā, 180
Darazī, 61
Dastagerd, 26
Daulat, 92
Dēnhā I, 155, 165
Dhimmī, 38, 44ff.
Dīnavar, 9
Diplomas, 41, 53, 150, 166
Diyārbakr (*see* Āmid)
Docetists, 6, 20, 75
Dress of Christians, 45, 47f., 54, 60, 62
Druzes, 62
Durqona, 54

Ebionites, 23
Edessa, 9f., 25, 32, 59, 67, 145
Edward II, 169
Egypt, 42, 154, 156, 174
Elias I, Melkite Patriarch of Antioch, 57
Ēlīyyā III, Catholicus, 103
Ēlīyyā Jauharī, 7
Ēlīyyā of Merv, 93
Ēlīyyā of Naṣībīn, 48, 68, 72, 82, 86, 123
Eucharist, 7, 17, 134, 158, 163
Euchites, 69

Faḍal b. al-Ḥadathī, 130
Fars, 9
Francis of Assissi, St, 144
"Frankish Protectorate of the Holy Land", 51, 141

Gaikhātu, 158f.
Garamaea, 9
Georgia, 147
Georgians, 149, 156, 169
Ghassān, Banū, 10, 13, 36
Ghāzān, 80, 161ff.
Ghaznavids, 139
Ghazzālī, al-, 132
Gilān, 9, 83, 90, 95

Ḥadramaut, 11
Haithon, 166f.
Hajar, 30
Hajarēn, 11
Ḥajjāj, al-, 36
Ḥākim, al-, 60ff., 141
Hallāj, al-, 131
Hamadān, 9, 165
Hanānīshū' I, 80
Hanīf, 19
Hārūn ar-Rashīd, 49, 51, 53, 59, 138, 141
Hāshimī, al-, 88
Ḥazm, Ibn, 20, 73n., 120
Hebrews, Gospel according to the, 21
Hephthalite Huns, 9, 93
Heraclius, 25, 39, 138
Herāt, 9, 51, 181
Hijra, 26
Himyarites, 11
Ḥīra, Banū, 13, 31
Honorius IV, 158
Hormizd IV, 24
Hūlāgū, 149ff., 162
Ḥulwān, 9
Ḥunain b. Iṣḥāq, 68, 81
Hungarians, 142

'Ibād, 13
Ibrāhīm b. Nūḥ, 54
Iconoclasm, 74
Īlak Khāns, 139
Īl-Khāns, 149, 171
Illingworth, J. R., 84, 113
Images, 74, 175
Imru al-Qais, 16
Incarnation, 6, 70ff., 86
'Irāq, 8, 31
'Īsā b. Nestorius, 61
Isfahān, 180
Īshū'dād of Merv, 21, 54
Īshū'yāb II, Catholicus, 41
Īshū'yāb III, Catholicus, 41, 73n.
Īshū'yāb b. Malkūn, 66, 69, 78
I-ssŭ, 96
Issus, 26
'Iyāḍ b. Ghanm, 32
Izd-buzid, 96

Jabalah, 37
Jacob Baradaeus, 10, 13
Jacobites, 5, 10, 39, 50, 148, 172
Jāḥiẓ, al-, 47, 69, 130
Jalāl ad-dīn ar-Rūmī, 133f.
James II of Arragon, 168
Jauzīyya, al-, 121
Jazīrah, al- (*see* Mesopotamia)
Jazī-at ibn 'Umar, 180
Jerusalem, 25, 39, 142, 145, 158
Jesuit missionaries, 173
Jews, 12ff., 22, 25f., 52, 61, 155, 158, 163f.
Jizya, 29ff., 44, 166, 168
John I of Antioch, 109, 114
John II of Antioch, 51
John de Monte Corvino, 105
John of Damascus, St, 72, 74, 110, 129
John XXII, Pope, 171
John (*see also* Yūḥannā)
Jundaisābūr, 8, 51
Justin I, 10, 50
Justin II, 138
Justinian, 1

Kailac, 104

Kanchau, 104
Kao Tsung, 100
Karakorum, 104
Karbalā, 180
Karkūk, 9
Kāshgar, 103f.
Kerait Turks, 101ff., 107, 150
Khaldūn, Ibn, 91
Khālid, 31
Khamārawaih, 134
Khānbāliq, 103, 105
Kharāj, 44, 169
Khubilai Khān, 105, 149, 152ff.
Khudābanda (*see* Uljāitū)
Khūzistān, 8
Khwārizm, 147, 181
Kindī, Apology of al-, 65, 80, 84, 88, 111
Konia, 134
Kūfa, 179f.
Kuyuk, 148

Labīd, 16
Labourt, J., 8
Law of the Christians, 115
Leo the Isaurian, 74
Leo, Tome of, 7f.
Lord's Prayer, parody of, 127
Louis, St, 148
Lyall, C. J., 15

Macarius, 69
Madā'in, al-, 4, 8
Mahdī, al-, 59, 95, 123
Maḥmūd of Ghazna, 139
Maishān, 9
Malabar, 79, 107, 173f.
Mālik, 31
Mālik Shah, 144
Ma'mūn, al-, 49, 52, 59
Manchuria, 104
Mangū, 148f.
Manichaeans, 69f., 93, 96
Manṣūr al-'Ijlī, 131
Manzikart, 142
Maphrianus, 11, 157, 172
Marāghā, 165, 167
Mārāma, 41
Marco Polo, 104, 152
Mārdīn, 171f.
Margoliouth, D. S., 15
Ma'rib, 11
Marwān I, 36
Marwān II, 51
Mary, Blessed Virgin, 20, 135
Mas'ūdī, 81
Mattai, monastery of Mar, 10
Maurice, 24
Māwardī, al-, 46
Medical school, 8, 11, 51
Melet, 5, 44f., 63, 141, 149
Melkites, 5, 24, 50, 141
Merv, 9, 51, 181
Mesopotamia, 8, 32
Messalians, 69
Michael III, 50
Michael VII, 142
Michael the Syrian, 39, 88
Ming dynasty, 173
Miracles, 80ff., 121f.
Missionary spirit, 85, 107, 111
Monasticism, Christian, 16, 22, 66, 69, 97, 143
Mongols, embassies to the, 148
Mongol embassies to Europe, 148
Monophysites, 5, 10, 24
Monotheism, 15, 18, 24
Monothelitism, 27
Mosul (Mauṣil), 47, 155, 164f., 172
Mu'āwiya, 36
Muḥammad, 15, 17, 22, 26, 28, 34, 46, 88, 90, 112, 117, 121, 125, 127, 183
Muqanna', al-, 95
Muqauqas, al-, 27, 40
Muqtadir, al-, 55

Muṣallīn, 69
Mu'tasim, 139
Mu'tawakkil, al-, 54, 59
Mu'tazilites, 59, 128, 130
Mystery Religions, 1

Naiman, 104
Najrān, 11, 34, 73 n.
Najrān, a monk of, 98
Nakhchivan, 147, 165
Naṣībīn, 9, 51, 180
Nāṣir Muḥammad, 176
Naurūz, 162 ff.
Nayan, 152
Nestorians, 5, 50, 57, 148, 172
Nicaea, Council of, 4, 7, 64
Nicephorus I, 37, 49, 59
Nicetas of Byzantium, 112
Nicetas, General, 25
Nīshāpūr, 9, 181
Nisibis (*see* Naṣībīn)
Northampton, 169
Number of Christians, 9, 36, 172
Nur Muḥammad, 128

Odoric, Friar, 105
Ogotai, 147
Öngüt Turks, 104

Passibility of God, 73 n.
Paulicians, 50
Peking (*see* Khānbāliq)
Pentapolis, 42
People of the Book, 29, 113
Pepin the Short, 141
Phocas, 25
Pilgrimage, 140 ff.
Pre-Islamic Arab poetry, 15
Prophecy, 116 ff.

Qādir, al-, 60
Qal'at ar-Rūm, 159
Qā'im, al-, 41
Qinnasrin, 58
Qur'ān, al-, 14, 17, 46, 115, 128, 182

Rāhib, Paul, 78
Rai, 9
Ramleh, ar-, 55
Raqqah, ar-, 32
Raymon Lull, 144
Relics of Saints, 53, 78
Rēvardashīr, 107
Ricoldus de Monte Crucis, 140
Ruhā, ar- (*see* Edessa)
Ruṣāfat, ar-, 60

Sabarīshū', 58
Sacraments, 77 n.
Sa'īd b. Ḥasan, 118, 175
Salīḥ, Banū, 59
Saljūq Turks, 101
Ṣalūbā, Banū, 31
Sāmānids, 139
Samarqand, 10, 101, 104, 139, 181
Sāmarrā, 11, 54, 180
San'ā, 11
Sapor II, 2, 4, 44
Schism, the great, 142
Seleucia, Council of, 5, 9, 45
Seleucia-Ctesiphon (*see* Madā'in)
Semiryechensk, 101
Sepulchre, Church of the Holy, 61, 141
Sergius, Patriarch of Constantinople, 26 f.
Shāfi'ī, ash-, 30
Shams ad-dīn, 134
Sharī'a, 63, 182
Shelēmōn of Baṣra, 159
Shi'a, 137 f., 179 f.
Shūbḥāl-īshū', 90, 95, 107
Sidon, 150
Sijistān, 51

Simeon of Rēvardashīr, 41
Sinai, Mt, 38
Si-ngan-fu, 93, 95 ff., 104
Sinjār, 11
Sophronius, 78
"Spirit", feminine gender of, 21
Spirit, power of the, 63, 80, 83, 101, 108
Suchau, 104
Sufism, 126
Sulṭānīyya, 171
Surra-man-rā'a (*see* Sāmarrā)
Susiana, 8

Ṭabarī, 'Alī, 90, 117
Tabriz, 147, 163 ff.
Taghlib, Banū, 13, 30, 32 ff.
Ṭai, Banū, 13
T'ai Tsung, 100
Taima, 13
Taimīyya, Ibn, 119
Takrīt, 10, 150, 172
Talmud, 19
T'ang dynasty, 101
Tangut, 104
Tanīs, 55
Tanūkh, Banū, 13, 58
Tashkent, 101
Tatars, 105
Theodore Abucara, 64, 70, 80, 110
Theodore of Studium, 76
Theodosius, 54, 97
Theological school, 9, 51
Theophilus, 50
Thomas, Jacobite Bishop in Baghdad, 58
Thomas of Marga, 67, 83 f., 90
Thornton, L., 76
Tiberias, 179
Tibet, 95
Timothy, 12, 57, 71 ff., 88, 95, 112, 116, 123
Tīmūr Lang (Tamerlane), 172
Transoxania, 9, 93, 95, 101, 139, 180
Trinity, 114, 122
Tripoli, 145
Ṭughril Beg, 139 f.
Ṭūr 'Abdīn, 10, 172
Turks, 9, 93, 138 ff.
Tyre, 179

Ubullah, 53, 180
Uigur Turks, 103 f.
Uljāitū, 168 ff.
'Umar I, 9, 33 f., 37, 41
'Umar II, 36, 58
Umayya b. abi 'ṣ-Ṣalt, 17 f.
Urban II, 143
'Uthmān, 35

William of Rubruck, 79, 104, 106, 144
Worldly success the criterion of divine favour, 87 ff., 178, 184

Yabalāhā III, 83, 103, 156, 158 f., 165 ff.
Yaḥyā b. 'Adī, 68, 81
Yaman, 11 ff., 34
Yang-chau-fu, 105
Yarkand, 104
Yazdegerd I, 45
Yazdegerd II, 2
Yazīd I, 36
Yazīd II, 74
Yūḥannā V, 56
Yūḥannā b. Bāzūk, 60
Yūḥannā b. 'Īsā, 12
Yun-nan, 104

Zara'a, Ibn, 65
Zindiq, 69
Ẓofār, 12
Zoroastrianism, 2, 30, 63, 96, 137, 182
Zuhair, 16